Culture, Rhetoric and the Vicissitudes of Life

Studies in Rhetoric and Culture

Edited by **Ivo Strecker,** Johannes Gutenberg University Mainz and Addis Ababa University, **Stephen Tyler,** Rice University, and **Robert Hariman,** Northwestern University

Our minds are filled with images and ideas, but these remain unstable and incomplete as long as we do not manage to persuade both ourselves and others of their meanings. It is this inward and outward rhetoric which allows us to give some kind of shape and structure to our understanding of the world and which becomes central to the formation of individual and collective consciousness. This series is dedicated to the study of the interaction of rhetoric and culture and focuses on the concrete practices of discourse in which and through which the diverse and often also fantastic patterns of culture—including our own—are created, maintained, and contested.

Volume 1
Culture & Rhetoric
Edited by Ivo Strecker and Stephen Tyler

Volume 2
Culture, Rhetoric, and the Vicissitudes of Life
Edited by Michael Carrithers

Volume 3
Economic Persuasions
Edited by Stephen Gudeman

Culture, Rhetoric, and the Vicissitudes of Life

∎ ∎ ∎

Edited by
Michael Carrithers

Berghahn Books
New York • Oxford

First published in 2009 by

Berghahn Books

www.berghahnbooks.com

©2009, 2012 Michael Carrithers
First paperback edition published in 2012

All rights reserved. Except for the quotation of short passages for the purposes of criticism and review, no part of this book may be reproduced in any form or by any means, electronic or mechanical, including photocopying, recording, or any information storage and retrieval system now known or to be invented, without written permission of the publisher.

Library of Congress Cataloging-in-Publication Data

Culture, rhetoric, and the vicissitudes of life / edited by Michael Carrithers.
 p. cm. — (Studies in rhetoric and culture ; v. 2)
 Includes bibliographical references and index.
 ISBN 978-1-84545-429-6 (hbk.) -- ISBN 978-0-85745-800-1 (pbk.)
 1. Culture. 2. Social evolution. 3. Rhetoric. 4. Life. 5. Social problems. 6. Philosophical anthropology. I. Carrithers, Michael.
 GN357.C849 2009
 306—dc22

2009012807

British Library Cataloguing in Publication Data

A catalogue record for this book is available from the British Library

Printed in the United States on acid-free paper.

ISBN: 978-0-85745-800-1 (paperback)   ISBN: 978-0-85745-816-2 (ebook)

Contents

■ ■ ■ ■ ■ ■

Preface	vii
Introduction *Michael Carrithers*	1
1. Internal Rhetorics: Constituting Selves in Diaries and Beyond *Jean Nienkamp*	18
2. Story Seeds and the Inchoate *Michael Carrithers*	34
3. The Diffuse in Testimonies *Stevan M. Weine*	53
4. Medical Rhetoric in the U.S. and Africa: The Oncologist as Charon *Megan Biesele*	69
5. 'As if Goya was on hand as a marksman': Foot and Mouth Disease as a Rhetorical and Cultural Phenomenon *Brigitte Nerlich*	87
6. The Palaestral Aspect of Rhetoric *F.G. Bailey*	107
7. Ordeals of Language *Ellen B. Basso*	121
8. Inventions of Hyperbolic Culture *Ralph Cintron*	138

9. Rhetoric in the Moral Order: A Critique of Tropological
   Approaches to Culture   156
   James W. Fernandez

Notes on Contributors   173

Index   174

Preface

■ ■ ■ ■ ■ ■

All research is based on the notion that the world is explicable, an idea with powerful attractions. The attractions were all the greater in the Colorado Springs of the late 50s and early 60s of the last century, which was dominated by the Cold War, evidenced to me every morning as I looked out over my breakfast cereal towards the entrance to the hydrogen bomb-proof headquarters of the North American Air Defence Command at the base of Cheyenne Mountain, plainly visible fifteen miles away. Colorado Springs then offered a choice of certainties and hopes in the face of instant annihilation. But the one that captured my imagination in high school was the scientific hope that we would develop the equations to understand things completely and, once we put in the initial conditions, we could predict and control the course of the future. I was encouraged in this by the scientific optimism of the period, and by the Foundation Trilogy of Isaac Asimov, which invented the idea of the predictive, and controlling, science of psychohistory. There went with this, too, the sanctioning of curiosity as a blameless and necessary emotion.

I have long since lost the megalomaniac certainties, but the convictions remain that curiosity is laudable and that authoritative explanation is worth the work. So far as I can see, without those convictions you can hardly engage in so peculiar an occupation as explaining the human world to people who always already have a way of understanding it.

University brought two discoveries that sharpened my curiosity. The first was that others might live in radically different *worlds*, by which I mean, they live among assumptions which force us to discover, and possibly overturn, the unsuspected grounds of our own world. This came to me first through reading the German Renaissance theorist of poetics, Martin Opitz, whose received Aristotelian ideas of poetry as a poor relation to philosophy were so very different from the Romanticism – poets as the unacknowledged legislators of the world – which I had imbibed with English lessons in school. The point was that thereafter the discovery of others' worlds and, through them, my own world, would turn out to be an abiding obsession.

The other discovery, that ideas and attitudes could change so profoundly with time (e.g. as between Renaissance and Romanticism) seemed then to be a natural accompaniment: you could find your source of challenging otherness in the past, or beyond your front door today, but surprise was there for the meeting. Only much later did I discover that the understanding and explication of *worlds* rubs painfully against the understanding and explications of *histories*. And even when I chose to study a world through its varying histories in *The Forest Monks of Sri Lanka*, or gave an account of the world surrounding the history of *The Buddha*, the practical problem of finding a way of talking about both worlds and histories made me uneasy, but did not alert me to the real difficulties.

The difficulties only became apparent when I came face to face with evolutionary anthropologists, in this case the very congenial and interesting people at Durham University, whose ideas of explication were for the most part profoundly opposed to my own. Here was yet another world, not so much beyond my front door as inside it. True, my fellow socio-cultural anthropologists had already practiced a defence against evolutionists' propensity to explain behaviour by some evolutionary advantage to be found in it, and that defence was this: since human beings have devised such an enormous array of different cultures, we can always show some variation of human behaviour which is not compassed in your ideas of human nature, so your explanation from general evolutionary advantage to the whole species must be wrong. But the problem was that, however useful that defence might be, socio-cultural anthropologists were depending entirely on the sheer existence of that vast variety of cultures, without any sense of the source or origin of those tremendous differences. Indeed, early in the twentieth century anthropologists, faced with the purely speculative histories of cultural differences that had gone before, gave up any systematic aspiration to account for cultural differences; and to top it off, the standard anthropological way of writing, in the ethnographic or habitual present, was in effect anti-historical in its implications and invited the assumption either that the people involved had no history because their culture and society were unchanging, or that historical explanation was in any case irrelevant. What this all meant was that, however I and my colleagues might routinely write our ways more or less gracefully around this impasse, we simply had no grounds on which to make sense of the cultural differences that lay at the root of our undertaking.

At this point it was far too late in the plot to resurrect Asimov's psychohistory, but there did seem to be one slightly more modest question whose answer might retrieve some sense, and make for some reconciliation between talking about worlds and talking about histories: given that there does exist such a wide variety of cultures among our species, what must generally be true of us to make that variety possible? To this there seemed an intertwined array of human attributes that make for constant changeability among us. We are intensely intersubjective; we respond rapidly and constantly to one another, with often unforeseeable consequences; our understanding of each other is often based more on interpretation and imagination than on certainty; we depend for understanding of our social environment on narrative and other more or less poetical means; we are, as a species, tremendously inventive in new and unexpected forms of symbolic reasoning and expression; and we are consequently also very fecund in the imagining and execution of new forms of social organisation and social action. To make this characterisation of human beings comparable to the evolutionary biologists' characterisation of other species, I used the word *sociality* as the keyword, so that our very volatile and mutable sociality could be compared in principle with the sociality of other species. And to describe the consequences of this volatility, I used the word *historicity*, referring to the fact of constant eventfulness and change among us. So even though there was nothing here to explain any particular case of cultural history and mutation, there was at least an explanation of human nature in general that would make us expect change and to allow for a sense that any explanation in the present tense would be just that, an explanation in the present which invites or demands an account of the past as well, and of change and instability, or at least of some good reason to find stasis and stability.

That is more or less the argument of the book *Why Humans have Cultures*. There is no significant mention of rhetoric in that book, however, and even though I had from the beginning been concerned with matters that fall easily enough under the heading of rhetoric, I had not thought to tap that reservoir of accomplished thought, not least because it is not one easily available on the British social science scene. The invitation from Ivo Strecker and Stephen Tyler in 2001 to join in the Rhetoric Culture project was therefore a turning point, because there I met, or re-met, many of my academic heroes and heroines, and found that, between us, we had always been speaking of rhetoric.

What does the notion of rhetoric do for, and to, the notion of culture and the practice of explaining cultures and societies? In the first place, it acts as another therapeutic corrective: our customary ways of talking and writing about society or societies had almost always assumed that there was something automatic at play, such that things could just go on and on without will. Rhetoric, on the other hand, places the will to make something happen, to make something change (or to make something abide against change), at the very foundation of our ideas about ourselves. It recognizes, in other words, the constant itch to adjust, move, improve, remove, and overcome the momentary and not so momentary conditions and needs which are a part of our, and indeed all animals', circumstances of life. So the urge among us, as a so very social species, to act on others, or to persuade others to act for or with you, is therefore foundational; it is to be expected, just as change is to be expected; and therefore the view we have across human life is one in which people are always seeking to convince one another for this purpose or that. F.G. Bailey, in his essay in this book, begins by invoking the image of the *palaestrum*, the wrestling-school, to understand rhetoric. This is too narrow an image to apply across all rhetorical occasions, but it does capture the sense of urge and energy on one hand, and the sense of the world's resistant material on the other, that is immanent in the notion of rhetoric.

Following from this notion of rhetoric, culture also invites us to see our repertoires of speech and expression as always having a rhetorical edge, as having reality and meaning only insofar as it is applied for some desired end in some particular circumstance. Rhetoricians speak of "the rhetorical situation", a sort of idealised and abstracted particularity (if there could be such a thing) in which the rhetor, the speaker, addresses others with a sense of *kairos*, that is, of the timeliness and fitness of his address to his particular audience and their present circumstances. And so it invites the anthropologist or fellow researcher in the human sciences to explain not just the general form of our cultural repertoire, but the actual circumstances of use such that our explications are put back into life (so far as that is possible in written discourse).

It might seem, of course, that this move to the rhetorical situation, with its emphasis on particularity, is too far away from that social science which has been so successful in delineating larger and slower precessions of social change. It might seem, in other words, that to prescribe rhetoric as a style of explicating culture is to recommend writing the academic equivalent of very short stories or *haiku,* rather than monographs. But the circumstances bearing on any given rhetorical situation are not always plainly present, and may require longer exposition; nor is there any limit in principle to the circumstances which might be relevant. So there is every reason to think rhetoric relevant to large and slow movements in affairs (as Cintron and Carrithers show here) as well as to suddenly arising emergencies. Moreover it is often in moments of difficulty – whether those moments arise and pass away swiftly or slowly – that rhetoric leads to the creation of culture, the fashioning of new instruments by which people are able to work out what to think and how to act, both individually and collectively. On this view persuasion and conviction reach into all corners of social life, and the tools and schemas of culture are continually created by human beings to formulate and work their will on one another. This perspective, we think, opens onto fresh discoveries across the whole of social and cultural anthropology.

When I speak of 'we', I refer not just to the contributors to the argument in this volume, but to all those involved in the Rhetoric Culture Project. To put 'us' in context, it is perhaps important to observe that, by about the 1980's, anthropologists had come to realise that our fundamental working ideas, deposited in the terms 'culture' and 'social structure', were too inflexible to capture the constant change that social and cultural life across the globe throw before us. New figures of thought such as 'process', 'construction', 'invention' and 'performance' crept into our conceptual vocabulary to capture some of this quicksilver movement, and the mysterious term 'agency' began to be used. The conviction grew too that social life does not move as in serried ranks or alone through plainly specifiable causal forces, but also through constant messy and mutual action, and that we needed some clearer way to think about these matters in a single idiom.

These and related questions were debated at the first conference on *Rhetoric Culture Theory*, which was held at Mainz in February 2002. In the next years further conferences followed on themes such as language, social relations, religion, politics and economics, spawning an abundance of papers that will be incorporated in different volumes of the Berghahn Books series *Studies in Rhetoric and Culture*. The fate of the contributions to general rhetoric culture theory was particularly varied. Originally they all were to be part of one volume entitled *Rhetoric Culture. Theory, Method and History*. In the event, that single volume was split into others, two of which are herewith published concurrently: *Rhetoric Culture Theory*, edited by Ivo Strecker and Stephen Tyler, and *Culture, Rhetoric and the Vicissitudes of Life*, edited by myself. It is my own understanding that all the authors of all these volumes have in fact investigated 'vicissitudes of life' and people's rhetorical responses to them, but the essays here show those vicissitudes and responses, and the lessons we may learn from them, with particular poignancy.

Another lesson in this, and the other, volumes is that no piece of rhetoric is authored by its manifest speaker alone. I would like in particular to thank Bob Hariman, Ivo Strecker and Steve Tyler for their insightful help.

Introduction

Michael Carrithers

■ ■ ■ ■ ■ ■

> The world is but a perennial movement. All things in it are in constant motion—the earth, the rocks of the Caucasus, the pyramids of Egypt.... Stability itself is nothing but a more languid motion. ... I do not portray being: I portray passing.
>
> Montaigne, 'Of Repentence'

> Whatever comes together passes away.
> From the last words of the Buddha, *Mahaparinibbana Sutta*

> Everything flows; nothing abides.
>
> Heraclitus, *The Fragments*

THIS BOOK IS ABOUT HUMAN expectations, vicissitudes and the ruin of expectations, and our human remedies, such as they are, against such ruin. The net of vicissitudes is cast very widely, across different societies and different scales of adversity, including a mother's death, exile to a strange land, an unwanted sexual advance, a surprise rebuff of a rich man's plans, the aftermath of the Holocaust, the events of 9/11, and a great slaughter of animals. What these have in common is that, because they are unanticipated and beyond routine, they test the nature and limits of cultural resources, call up inventive answers, and, in so doing, demonstrate the very nature of both culture and the human imagination. If this book has only one lesson – and I believe it has many – it is that it will never be enough to understand human beings as culture-bearing animals unless we also understand that they are rhetorical animals who need constantly to persuade not just others but also themselves.

Let me first say something about expectation, which is the implicit ground before which the arguments set out here are the explicit and articulated figures. Unlike our cousins the other primates (so far as we know), we human beings routinely entertain conscious plans and dreams for a future, sometimes many years ahead. Expectation is in part a matter of conscious thought, but also of implicit assumption, being built into the collective acquired sensibilities of our various societies. A Navaho newborn girl is likely to be welcomed with celebration of her eventual maturity and fertility as the matrix of continuing Navaho life; many North Indian newborn girls, however, are greeted grimly, a leaden weight on their family's fortunes because of the crippling dowry payment which will have to be made at the girl's eventual marriage. So in that respect you could say that having certain expectations is a constituent part of understanding what it is to be Navaho or North Indian.

There are also even more generalized expectations, common across many societies: for example grief at someone dying in old age after a full life is frequently regarded as a lesser occasion for grief (or anger) than death at a younger age. So expectations may routinely stretch across the whole of a life, making judgements about what is an auspicious or inauspicious future, or a timely or an untimely death. And of course expectations may blend into a hope, or fear, which organizes the collective life of many: you may expect the revolution, independence, the saviour, or Armageddon to come, democracy finally to be established or the state to wither away, the magical cargo to arrive, or your creed to reign across the world.

The net of expectations works at finer scales as well, such that we may have routine hopes for the timely coming of spring; for recovery from a common cold; or that traffic around the next corner will be running smoothly. Indeed many of the procedures and more or less scripted encounters that are the stuff of anthropological enquiry – a wedding ritual, the coronation of a monarch, an induction into a secret society, or, at finer scales, an exchange in a shop, an enquiry for information, a formula of greeting, of departure – have among their possible descriptions the management of expectation. These procedures are, so to speak, social and cultural machines which at once guide and consummate our anticipation of events and outcomes.

There is, however, a dark and inescapable corollary of this ubiquitous regime of expectations, namely that anticipation, hope and preparation are no guarantee. Human beings – along with the rest of creation – are chronically vulnerable and exposed, despite their best attempts. From the small and passing (the bottle dropped and smashed in the street or the theft of a wallet) to the great and momentous (the collective catastrophes of war, famine, inflation and plague) we are faced constantly with emergencies and unaccounted situations. These are all vicissitudes, that is, 'difficulties or hardships erupting into a life, a career, a course of action or an ordered scene and usually beyond one's control,' (the definition of 'vicissitude' is my adaptation from the Merriam-Webster version). If expectations and routines are a constant feature of human life, then so are emergencies and crises. And I will add, too, that though many vicissitudes may be *expectable* – and here I offer the example of the death of loved ones and oneself – that does not mean that they are necessarily *expected*, especially in the sense of being prepared for and under control. Some eventualities may fall relatively easily under a more or less automated response, but others, those we experience as vicissitudes, may leave us speechless and confused, without a ready interpretation of what has happened. Some eventualities may be routine to some participants, such as the undertaker, but not to others, the family of the deceased. The cases treated here certainly challenge those affected for an appropriate response. Such vicissitudes require a sustained, even strained, marshalling of resources, and particularly of moral, emotional and imaginative resources to understand and interpret the event. Moreover – and this is the devilish side of the matter – our very responses to a vicissitude may deepen the crisis, create more vicissitudes, and require yet further marshalling of ideas and interpretations.

So the topic of this volume is less the vicissitudes than the nature of the culture and rhetoric mobilized to deal with them. Put very briefly, we maintain that 'culture' (or any related notion such as 'discourse') exists as a set of potentials and possibilities. A fruitful analogy might be with a set of tools which, strictly in themselves, are inert and inactive, but which also offer an indefinite but broad set of potentials and possibilities in the hands of people addressing one task or another. 'Rhetoric', then, is the use of those tools in critical and unclear situations to achieve some desired understanding, some policy and orientation, and with that orientation a deflection of minds, hearts and events into a desired, or at least less disastrous, direction. Or to put it another way, we cannot understand culture as a human endowment (or a human fate) unless we understand culture's rhetorical edge, its pointed use. As I will argue in the rest of this introduction, this represents for social and human scientists a more methodically fruitful way of regarding the historicity, changeability, and the evident creativity of human cultures and societies; and from a rhetorician's perspective this represents a deeper and more widely applicable interpretation of 'the rhetorical situation' than has usually been the case.

Culture

Let me take each of our keywords, culture, rhetoric and vicissitudes, in turn. I begin with culture because it is perhaps the most troubled of our three terms.

Culture is what W.B. Gallie famously called an 'essentially contested concept', that is, a concept with no essential single meaning but rather a series of disputed meanings, like Democracy, Christianity or Sustainable Development. And indeed the concept is hardly mentioned by name in the essays in this volume. Nevertheless a concept of culture is implicit and necessary here, as in all the contributions to the Rhetoric Culture series.

Let me say first what people writing here do *not* assume: they do not assume that an explanation of 'culture', or for that matter 'social structure', or 'discourse', or any other sociological or anthropological master term can, in itself, suffice as a global explanation of people's behaviour or utterances. They are aware that no single system of explanation is adequate to clarify the raw materials from which the social sciences are made, namely the interweaving of (1) human actions, (2) reactions to those actions, and (3) accounts of those actions and reactions. They would probably assent to something like this, however: culture comprises a repertoire of things learned, including mental schemes and images, values and attitudes, dispositions, forms of speech and organization, narratives, and commonplace knowledge. These things are doubtless a guide to people, a resource, and they certainly require our explanatory efforts. But they are not active in themselves, not the single source of what people do. As F.G. Bailey and James Fernandez point out in their essays here, any culture has plentiful alternative schemas, narratives and values, so that no one is able simply to read off the appropriate actions or statements from some table of right things to think, do and say which they have learned. Indeed, as Ellen Basso describes here, conflicting demands within a culture can lead to an embarrassing and painful impasse.

This means that the world of pressingly real things which we need to account for must have in it not just the mental and dispositional things of culture, but also people, relationships, events and situations. These stand apart from, and are to a degree resistant to, patterning by cultural ideas and dispositions: as Louis Dumont was fond of pointing out, values would not be values if everybody acted according to them automatically. Any anthropologist or other social scientist might be justly proud to discern in some knotty flow of events the local cultural schemes playing beneath the surface. By displaying such discernment to the non-cognoscenti, the anthropologist could dispel much ignorance and confusion among onlookers from afar. Or, as Ralph Cintron does here when talking about the culture of hyperbole in the United States, one can lay bare a feature of society and events so plainly taken for granted that it sinks below awareness and even natives, in this case Americans themselves, might recognize it with surprise. But we cannot take such cultural accounts by scholars as the exhaustive truth about why people do what they do; they are rather a guide to the perplexed that might allow us to begin to find our way about among the actual people, relations, events and situations, as Cintron gives us a thread to follow in thinking about the Twin Towers.

So on one hand, culture is, in the general perspective taken here, a fund of mental materials and dispositions which are in themselves inert except as they are grasped and used in some particular situation. On the other, those mental materials and dispositions are current among some set of people. One might say: their use resonates among that set. I use the word 'set' advisedly, since it is as vague and general a word as I can think of to designate those among whom a cultural understanding may resonate. For example, in this volume Megan Biesele contrasts Americans with the Ju/'hoan San of the Kalahari Desert, and Ellen Basso contrasts the Japanese with the Kalapalo of the Amazonian rainforest. For most purposes the more embracing designations (Americans, Japanese) are not commensurable with the less embracing (Ju/'hoan, Kalapalo), and that for many reasons, including differences of scale, internal homogeneity or disparity, and character of social organization. But they are comparable, at least if rounded off at the edges, in that each set possesses a cultural repertoire which is mutually intelligible among its members.

I have adopted this peculiar language of 'set' and 'repertoire', rather than 'society' and 'culture', largely as a sign that here we make considerably more modest claims for the idea of culture in itself than have been made in the past. And now I want to make those claims even more modest by pointing out how relatively little is assumed by saying that a cultural repertoire is mutually intelligible among a set of people. The lead is given by Bailey's essay here, which shows a peasant talking to a wealthy citified gentleman: their talk is mutually understood, but hardly agreed. Similarly, Carrithers discusses a distinctively German term concerning the German past, but not all Germans, even though they understand its meaning, would assent to its import. Perhaps I can make the general point clearest with reference to an exercise I carry out with my students in the university here. I write the word 'whore' on the blackboard, and ask students to discuss what it means, to whom it applies, and whether, and how, they have used the word. The result is that all, in their capacity as native English speakers, understand the word. Some have reported that they have never used the word at all. Others have reported that they have never used it, and would never use it. Others have reported that they use it, but in the form 'ho', as an ironic and derogatory term for 'woman' or 'girl', derived probably from the word's pronunciation in American Black hip-hop music – speaking in quotation marks, if you will. And yet others, speaking apparently from an all-male boarding school setting, report that they have used it, in its spoken form as 'whore', or indeed 'man-whore', as a form of insult, again perhaps in quotation marks. And these are just some of the disparities issuing from that simple word among this more or less homogeneous group of educated middle-class English persons. So to say that 'whore' is intelligible as an item of culture, i.e. not just a word but also a set of associations, does not yet specify, and never could fully specify, the uses to which it will be put or the variety of responses to it.

Rhetoric

And that is where rhetoric, our second term, comes to the rescue. For rhetoric, in the broad sense meant here, is the moving force which connects that which is learned, culture, to that which happens. To use the concept of rhetoric in this way involves three initial steps. First, rhetoric cannot mean only 'mere rhetoric', i.e. words or displays which are hollow or deceptive ... though those, too, are included under this more capacious understanding. Second, rhetoric is not associated solely with either the Classical world, or with the practice of politics alone. It is true that we derive our basic ideas of rhetoric from the ancient Greeks and then the Romans. In their practice of rhetoric, public political speaking and acting were central. But here our concern is with rhetoric in a more general usage, which in Cicero's terms is 'to move' (*movere*) or 'to bend' (*flectere*) the mind of the audience, with the aim of making them act or respond in line with the rhetoric. And third, rhetoric need not be limited to speech alone. Last spring I watched two young gardeners digging in a sullen desultory way in the herbaceous border outside my office. When they heard the boss's truck come up the driveway, though, they doubled their efforts and when the boss came around the corner he was treated to the sight of two hard-working labourers, no effort spared. So in that case, I would say, the culture lay in their ability to dig the border, but the rhetoric lay in their sudden display of horticultural dynamism.

This example also allows us to see why we may speak of rhetoric culture – or perhaps just as appropriately, *the rhetorical edge of culture*. On one hand, the skills of digging over a herbaceous border are learned and, considered in isolation, the use of such skills need not possess a rhetorical edge. Digging is allowed to be just digging. However, the moment we begin to consider that such digging may be *addressed* to someone, then the rhetorical edge begins to show. In the incident I witnessed, the digging was (momentarily at least) addressed to the boss, and so it became rhetorical, aimed at moving the boss to think that the diggers were industrious. And there is another sort of address here as well, if we consider the role of the boss as head gardener. This digging is designed to 'make a display', in the terms my English parents-in-law might use to praise an attractive garden. So as far as the head gardener is concerned, this digging is most certainly addressed to someone, including his boss, his boss's boss, and the general public, all of whom may like a well-turned border and may be persuaded thereby that the university is a well-run concern. So even though we may let digging just be digging, the whole project in which it is involved may be rhetorical (among its other characteristics).

Bakhtin used the term 'addressivity' to capture this character of human expression, its nature as being necessarily oriented to some other person or persons. When we express ourselves – by speech, writing, song, dance, or especially fervent excavation – that expression is to be understood not only in relation to oneself, but also in relation to an audience. Addressivity is, so to speak, the articulate face of our pervasive human intersubjectivity, the deeply affecting and mutually constituting awareness that we have of one another as intensely social primates. And intersubjectivity involves incessant action, or better, *inter*action – the busy-ness of everyday life, the incessant exchange of words, things, glances, blows with each other. This constant activity means, too, that our situation is constantly changing in relation to others, and so constantly needing attention, constantly needing to be *addressed*, to be adjusted, or at least to be coordinated with others. And in fact this deep propensity to address is sunk so deep in us that we not only address other people, but ourselves as well: we discuss, cajole and argue with ourselves to achieve clarity or at least some sense of purpose in what is sometimes a testing world, as Jean Nienkamp shows so well in her essay here.

Implicit in this understanding of everyday rhetoric is that it involves a charge of energy, a potential, as there is energy between the top of a waterfall and the bottom. In James Fernandez's pregnant phrase, rhetoric 'makes a movement and leads to a performance', that is, a rhetorical expression effects a change in the addressee's mind, leading to some form of action. Or that at least is the ideal. Just now my son is approaching a set of examinations, for example, and on occasion I ask him how the work is going. Sometimes this is just solidarity talk, but occasionally – as when he is going out of the door into town when I suppose he should be studying – the question takes on rhetorical energy: it is meant to 'make a movement', i.e. remind him of the situation, and 'lead to a performance', make him come back soon and work. This example shows, too, that rhetoric does not automatically succeed, just as cultural learning does not automatically mean that people behave according to their acquired values. And indeed there would be no need for rhetoric if there were not constantly a difference between affairs as they are and as the rhetor (the speaker, or better, the 'addresser') wants them to be.

Rhetoric to Rhetoric Culture

So what is the effect of multiplying culture by rhetoric and producing rhetoric culture?

In the first place, rhetoric culture emphasizes the interactive character of life: through the glass of rhetoric we can see that, in any moment of interaction, some act to persuade, others are the targets of persuasion; some work, others are worked upon; some address, others are addressed. Or one could speak of both agents and patients, the latter to designate those who are the object, rather than the initiator, of action. This stress on the dyadic or plural character of social and rhetorical action – the fact that some do, while others are done to – is an important adjustment of the idea of 'agency' whose salience in social science writing has soared in the last decade or so. We would do better to speak of 'agency-cum-patiency'. And of course one may be an agent one moment, and a patient the next. It is the sort of thing that happens in a conversation, for example.

Moreover, by thus placing interaction at the heart of the interpretative enterprise, rhetoric culture challenges social scientists not only to fit things into recurring patterns, but to be sensitive to the possibility that things may fall out of a pattern, may erupt into the new and different … indeed to the possibility that out of old materials lying to hand new materials can be fashioned. Rhetoricians speak of 'the rhetorical situation' in general, i.e. any occasion when someone taking the role of rhetor intervenes, hoping to address an audience appropriately, in a timely manner, with energy and effect – whether before the United Nations or across the kitchen table. In that sense rhetoric culture is designed to address the historicity of things, the fact that human life is, in the longer run, mutable and metamorphic, constantly producing new forms of life, culture and organization in adaptation to new situations. And if rhetoric culture moves rhetoric into the kitchen, so to speak, then it also moves the study of culture into the sphere of the singular – the Gettysburg Address, the promulgation of the Universal Declaration of Human Rights, the declaration of War on Iraq by the United States and Britain – where we find cultural materials fashioned to new ends in extraordinary situations.

The notion of rhetoric culture also invites us again to look closely again at the foundation of human beings' understanding of experience overall. Tropologists, studying figurative thought and language (including the ancient Greek Isocrates, the early modern Giambattista Vico, the twentieth-century polymath Kenneth Burke, as well as contemporary psycholinguists such as George Lakoff, and those writing here), have shown how human thought is shot through with the use of poetical and rhetorical imagery and narrative. Such thought penetrates everyday talking and thinking to such an extent that we might best think of ourselves as speaking, not prose, but poetry. Here's an everyday example: a German colleague was recently much amused when she heard the English word for those receptacles we hang on the wall in the department to receive letters: pigeonholes. A routine word to Anglophones here, but the imagery translated into German invites wild speculation (she said, 'Does that mean *Tauben? Löcher?* Pigeons? Holes?'). It makes no sense whatsoever ... or rather, it makes only figurative sense, by bringing the housing of pigeons to explain the housing of the Royal Mail. A dead metaphor is still a metaphor; a familiar narrative is still a narrative.

Figurative thought extends to the horizons of human experience as well. The philosopher Hans Blumenberg devoted his life's work to understanding what he called 'absolute metaphors'. A non-absolute metaphor, so to speak, is one in which we know both legs of the comparison: 'the king is a lion' works because we know something of kings, and something of lions, and find it illuminating and mind-moving to connect them. An absolute metaphor, on the other hand, is one where the figurative side is known, but the other is unknown or difficult to grasp. 'Death is a journey' is such an absolute metaphor – for who knows death? – but so is 'life is an journey', for how otherwise (as Virginia Woolf so comprehensively demonstrated) are we to understand so complex, comprehensive and varying an experience? Stories are pressed into service as absolute metaphors as well. Consider Adam, Eve, the snake and the apple as proposing a view of the difficult relation of the sexes, or the story of the Buddha's struggle towards enlightenment as a view on how to find an abiding sense of well-being in this often troubled life. These are all materials that have been applied, and will continue to be applied on one occasion or another, to orient people among the vicissitudes of life ... to which I now turn.

VICISSITUDES (AND CULTURE AND RHETORIC AS WELL)

The argument of this book as a whole lies in the tension between rhetoric/culture on the one hand and the 'vicissitudes of life' on the other. Now the phrase 'vicissitudes of life' is a rich one which extends deep into European cultural history, but also rhymes with many other – indeed arguably, with *all* other – cultural traditions. Let me follow Jean Nienkamp in her chapter here, and adopt Kenneth Burke's term 'terministic screen', which describes from the viewpoint of language – he uses the word 'terminology' – everything I have here called the rhetorical edge of culture. Burke writes that 'if any given terminology is a *reflection* of reality, by its very nature as a terminology it must also be a *selection* of reality; and to this extent it must function also as a *deflection* of reality' (Burke 1966: 45). 'Vicissitudes of life', as a terministic screen, is indeed a selection of reality: it concentrates (in modern usage at any rate) on events that are breaks with the expected, the desired and the comfortingly routine, and not (as would be justified by older usages of the word) on any event which represents change. So it both *reflects* reality, in that the unexpected and the unwanted will erupt into everyone's life, and *selects* a part of reality for our attention.

It is also a *deflection* of reality in two senses: first, it collects under a single heading a series of occasions which we might otherwise regard in different lights. In this volume the writers consider a mother's death, exile to a strange land, an unwanted sexual advance, a rebuff of a rich man's plans, threatened arrest and torturous murder during the Holocaust, the events of 9/11, and a great slaughter of animals. (Other terministic screens would deflect reality in other directions: for example, there is now a strong current of opinion in both Israel and Germany that the Holocaust is in some sense incomparable, beyond history, the epitome of an evil which is nowhere else so purely manifest. So with that terministic screen the Holocaust would be quite misplaced in our list.)

Second, the very act of using the phrase 'vicissitudes of life', and so of categorizing these and myriad other fractures and violations together, is to take a step towards seeing them *sub specie aeternitatis,* from afar, with at least some tranquillity and mended reflection, at a distance from the raw shock of events themselves. There is a rhetoric of generalization which, by moving events from their immediate particularity to the general also moves them from the sphere of feeling (*pathos,* as Aristotle put it) towards the sphere of dispassionate thinking (*logos*). Similarly the apothegms from Montaigne, the Buddha ('whatever comes together passes away'), and Heraclitus ('everything flows; nothing abides') with which I began this introduction lift any particular unexpected event or trauma away from their actual circumstances and invite the listener/reader to regard the episode as but one of a countless number of similar occasions, rendering what was painfully specific into something general and more tranquil, a typical example of perennial wisdom. Yet it is important to recall again that it is not the vicissitude which has already been denatured by the operation of rhetoric that stands to the fore here, but the thing itself, the raw shock, the sting, the unbridged loss, the rip in the fabric of hope and expectation. So in the view taken here, human beings are constantly vulnerable to accident and the unforeseen, and wield rhetoric and culture against those accidents in order to render intelligible and operable what may at first seem incomprehensible and incomprehensibly disastrous. It is not that rhetoric culture could in itself provide the skills to rebuild a house after a flood, assemble arms against another attack, or eradicate the mosquitoes which have brought the disease, but it can move oneself and others to a common understanding and a common policy, which may then lead to house building, arms assembling, or mosquito eradication.

From this point it is not difficult to move a step further, namely to see the opposition of rhetoric culture to the vicissitudes of life as a corollary of that basic trope of contemporary thought, the opposition between nature and culture (a trope so very similar to the ancient Greeks' opposition of human and natural law, *nomos* and *physis*). This basic trope is worked out in many ways, for example in the idea that the evolution of human intelligence has given human beings supposed mastery over nature, or in the inverse of this idea, that our manipulating materialism threatens both ourselves and the world we seek to manipulate. This opposition has been especially effective in setting the debate – or narrowing the mind – in the matter of 'nature vs. nurture', the supposedly contravening forces of genetic inheritance and cultural shaping as they affect human dispositions and behaviours.

The Argument(s) Carried On

My colleagues and I carry on the argument from here in the rest of the book, but let me here draw out these further lessons in brief. In the first place, these papers demonstrate the rhetorical edge of culture at all scales of human events. Jean Nienkamp, in the first chapter, makes a point which establishes one extreme of rhetoric's reach, in what she calls 'internal rhetoric', conversations and arguments that people have with themselves. The material she adduces in this case are diaries of women in precarious situations, women who are attempting to make sense of, and find a policy for, dangerous and unbalancing events. The larger point, however, is that the sense of addressivity, or of interaction, or of dialogue is not a matter just for audible or legible exchange between persons, but also for the inner argumentation through which people manage by themselves to understand their world and guide their actions. From one perspective, this stands to reason: if I can be moved or guided by others, why not by myself? But that other powerful trope of our culture, the spatial metaphor that 'private' means something happening *inside* your head, while 'public' is what happens *outside* it, makes it difficult for us to realize how pervasively interactive and dialogical we are as animals, such that conversation or debate is no respecter of the skin's boundary. This point has been powerfully prepared by Nienkamp herself (2001) and by the psychologist Michael Billig (1987).

The opposite end of rhetoric's reach, which might seem more its natural home, is the body politic, the public sphere, the realm of mediated speech, writing and performance, which is the contemporary equivalent of the public arena of the ancient world in which the explicit cultivation of rhetoric was born. The second paper concerns Germany, which, immediately after the Second World War, sought to forget or bowdlerize German deeds in the Hitler period. Carrithers shows that some Germans drew from the matrix of available stories and images a new and quite powerful narrative idea, that of an 'unmastered past', a disastrous recent history whose aftermath, if not brought fully to consciousness, would continue to infect the body politic. The idea then went on to become a keyword which oriented a broad range of investigative, juridical and commemorative public acts, aimed at unearthing and displaying for all to see the Germans' responsibility for the enormities of the Hitler era. This essay illustrates, too, another facet of the rhetoric culture idea, namely that, in applying the raw materials given by culture to new situations, the rhetorician can create new cultural forms and a new language of imagery and story.

And it also typifies a point made in all three of the first papers, namely that the creation of a narrative across events and people is one of humanity's most powerful means for interpreting chaotic events, for giving them a sense and preparing a policy, or at least an attitude, for future occasions. Stevan Weine's paper concerns the experience, and the narrating of experience, among refugees from Bosnia and Kosovo in Chicago. He suggests from his clinical experience that the effect of traumas leading to exile is 'diffuse', to use a term from W.G. Sebald, permeating experience and awareness and not deriving from any single event or perpetrator. He argues, though, that the narrative solutions, the 'talking cures', which are routinely used by clinicians to ameliorate the effects of such traumas, are not adequate, because they constrict the occasion of speaking and miss the diffuseness of both the source and the consequences. He suggests – and goes on to demonstrate – that a diffuse narrative may be just the therapeutic means to address such psychic repercussions. Taken together, these three papers display the pervasiveness of narrative as human endowment, and the effectiveness of narrative when it is applied rhetorically to orient and to move. And of course 'narrative' covers a whole genus, or perhaps better, a superfamily, of devices through which we project expectations or mend broken expectations.

Or, to put it another way, narrative is one of humanity's most common ways of linking and connecting things, in this case, linking past events to one another, to the present, and to an anticipated future. Another superfamily of connecting devices is metaphor: the linking of two different spheres of experience to throw light on one or the other, or both. The next two papers concentrate on metaphor, or perhaps better (as Robert Hariman has usefully suggested to me) metaphoric containment, the reaching into another sphere of experience to find a way of containing something threatening and out of control. Megan Biesele addresses the rhetoric of dying through comparing two rhetorical complexes around the healer. One is that of the Ju/'hoan San ('Bushmen') hunter-gatherers of the Kalahari Desert of Southern Africa, where the healer is metaphorically identified through vulnerability, as a 'little bird' beside God, a child, but also as a trickster, one who uses cunning in the face of God's compulsions, and in any case is throughout a support, and a fighter on the side of the patient, up to the last moment, up to death. In contrast the

American biomedical system stands partly alienated from the patient; and the cancer specialist, the oncologist, has come recently to be identified as one who decides on the prediction of death and then prepares people for death, encouraging them towards a 'good death' as it is understood by him: he becomes metaphorically a sort of Charon, the boatman ferrying souls to Hades. Biesele argues that, at the very least, the American rhetoric, and with it the practice, places an increasingly difficult burden on both the oncologist and the patient. The oncologist is forced both to make the judgement of death, and to prepare the patient through rhetoric to abandon hope, while the patient is shorn of both agency and hope. So, by comparison with the Ju/'hoan complex, American rhetorical demands make the process of dying harder, not easier, despite the expressly ameliorative sense of the rhetoric now attached to the healer.

In Nerlich's case, the threat faced by the rhetors was the foot and mouth disease epidemic which struck U.K. farm animals in 2001. The U.K. government hit upon the metaphor of *war*, with its rich links of stories and images, to describe their efforts to deal with the epidemic; they reinforced the aptness of this image by the large-scale (and not really necessary) slaughter and immolation of all those animals which were, or could have been, infected; and the images of a holocaust, a vast burning of sacrificial victims, became the iconic representation of the *war* idea for the British public. But as the links and associations spread from the idea of war and the practice of slaughter, another feature of rhetoric came to the fore, namely, that once let loose, rhetoric may lead to consequences unforeseen by the rhetor. In this case, the public's general affection for animals, their sympathy with the farmers whose herds were slaughtered, and their alarm at the scenes and ideas released into the public domain led from a general support for the slaughter policy to general revulsion.

So the larger lesson from these two cases is this: what is first set out as effective rhetoric can become, with the turn of events or the materialising of further links in the chain of suggestion, a new vicissitude in itself, a disaster not of physical events but of words and images, and eventually of performance. In terms of the book as a whole, this is a turning point. For the initial image, that rhetoric and culture stand on one side, and the incursions of deleterious events which must be countered on the other, must now be modified. The stuff of culture in its rhetorical use may be a fine thing, but that rhetorical edge may come to cut against the rhetor as well as for her.

The next two essays reveal another twist in the tale. 'All rhetoric is palaestral', writes Bailey. 'The metaphor of the wrestling-school is a vehicle for the rhetorical struggle to pin down another person and make him/her accept a definition of the situation.' The case set out concerns a rich man in an Italian village who makes an offer to buy a derelict shack from a poor peasant, but is rebuffed instantly with grace and consummate skill, such that no comeback is possible. This is certainly palaestral in character, a man-to-man struggle with a winner and a loser. But from this plain case two further corollaries of the rhetoric/culture perspective come to light.

First, there is what Bailey calls a 'plurality of structures' – and he is clear that these 'structures' are things of the imagination, mental materials, collective representations, fashioned of the airy matter of culture – that bear on the case. There is the 'structure', the rhetoric, of the marketplace in the offer of cash for goods, in this case 'money for old rope', as the English might say. A rhetoric of family and family obligations is part of the encounter as well. And then too a colouring of class conflict and differentiation passes over the event, as does gift-giving and its associated ideas. Each of these complexes of ideas, images and storylines, and others as well, are available to the participants, and come into play, leaving the rich man without a leg to stand on. This is a vivid, detailed and explicit demonstration of what is implicit in the other cases so far, namely that the things of culture, the ideas, figures, stories, values and schemas, are in no case unified and consistent such that a single response is deducible in a situation. There are always alternatives to an utterance, a response, an expression, a gesture. So by designating rhetoric as that which finds in culture a cutting edge for a situation, we also recognize that rhetoric is a *necessary* art, an *inescapable* art, the ability to assemble of disparate materials a more or less fitting and timely utterance, even in the most everyday of occasions. And, being an art, rhetoric may be wielded well or badly. In this case the peasant showed himself to be a master.

The other corollary is that rhetoric, in this and the other cases adduced here, seems closely related to moral evaluation. Nienkamp's diarists, the German rhetors facing the German past, the Bosnian refugees recounting their histories, Biesele's oncologists, Nerlich's government spokesmen, as well as Bailey's peasant, are all trying to put themselves, or their case, *in the right*. It is not just that people are trying to make others (or themselves) 'accept a definition of the situation', as Bailey says, though that is true enough; they are also trying to make others accept an *evaluation* of the situation, so that the rhetoric is morally compelling.

Now rhetoric is not inevitably moral in tone, since there can be rhetorics, such as the rhetoric of the market, that use other criteria, in this case utilitarian good or profit. But that rhetoric so often involves moral evaluation is a consequence of the pervasiveness of moral judgement in human life. I remarked at the beginning that humans were unique as a species in their sense of expectation, anticipation and planning. But we are unique for another reason as well, namely that we, unlike other animals, teach our offspring a *moral aesthetic* sense, that is, a sense of how to comport ourselves with others, and with it, a sense of how to judge others' comportment (Premack 1991; Carrithers 1992).

This moral pedagogy is pursued in different ways by different sets of people, but it is a universal trait of our species, affecting people from very early in their lives right through the whole life's course.

Moreover there is an affinity between our capacity for expectation and for a moral aesthetic, since we come to expect certain morally constrained behaviours from others and ourselves, and find the breach of those moral expectations a problem, a vicissitude. In Ellen Basso's essay, she shows in the first place how a rhetoric of civility, of shame, of self-constraint, of politeness – in other words, a moral aesthetic of comportment – is acquired with the acquisition of language, extending the earlier point that to learn language is to engage with rhetoric. Basso uses examples drawn from European, American, Japanese and Kalapalo (South American Amerindian) societies, and shows how, despite radically different constructions of civility, shame, or moral constraint in these different societies, all these early acquired and omnipresent rhetorics of civility lead to what Basso calls 'ordeals of language'. These are situations in which people find themselves disastrously at odds with the reigning moral aesthetic; or facing the consequences of a breach of the code; or perhaps even forced into self-inflicted silence or social exile by the internal contradictions of the moral aesthetic – since, just as with Bailey's 'structures', there is no guarantee that a moral aesthetic is internally consistent, or that the rhetoric of moral comportment may not conflict with actual situations in social life. So here again rhetorics, so powerful in defining and orienting human life against vicissitudes, may become themselves a source of vicissitude. And we can see, too, that the addressivity of rhetoric can again be aimed at oneself as well as others, and that rhetoric – speech or expression to make a movement of mind – may reach into the most intimate corners of experience.

The last two essays address the omnipresence of the rhetoric/vicissitudes pair from an altitude, finding them not in the constant everyday interpersonal intimacies of life, but in larger but no less pervasive forms of the world. In writing of the World Trade Center (WTC) and 9/11, Ralph Cintron carries on the theme of morality and rhetoric, but now with a markedly critical commentary, a moral assessment of the rhetorical and cultural currents leading to both the WTC itself, and to 9/11. He diagnoses a persistent feature, and malady, of modern life, distributed across the world but concentrated in the United States, namely the hyperbole of modern culture, the constant straining for the newer, the larger, the better. Invention has become, he argues, a value in itself, an ideology. It is a *doxa* which governs public life but reaches into our homes and our dreams. The Twin Towers were spectacular evidence of a rhetorical achievement by the builders, who overcame resistance to their building by making the towers ever bigger and ever newer. But by becoming the visible testimony of our urge for the giant and for tomorrow's creations, they also became the target of those who, reading our modernity in their own way, recognized that their gigantic destruction of the towers, and of the lives in them, would address the world, and ourselves, just as effectively as the Twin Towers themselves, though with a very different message. Cintron notes, too, that the hyperbole of this hypermodernism hardly stopped with that destruction, but went on to the 'shock and awe' of the Iraq war, with its monumental rhetoric, its monumentally clever technology, and its monumental destruction in turn.

This brings us to a point close to Biesele's critical evaluation of a rhetoric, and suggests that we, the scholars and readers, are entangled as well in such rhetoric and its moral evaluation. In fact a keener eye would see that some moral stance has been involved in all the essays here. And I think the logic is this: just as Cintron's treatment of the Twin Towers and 9/11 would hardly be credible, or likely, or indeed possible, without some comment on the comportment of those who built them and those who destroyed them, so the same observation applies, if with less immediacy, to our other cases. And the underlying reason is, again, addressivity. As scholars and researchers of the human world, those we discuss here in print are still addressed by us, partly as one addresses an issue, i.e. turns one's attention to it, but also as one addresses a person, even though they appear here in the third person and not the second. For by writing of them we are comporting ourselves towards them, and any comportment between members of our species is, from the ground up, always already moral in its implications. None of this, either our subjects' ordeals or our own reflections, is pre-programmed or deducible, for no rhetoric which guides action is the only one possible. So it is appropriate, both as regards our third-person subjects, ourselves and our readers, to speak of the *moral imagination*. Just as our subjects are forced, in the course of events, to find a rhetoric which fits from among those possibilities presented to their imaginations, we must likewise imagine any rhetoric, and any action, as existing among an array of other possibilities and other evaluations. We have no choice, for that is our situation.

So it is fitting to end with Fernandez's essay on the moral imagination, which looks across both our globe of moral rhetorical struggles, and our world of scholarship which seeks to interpret those struggles. 'Moral', he notes, derives from *mos*, 'a way of comporting oneself', and he goes on to speak of the 'complexities and contrarieties of comportment' which need to be 'figured out' (in the rhetorical sense of the word 'figure' as in 'figure of speech') as *aides-pensées* and as actual guides to comportment. So Fernandez begins his observation of the contradictions among the airy structures within each of our many cultures, and of the necessity of rhetoric to assemble, from among the possibilities available, some way of thinking, speaking and acting in a timely and appropriate manner in the face of vicissitudes. On this basis he then surveys some of the ways in which scholars have recently addressed the moral rhetorical imagination, and suggests that these scholars' views themselves are entangled in challenges to the moral imagination, especially as they arise not in a vacuum, but in particular historical existential circumstances that press on them particular vicissitudes and exigencies. In this perspective the vicissitudes that crowd in on all of us may be far from evanescent, but may in fact irrupt into our worlds and our expectations with endurance and longevity, forcing us again and again to try to restore our moral expectations with timely and energetic rhetoric.

References

Billig, M. 1987. *Arguing and Thinking: A Rhetorical Approach to Social Psychology.* Cambridge: Cambridge University Press.
Burke, Kenneth. 1966. 'Terministic Screens,' In *Language as Symbolic Action.* Berkeley: University of California Press.
Carrithers, M. 1992. *Why Humans Have Cultures: Explaining Anthropology and Social Diversity.* Oxford: Oxford University Press.
Nienkamp, Jean. 2001. *Internal Rhetorics: Towards a History and Theory of Self-Persuasion.* Carbondale and Edwardsville: University of Southern Illinois Press.
Premack, D. 1991. 'The Aesthetic Basis of Pedagogy.' In *Cognition and the Symbolic Processes: Applied and Ecological Perspectives,* ed. R.R. Hoffman. Hillsdale, NJ: Lawrence Erlbaum Associates.

CHAPTER 1

INTERNAL RHETORICS
CONSTITUTING SELVES IN DIARIES AND BEYOND

Jean Nienkamp

■ ■ ■ ■ ■ ■

WHAT IS INTERNAL RHETORIC?

Internal rhetoric is my term for the way that we persuade ourselves – talking ourselves into (or out of) things, arguing with ourselves, berating ourselves. It is taken for granted in common parlance, but little studied in academia. Such self-talk is rhetorical insofar as it affects our actions, attitudes or beliefs, consciously or unconsciously. I thus coin the term 'internal rhetoric' as a deliberate 'terministic screen'[1]: to call attention to the persuasive or rhetorical nature of much of our thought.

The ways that we consciously talk to ourselves mentioned above are often deliberately cultivated to affect our actions, attitudes and beliefs in culturally and personally acceptable ways.[2] There are even professions whose purpose is guiding the internal rhetoric of others, including those of coaches, therapists, educators and the clergy. Such culturally endorsed self-talk has been compared to public rhetoric over the course of Western rhetorical history. Thus, rhetoricians as diverse as Isocrates (fourth-century BCE Athens) and Richard Whately (nineteenth-century Britain) defend the teaching and practice of public rhetoric as being the same thing as wise people do in their own heads. Francis Bacon's discussion of rhetoric in *The Advancement of Learning* (1605) is fundamentally about internal rhetoric, and makes a cogent argument that the only way people can act ethically is to consciously practise internal rhetoric. Since most of this history predates the recognition of the subconscious mind, discussions of self-talk are focused on internal rhetoric that people deliberately engage in, although there are also discussions of the suasive nature of the emotions that are not under conscious control. Thus, one end of the spectrum of internal rhetoric might be called cultivated internal rhetoric, insofar as it is a learned and deliberately cultivated practice of intentional self-persuasion towards a desired end.[3]

At the other end of the spectrum of intentionality is the deeply subconscious mental activity that I call primary internal rhetoric. Much, perhaps most, of our internal rhetoric is unconscious – hortatory mindsets internalized from the 'thou shalts' and 'thou shalt nots' we have heard from our youngest age. Unconscious or primary internal rhetoric correlates to contemporary definitions of rhetoric that stress the diffusive nature of much cultural rhetoric, as opposed to the conscious manipulation of language by a single orator:

> Rhetorical studies are properly concerned with the process by which symbols and systems of symbols have influence on beliefs, values, attitudes, and actions, and they embrace all forms of human communication, not exclusively public address nor communication within any one class or cultural group. (Bitzer and Black 1971: 208)

Primary internal rhetoric, then, focuses on the influencive nature of language and symbols that have been internalized without our awareness. A study of internal rhetoric attempts to peer into the 'black box' that rhetoricians have allowed to escape analysis with our bifurcated concerns of person as rhetor/language user and person as audience/language recipient. It allows us to see that people are 'complex agents that take in cultural and direct rhetorics; reject, manipulate, or swallow them whole; and re-create or respond to them in personal utterances and actions, intentional or not' (Nienkamp 2001: 4).

This distinction between cultivated and primary forms of internal rhetoric is not intended to indicate a sharp delineation between the two. Internal rhetoric ranges along an entire spectrum of being deliberate and deliberately cultivated to being unconscious, so deep in our psyches that we are not aware of the powerful influence that enculturated inner voices have on us.[4] Thus, Kenneth Burke extends his 'range of rhetoric' to reflect this variability of levels of intent:

> There is a wide range of ways whereby the rhetorical motive, through the resources of identification, can operate without conscious direction by any particular agent. ... One can systematically extend the range of rhetoric, if one studies the persuasiveness of false or inadequate terms which may not be directly imposed upon us from without by some skillful speaker, but which we impose upon ourselves, in varying degrees of deliberateness and unaware-

ness, through motives indeterminately self-protective and/or suicidal. (1969 [1950]: 35)

Burke thus argues that the distinction between cultivated, conscious internal rhetoric and primary, subconscious internal rhetoric is a matter of degree rather than opposition: internal rhetoric occurs along a continuum from the most deliberate acts of self-encouragement or – chastisement to the most deeply buried exhortations that form our very selves.

If internal rhetoric encompasses such a broad range of mental activity, why is it a useful terministic screen? First, it gives us the tools of the entire history of rhetorical theory with which to describe and analyse mental and ideological phenomena. From Aristotle's distinction among *ēthos, logos* and *pathos* to Perelman and Olbrechts-Tyteca's analysis of the 'universal audience' and hierarchies of value, rhetorical theories explicate how language and other symbol systems affect human beings. Again I return to Kenneth Burke's concept of a 'terministic screen': 'Even if any given terminology is a *reflection* of reality, by its very nature as a terminology it must also be a *selection* of reality; and to this extent it must function also as a *deflection* of reality' (1966: 45). Rhetorical theory, as a body of terministic screens, allows us to understand the extent to which internalized language use affects our attitudes, beliefs and actions – constructs our very selves, in essence. I do not, as Burke does with his dramatistic screen, posit that a rhetorical terministic screen supersedes others; rather, I argue that its purpose is to highlight a particular function of internalized language – the rhetorical – among the many other functions language accomplishes.

What is interesting is that once you have this terministic screen, you start seeing internal rhetoric everywhere – not just in contemporary culture, but in historical accounts from ancient times to the present. Literary accounts might not be considered the best evidence for a psychological phenomenon, but when Ernest Hemingway has Robert Jordan think: 'Listen, he told himself. You better cut this out. This is very bad for you and your work. Then himself said back to him, You listen, see? Because you are doing something very serious and I have to see you understand it all the time' (1940: 265), is there anyone who cannot recognize from personal experience the feeling of debating with oneself, the feeling of having two or more 'selves' at odds with each other?

Internal Rhetoric and the Constitution of Selves

The psychological effect of these continuously internalized and interacting discourses is the rhetorical self, a colloquy of voices that interact 'rhetorically to adapt attitudes and behaviour to personal, cultural, and environmental demands' (Nienkamp 2001: 126). These voices are not strictly verbal, but are rich mental representations of the ideologies, subjectivities, roles and expectations that we have been subjected to and have internalized, adjusted and assumed. George Herbert Mead calls these internalized representations of the attitudes of others the 'me', which is what creates self-consciousness (1934: 175). While Mead did not call these internalized social attitudes 'rhetorical', it is easy to see the rhetorical force of the internalized language he discusses: 'What goes to make up the organized self is the organization of attitudes which are common to the group. ... [Common responses] give him what we term his principles, the acknowledged attitudes of all members of the community toward what are the values of that community' (1934: 162). Values, attitudes – these are the stuff of rhetoric, and thus the substance of the thoroughly rhetorical 'self' described by Mead.

What the theory of internal rhetoric adds to this concept of the rhetorical self is the dynamics of that self as a *product* of internal rhetoric continuously in *process*. Acting as what Burke calls a 'parliamentary wrangle' (1969 [1950]: 38), the rhetorical self is not a static entity, but is constantly negotiating among its constituent voices in order to respond to exigencies in the personal and socio-historical environment. Moreover, new voices are internalized as a person matures and encounters new situations and role expectations: thus, a child adds to early gender and familial voices (son, niece, grandchild) those of playmate, student, ethnicity, nationality, etc. Adults assume additional professional, civic and familial roles, but the earlier voices are not erased with the assumption of new voices. There is no continuous, overarching monitor that eliminates obsolete voices and makes new voices dominate ('You're no longer a child! Quit needing parental approval!'). For this reason, 'the primary internal rhetoric that shapes the rhetorical self is typically a conservative mechanism, adhering most to the most deeply ingrained voices and often taking years (if ever) to internalize or adhere to new voices that are called forth when people enter new social situations or discourses' (Nienkamp 2001: 129). The rhetorical self, then, exists in a state of tentative equilibrium, changing according to the different personal exigencies, roles, social discourses and cultural situations people are exposed to throughout their lives. What we experience as a continuous self is the 'result of the ongoing primary internal rhetoric that negotiates "normality" among voices acquired at and persisting through various times in our lives' (Nienkamp 2001: 130).

Internal Rhetoric and Diaries

One way of accessing internal rhetoric and the shaping of the rhetorical self without the use of introspection is to look at private diaries. I am not arguing that diaries represent the exact moment when societal discourses interact with the experientially shaped individual psyche to produce internal rhetoric and the rhetorical self. I do argue, however, that a good place to look for textual traces of internal rhetoric is in diaries, where experiences are sifted through, selected, and translated into words – whether for a public or private audience, whether by a professional writer or a frontier woman. Although most of the work of internalizing and reshaping cultural rhetorics takes place subconsciously, private diaries provide a venue for their authors to work out areas of problematic discourse.

An explanation of when the work of self-construction needs to rise to a level that is conscious enough to be revealed in diaries parallels the work of Lev Vygotsky, the Russian social psychologist. Vygotsky, in studying the development of inner speech from the egocentric speech of children, found that they engaged in egocentric speech twice as often when an element of difficulty was introduced into children's activities (Wertsch 1985: 116). This finding supported Vygotsky's argument that 'the function of egocentric speech is to plan and regulate human action' (Wertsch 1985: 116). What this suggests about the rhetorical function of diaries for their authors is that we see the working out of problematic internal and social rhetorics, the testing and application of events in the authors' daily lives against the selves they inhabit or aspire to inhabit.

In the following sections, I look at two diaries, written at very different points in American and European history. First, I argue that the diary of Martha 'Patty' Rogers, kept in 1785 in Exeter, New Hampshire, serves as a venue in which she can insert her experiences into a social context and thus understand them better. Secondly, I examine Anne Frank's famous diary (1942–44), which presents a much more intense example of the diary as a venue for both internal rhetoric and self-construction. What binds these diaries together is that each author experiences discord between their situations or society and their internal voices and expectations – discord that must be negotiated through in their diaries. In rhetorically working through these clashes between self and other, the diarists also construct the meanings of themselves and their societies.

Patty Rogers and the Social Orientation of Experience

Martha 'Patty' Rogers (1761–1840) was the youngest daughter of a 'New Light' minister and follower of George Whitefield, Reverend Daniel Rogers of the Second Church in Exeter, New Hampshire. In her 1785 diary, she uses two seemingly incongruous social rhetorics with which to understand her life: New Light religion and romance novels. What joins the two is the importance and fomenting of the proper emotions, anticipating Richard Whately's prescription for internally directed *pathos*: 'Not only in the case of Religion, but in many others also, a man will often wonder at, and be rather ashamed of, the coldness and languor of his own feelings, compared with what the occasion calls for:

and even makes efforts to rouse in himself such emotions as he is conscious his reason would approve' (1963 [1828]: 181). Often on Sundays, Rogers writes of the state of her soul: 'Sunday–March 27th ... read and wrote & had a peaceful day – O! may all my days be Tranquil! – may each morning see me devoting my all to that Being by whom I am supported!'; 'Sunday – April 17th – fine day – felt unhappy to be so long from meeting – Wished to spend my time profitably – but O! the coldness of my heart! the want of love to Christ!' In these, she judges her emotional states by the expectations of her father's church, which practised a particularly emotion-laden form of evangelicalism. Emotions are not value-neutral; rather, they are indices for the state of Rogers' soul.

The most prevalent social rhetoric that Rogers uses in the diary to understand her experiences, though, is that of romance novels. It may seem odd to consider the language of romance novels a discourse that might seriously be internalized by their readers, but this was precisely the fear of the many writers – including novelists – who inveighed against novel reading in eighteenth-century America. For example, the prefatory letter to the novel *Female Quixotism* characterizes the book as 'a true uncoloured history of a romantic country girl, whose head had been turned by the unrestrained perusal of Novels and Romances' (Tenney 1992 [1801]: 3). Rogers names only two novels that she is reading over the course of the diary, *The History of the Human Heart* and *Yorick's Sentimental Journey*, but she frequently mentions reading and it is evident that novels are not only passed among friends but used as an effective means of courting: 'Read in a sweet novel the D—r brought me. it affected me so, I could hardly read it, and was often obliged to drop the Book to suppress my greif!' (10 January 1785).

That Rogers constructs herself as a romance heroine, or at least using the language available to her in romance discourses, is evident in many of the diary entries. For example, she records her current emotional state in very flowery language: 'I now at this moment feel every tender emotion arising in my Bosom!' (7 January 1785). Her recording of emotion is not purely descriptive, but often intentionally self-persuasive:

> But take care little fond foolish Heart remember the pain – the keen tortures which recently sunk the[e] to the depths of malancholy /^{5} drive from thee thy too great susceptibility! Shut every avenue which lays open the tender mind to soft distress! – My heart felt the gentle tho well-timed caution & assured me by its peaceful steady Vibration its fidelity to its owner. (2 October 1785)

Rogers' entries about her emotional states thus not only record the experience of emotion, but also reinforce and foster emotions that she feels are appropriate to a given situation. She also writes about her responses to reading letters from a man she loves who is engaged to another woman: 'Break asunder the seal of my private papers & with feelings most exquisitely <u>tender</u> perused <u>his</u> [letters] & <u>mine</u> / shed a torrent of tears at <u>reperusal of my past struggles</u> – found it almost <u>too</u> much for me! Spent the evening in tears – O! why was I thus <u>attached</u> to <u>one</u> who was <u>never designed</u> for me?' (12 March 1785). The tender feelings or heart, torrents of tears, and fetishization of letters are all characteristic of romance sentimentality, the dominant rhetoric available to Rogers to express heightened emotions.

Romance discourse does not always provide a rhetoric that Rogers is comfortable applying to the events in her life, however. At times, the roles offered by the romance discourse do not correspond to Rogers' understanding of the events in her life, and she struggles to understand her own story in the terms offered by her society. One example of such a mismatch is found in her entry on 4 August 1785:

> In the course of the evening he took some liberties that would not have been <u>strictly decent</u> had they come to light – It gave me <u>pain</u> – Surely thought I he must have mistaken my Charicter – Dont you <u>hate</u> me said I? ... If I <u>Conduct</u> well no doubt I shall meet with Civil treatment! – 'If I had tried to get your heart, I should think I treated you Ill' *Well thinks I <u>what does all this mean</u>? If I had tried to get your heart – what then, you could not thought I – & the method of gaining a heart could not be treating me Ill – It must be with <u>tenderness</u> & <u>attention</u> that hearts are gained – I suppose he thought he could easily make a conquest of mine, & then <u>torment</u> me with <u>neglect</u> & <u>coldness</u> – But <u>thank fortune</u> my <u>heart fears no such assaults</u>!* (emphasis added)

'Philammon's'[6] (Dr Samuel Tenney's) behaviour does not fit with her sentimental ideology, in which the heroines are treated with respect by their suitors. Her initial reaction, then, is questioning the significance of Philammon's actions and comment, and a rehearsal of what the approved behaviour should be. She then reaffirms her own planned behaviour and emotions: '... *Well, Ill not go an <u>inch</u> out of my way see him or not for I am detirmind no person shall have one <u>corner</u> of my heart till they <u>surrender the whole of theirs</u> to me–*' (emphasis added). This is the selfhood dictated to women by romance novels, a defensive passivity in love that seems incompatible with the acute sensibility required at all other times. Again, she is intentionally bolstering the emotions that her society tells her – and that she therefore feels – are appropriate to the situation. But whatever Rogers' resolution, it does not seem to help her much in the current crisis. She continues:

> ... he put his hand on my Bosom, I with <u>avidity</u> attempted to snatch it away but found he was too strong for me. so I came to <u>entreaties</u> / one good argument P—y for taking of it, & it shall be amcaditaly[?] done – & a great <u>peice</u> of <u>immodesty</u> Sir – he took it away, and said no, not between two friends. ...

you did not think I could dare to put my hand here puting it on my handkercheif – no to besure not! ... We chatted familiarly on a few matters afterwards, & parted – *now I intend to see who will throw themselves in the way first & shall esteem him if I don't never see him again – Our conversation I think for friends was a little <u>misterious</u> – here matters rest.* (emphasis added)

The sections I emphasize are her commentary on the conversation she is recording; she attempts to critique Philammon's behaviour through the normative discourse of the sentimental novel and ends up calling the situation 'mysterious'.

But she has an explanation available to her, one that she offers immediately to Philammon – that she must have done something to invite his crude advances. In the discourse of sentimental novels, there is no sexual abuse or harassment – twentieth-century terms, of course – without the complicity of the woman involved. So, while she is clearly angry with him, she begins to internalize guilt for the situation by assuming that she must have 'thrown herself in his way'. Two days later, the guilt has outlived the anger: 'Philammon was bobing about my foolish heart all day – I was afraid I had offend him' (6 August 1785). In our cultural milieu, we might argue that Philammon was taking advantage of her father's illness and brothers' absence to abuse a defenceless woman, but all of the social discourses available to Rogers told her she was at fault – not just the romance discourse, but other religious and social discourses told her that 'good girls' did not get treated this way. Rogers cannot assume to herself an identity as anything other than a 'good girl', so she attributes his behaviour to some unconscious actions on her part that must have misled him.

This, then, is one of the rhetorical functions that diaries serve: they are a forum in which their authors can narrativize their experiences and thus shift them from poorly understood events to fully articulated and encultured narratives. Such an extended narrativizing takes place when a clash occurs between the author's sense of self – in this case, a self that is reinforced by multiple discourses in her life – and an event that takes place in her life. Not all such clashes are so easily resolved, however. Rogers' life, post-American Revolution, is in a relatively stable society with stable role expectations for women, despite the possibilities foreseen by Abigail Adams. In the case of Anne Frank, clashes between outside events and her developing sense of self only intensified as the diary progressed, and it is here that we see the intense internal rhetoric out of which the rhetorical self is shaped.

Anne Frank and the Rhetorical Construction of the Self

Anne Frank needs little introduction, since her diary has been in print since its initial publication in 1947 by her father, Otto Frank. The Franks, originally from Frankfurt, Germany, were living in Amsterdam when Nazi Germany invaded the Netherlands in 1940. Persecution of Jews began immediately, with increasing restrictions on their activities over the next two years.[7] The requirement that they wear a yellow Star of David was passed on 3 May 1942: 'The fate of the Jews in the Netherlands is now sealed, for, as the historian Jacob Presser would write, it "marked them out for slaughter"' (Lee 2003 [2002]: 330). The first deportations began in July of that year, and Anne Frank's older sister Margot was among the first group called up to go (Lee 2003 [2002]. 96). Otto Frank had already begun preparing a hiding place for his family in an annexe to his spice business, and they moved there on 6 July 1942. The final entry of Anne Frank's diary was dated 1 August 1944[8]; the Gestapo raided the annexe on 4 August 1944 and all of its inhabitants except for Otto would subsequently die in Nazi concentration camps. Miep Gies, a former employee of Otto's who had been helping the Franks during their period of hiding, found Anne's diary notebooks and loose pages scattered around the annexe after the raid and saved them in a desk drawer for the return of the family.

Anne Frank had received her first diary as a present for her thirteenth birthday on 12 June 1942. While the increasingly grim situation for Jews is described in the diary (20 June 1942), her early, pre-hiding entries are primarily gossip about school and friends, often elaborated with recorded conversations and characterizations of the people she's writing about. The nature of the entries changes once the family goes into hiding, as the pressures of living in a small annexe with seven other people during critical developmental years shape Frank's internal rhetoric and rhetorical self. In the following, I analyse Frank's responses to the discourses that attempt to shape her and argue that the clash between these discourses and the growing sense she has of herself as different from them gives her a larger, adult sense of self with a purpose in the world.

Even before the Franks go to the annexe, Anne's diary evinces a couple of identities that become complicated as she develops over the course of the diary. Most of the pre-annexe diary entries are breezy descriptions of her friends, flirtations with boys, and getting into trouble at school for being a 'chatterbox' (21 June 1942). These entries accord with her father's later descriptions of her as "'always gay, always popular with boys and girls ... she was ebullient – and difficult'" (quoted in Lee 1999: 32). What was challenging for her parents was channelling all this energy productively and disciplining Anne without crushing her spirit.[9]

At the same time, Frank was growing up Jewish in a Europe increasingly dominated by Nazi Germany, and while the Franks tried to give Margot and Anne as normal and happy an upbringing as they could, it was inevitable that the girls were somewhat aware of the political situation in which they found themselves. By the time the diary starts, the Jews in the Netherlands had already had two years of increasing restrictions on their behaviour, reflected in a remarkable diary entry that Frank writes when she is thirteen years old. It includes thirteen statements beginning with the phrase 'Jews were forbidden to' or 'Jews were required to' – e.g., 'Jews were required to wear a yellow star; Jews were required to turn in their bicycles; Jews were forbidden to use streetcars; Jews were forbidden to ride in cars, even their own ...' – an anaphoric tour de force that underlines vividly how 'our freedom was restricted by a series of anti-Jewish decrees' (20 June 1942).[10] So despite the apparent normality and happiness of her childhood, she had had this threat hanging over her virtually her entire life, and it is perhaps a testament to the strength of her parents that she had grown up so far to be as happy a person as she had been.

Frank's confinement in the 'Hidden Annexe' did not shield her from the cultural rhetoric around her various identities as being Jewish, adolescent and female; rather, they concentrated those discourses to a sometimes almost unbearable degree. Frank's identity as a Jew does not come into question in the diary: she agonizes about the treatment of Jews she hears about outside of the annexe and realizes that her Jewish identity excludes other possible identities: 'Fine specimens of humanity, those Germans, and to think I'm actually one of them! No, that's not true, Hitler took away our nationality long ago. And besides, there are no greater enemies on earth than the Germans and the Jews' (9 October 1942). As the German pressure on the Jews and the Dutch increase over the two years covered by the diary and the Franks hear about increasing anti-Semitism among the Dutch people, Frank becomes more defensive about the Jews, calling them 'the most oppressed, unfortunate and pitiable people in all the world' (22 May 1944). She hopes that she will be able to combine her Jewish identity with a Dutch nationality, but hopes and fears chase each other in tight circles in such a tense situation.

Of more immediate daily presence to Frank are the identities thrust on her by the others in the annexe. Under constant threat of exposure and death, being the youngest and liveliest among the annexe's occupants and therefore taking the brunt of five adults' conflicting orders and priorities, it is no surprise that relief from the emotional pressures of confinement is a major rhetorical use of the diary for Frank. Thus she writes,

> So many things bubble up inside me, as I lie in bed, having to put up with people I'm fed up with, who always misinterpret my intentions. That's why recently I've always come back to my diary. That is where I start and finish, because Kitty[11] is always patient, I'll promise her that I shall persevere, in spite of everything, and find my own way through it all, and swallow my tears. (7 November 1942)

What evidence, then, does the diary give us about the identities assumed by Frank in her life in the annexe?

Frank's identity as a family member is a source of both frustration and solidarity. She complains about not being able to understand her mother and sister, and about not being understood by them. She feels closest to her father, at one point commenting, 'he understands me perfectly, and I wish we could have a heart-to-heart talk sometime without my bursting instantly into tears' (28 September 1942). As she matures, she is less satisfied with her father's understanding:

> He always talked to me as if I were a child going through a difficult phase. It sounds crazy, since Father's the only one who's given me a sense of confidence and made me feel as if I'm a sensible person. But he overlooked one thing: he failed to see that this struggle to triumph over my difficulties was more important to me than anything else. I didn't want to hear about 'typical adolescent problems', or 'other girls', or 'you'll grow out of it'. I didn't want to be treated the same as all-the-other-girls, but as Anne-in-her-own-right, and Pim didn't understand that. (15 July 1944)

Between these poles of emotional identification and division, Frank has the typical adolescent process of individuation from the family – so intensely and personally felt by each teenager experiencing it – intensified further by the pressured confines and danger of their situation.

In relation to the van Daans, Frank shows her familial loyalties by taking her mother's part against what she sees as the selfishness of Mrs van Daan: 'Mrs van Daan is sulking. She's very moody and has been removing more and more of her belongings and locking them up. It's too bad Mother doesn't repay every van Daan "disappearing act" with a Frank "disappearing act"' (27 September 1942). She also appreciates her parents taking her part against the criticisms of the van Daans: 'Father and Mother always defend me fiercely' (27 September 1942). By her own account and that of her father and biographer, Frank's upbringing was quite progressive: she attended a Montessori school before being forced into a Jewish school, and her father wrote a letter to her in which he reminded her that '"I have often told you that you must educate yourself. We have agreed the 'controls' with each other and you yourself are doing a great deal to swallow the 'buts.' ... But the main thing is to reflect a little bit and then to find one's way back to the right path"' (quoted in Lee 1999: 44–45; also Frank 2003: 211). Mrs van Daan, however, considers Anne spoiled: '"you should have been at our house, where children were brought up the way they should be ... If Anne were my daughter..."' (27 September 1942). Not only is this a criticism of Anne, however, it is a criticism of her parents, and Frank triumphantly reports, 'a silence fell after Mrs van Daan finished her little speech. Father then replied, "I think Anne is very well brought up."... Mrs van D. was soundly defeated' (27 September 1942). So in the early part of the diary especially, we get a picture of two families thrown into uncomfortable proximity, struggling to find their boundaries – largely on the back of the youngest inhabitant of the annexe.

Frank also writes about her growing sense of womanhood over the course of the diary. Early on, we see her approvingly quoting her mother's defence of Margot, her older sister, reading adult books: '"To begin with, Margot's a girl, and girls are always more mature than boys. Second, she's already read many serious books and doesn't go looking for those which are no longer forbidden. Third, Margot's much more sensible and intellectually advanced"' (2 September 1942). Later, Frank associates her desire to write professionally as a journalist with the desire to go beyond traditional women's roles:

> If I don't have the talent to write books or newspaper articles, I can always write for myself. But I want to achieve more than that. I can't imagine having to live like Mother, Mrs van Daan, and all the women who go about their work and are then forgotten. I need to have something besides a husband and children to devote myself to! (5 April 1944)

Frank does not necessarily (or always) see herself as exceptional, though; she also writes about women's rights in general, exclaiming with approval that 'Modern women want the right to be completely independent!' (13 June 1944). By the end of the diary, she clearly perceives herself to be a woman: 'Let me be myself and then I am satisfied. I know that I'm a woman, a woman with inward strength and plenty of courage!' (9 April 1944).

Frank also sees herself as a writer, not only of the diary but also of short stories and 'fairy tales' over the course of their confinement in the annexe. After hearing Gerrit Bolkestein, the Dutch Minister of Education, Art and Science call for '"ordinary documents"' such as '"diaries"' to enable '"our struggle for freedom [to] be painted in its full depth and glory"' (quoted in Frank 2003: 59), Frank began to revise her diary for possible publication after the war. Although she recognizes the possibility that she may never actually write for publication, that is certainly not her plan, and she is clearly serious about her writing: 'I am the best and sharpest critic of my own work. I know myself what is and what is not well written' (5 April 1944). Frank sees her goal in writing 'to be useful or give pleasure to the people around me yet who don't really know me', as well as 'to go on living even after my death!' (25 March 1944). Beyond what Frank says about being a writer, though, the diary itself is testament to her identity as a writer, with its long, thoughtful entries and often eloquent writing.

A related self that the diary brings out is Frank's reflective self, the one that comments on her own feelings and behaviour throughout her discussions of other events and conversations. Early in the diary she's worried that she may be a bit too reflective: 'So far I have put almost nothing in my diary other than thoughts and have never got round to nice stories I might read out loud one day. But from now on I shan't be so sentimental or a bit less and keep closer to reality' (28 September 1942). But that doubt is soon overcome by the usefulness of having the diary in which to express both her moods – 'my head is haunted by so many wishes and thoughts, accusations and reproaches' – and her ongoing attempts to mould herself into the person she wanted to be – 'I know my own faults and shortcomings better than anyone else does, but the difference is that I also know that I want to improve, shall improve and have already improved a great deal!' (13 June 1944). As the tedium and tension of being in hiding wear on, the 'nice stories' become less important than the personal development Frank is undergoing over the course of the diary.

Finally, by the end of the diary, two dominant selves emerge, reminiscent of the two selves evident at the beginning of the diary. Her outward self 'contains [her] exuberant cheerfulness, [her] flippancy, [her] joy in life, and, above all, [her] ability to appreciate the lighter side of things' (1 August 1944). Frank characterizes this self as 'a mere diversion, a comic interlude, something that is soon forgotten'; 'the "lighthearted" Anne'; 'the happy-go-lucky Anne'; and, finally – 'the bad part' (1 August 1944). This final entry of the diary is a poignant and perceptive explanation of why Frank is such a 'bundle of contradictions' (21 July 1944; 1 August 1944) that supports her earlier characterization of herself as having 'a great deal of self-knowledge' (15 July 1944). She acknowledges that one meaning of 'contradiction' is 'not accepting other people's opinions, always knowing best, having the last word; in short, all those unpleasant traits for which I'm known' (1 August 1944).

The other self that Frank owns to in this passage is less fully articulated, perhaps because more deeply felt. This is the 'purer, deeper and finer' side of her that she does not show to anyone else, 'Anne's better side' (1 August 1944). Frank sees these two selves as polar opposites in terms of their *ēthos*: the lighthearted Anne is used to being 'on stage' and not taken seriously by other people; Anne's better side is 'too weak' to allow herself to be laughed at by others, and so appears only in solitude. Clearly, the light-hearted Anne is a protective self developed by Anne to allow the growth of the private, 'finer' self:

> If I'm quiet and serious, everyone thinks I'm putting on a new act and I have to save myself with a joke, and then I'm not even talking about my own family, who assume I must be sick, stuff me with aspirins and sedatives, feel my neck and forehead to see if I have a temperature, ask about my bowel movements and berate me for being in a bad mood, until I just can't keep it up any more, because when everybody starts hovering over me, I get cross, then sad, and finally end up turning my heart inside out, the bad part on the outside

and the good part on the inside, and keep trying to find a way to be what I could be if ... if only there were no other people in the world. Yours, Anne M. Frank (1 August 1944; end of diary)

This finer, deeper self can be identified with the reflective self discussed above. The diary is Frank's venue for the development of this self in a place where there are 'no other people'; while at times this results in unfair judgements of others, Frank notes that she is her own worst critic: 'I scold and curse myself much more than anyone else does. ... Sometimes I'm so deeply buried under self-reproaches that I long for a word of comfort to help me dig myself out again' (13 June 1944).

What happens in the annexe, then, is that to some extent the adults want her to keep this identity at the same time that the pressures of the situation in both the larger society and inside the annexe were forcing her to grow up much faster than she normally would have done had she been growing up in a normal situation. And Frank herself felt an increasing split between the carefree girl she had been and that the adults wanted her to remain and the budding woman that she herself felt was arising out of her situation. In working through that split, Frank does not necessarily seek to narrativize her experience within the dominant cultural discourses offered her, but to hold to an alternative discourse. This alternative is still offered by her readings and other cultural messages she receives, but it allows her an identification with ideals and goals that overreach the stifling confines of the annexe.

Conclusion

These brief readings have barely scratched the surface of the rich and complex internal rhetoric of the two diaries discussed. What I have tried to show, however, is the role that diary rhetoric has in helping their authors inscribe and accommodate themselves to their cultural milieux. Patty Rogers uses her diary, in part, to understand experiences in her life by enculturating them into accepted narratives. Anne Frank, confronted with a more bewildering array of cultural expectations as well as a grim personal and sociohistorical situation, uses her diary to write her way beyond that situation into a longer-term, independent identity. Regardless of whether the 'longer-term' actually came about for Frank, which in fact it did not, the diary still provided the rhetorical space for its construction, and thus it served a critical function for its author through the process of its being written.

Diaries, then, constitute a valuable quarry for mining traces of internal rhetoric from people and cultures of the past. They allow us to look inside the tangled web of discourse reception and production to see how people transform or replicate the cultural rhetorics to which they are exposed. Analyses of the internal rhetoric found in diaries can be combined with analyses of concurrent cultural and political rhetorics to get a fuller picture of how internal and external rhetorics are produced, received and embodied in a particular sociohistorical moment. As scholars of the intersection of rhetoric and culture, we are in these diarists' debt, because it is through their creative transformation of their cultures within their diaries that we can see meaning in the larger structures of their lives.

Notes

1. Burke describes terministic screens as follows: 'any nomenclature necessarily directs the attention into some channels rather than others' (1966: 45). Thus, the terminology surrounding internal rhetoric 'directs the attention' towards the rhetorical nature of much of our thought.
2. Nienkamp (2001) Chapters 1 and 2, develops this history of internal rhetoric further.
3. Michel Foucault calls such cultivated internal rhetoric 'techniques of the self'; 'which is to say, the procedures, which no doubt exist in every civilization, suggested or prescribed to individuals in order to determine their identity, maintain it, or transform it in terms of a certain number of ends, through relations of self-mastery or self-knowledge' (1997: 87). He considers such techniques the methods by which subjectivity is established in any given society.
4. What I am calling voices, James Paul Gee calls 'Discourses', which he characterizes as 'amalgam[s] of ways of acting, interacting, talking, valuing, and thinking, with associated objects, settings, and events, which are characteristic of people whose social practice[s] they are' (1992: 91). Gee argues that 'each of us is a member of many Discourses', and further that 'each discourse incorporates a usually taken for granted and tacit "theory" of what counts as a "normal" person and the "right" way to think, feel, and behave' (1996: ix).
5. Slashes (/) in quotations from Rogers' diaries indicate line breaks that coincide with the unpunctuated end of a thought. Underlines and spelling are original.
6. One of the characteristics of romance literature that Rogers imitates is to give the men she is interested in pastoral pseudonyms.
7. I am taking this sketch of events in Nazi-occupied Netherlands from Lee's 'Chronology of the Jewish Persecution in the Netherlands' ([2003]: 32–38).
8. I refer to Frank's diary entries by date only, so readers can refer to passages regardless of what edition they consult. I use both the 1995 'Definitive Edition' and the 2003 'Revised Critical Edition'.
9. For a more thorough discussion of the relationship between Anne and her parents, see Lee (2003 [2002]: 60–61).
10. Reflecting the relatively sheltered perspective of a thirteen-year-old, all of the restrictions she lists are ones that would overtly affect her life, and do not include business restrictions that resulted in the desperate machinations her father was taking to try to keep his business out of the hands of the Nazis. She does realize that her father is being excluded from his business, however: 'Father has been home a lot lately. There's noth-

ing for him to do at the office; it must be awful to feel you're not needed. Mr Kleiman has taken over Opekta, and Mr Kugler, Gies & Co., the company dealing in spices and spice substitutes that was set up in 1941' (5 July 1944). See Lee (2003 [2002]: 66–68, 84–89).
11. 'Kitty' is one of Frank's fictional addressees in the diary; see Frank (2003: 243, footnote).

References

Bitzer, Lloyd F. and Edwin Black, eds. 1971. *The Prospect of Rhetoric.* Englewood Cliffs, NJ: Prentice-Hall.
Burke, Kenneth. 1966. 'Terministic Screens'. In *Language as Symbolic Action.* Berkeley: University of California Press.
———. 1969 [1950]. *A Rhetoric of Motives.* Berkeley: University of California Press.
Foucault, Michel. 1997. 'Subjectivity and Truth'. In *Ethics: Subjectivity and Truth,* ed. Paul Rabinow, trans. Robert Hurley et al. Vol. 1 of *Essential Works of Foucault 1954–1984.* New York: The New Press.
Frank, Anne. 1995. *The Diary of A Young Girl: The Definitive Edition,* ed. Otto H. Frank and Mirjam Pressler, trans. Susan Massotty. New York: Bantam.
———. 2003. *The Diary of Anne Frank: The Revised Critical Edition.* Prepared by the Netherlands Institute for War Documentation, ed. David Barnouw and Gerrold van der Stroom, trans. Arnold J. Pomerans, B.M. Mooyaart-Doubleday and Susan Massotty. New York: Doubleday.
Gee, James Paul. 1992. *The Social Mind: Language, Ideology, and Social Practice.* New York: Bergin and Garvey-Greenwood.
———. 1996. *Social Linguistics and Literacies: Ideology in Discourses,* 2nd edition. London: Falmer.
Hemingway, Ernest. 1940. *For Whom the Bell Tolls.* Philadelphia: Blakiston-Charles Scribner's Sons.
Lee, Carol Ann. 1999. *Roses from the Earth: The Biography of Anne Frank.* London: Viking-Penguin.
———. 2003 [2002]. *The Hidden Life of Otto Frank.* New York: William Morrow-Harper Collins.
Mead, George Herbert. 1934. *Mind, Self, and Society from the Standpoint of a Social Behaviorist,* ed. Charles W. Morris. Chicago: University of Chicago Press.
Nienkamp, Jean. 2001. *Internal Rhetorics: Toward a History and Theory of Self-Persuasion.* Carbondale and Edwardsville: University of Southern Illinois Press.
Rogers, Martha 'Patty'. 1785. Diary. Rogers Family Papers. American Antiquarian Society, Worchester, MA. Also available in the microfilm collection *American Women's Diaries: New England.*
Tenney, Tabitha Gilman. 1992 [1801]. *Female Quixotism.* New York: Oxford University Press.
Wertsch, James V. 1985. *Vygotsky and the Social Formation of the Mind.* Cambridge, MA: Harvard University Press.
Whately, Richard. 1963 [1828]. *Elements of Rhetoric,* ed. Douglas Ehninger. Carbondale: Southern Illinois University Press.

CHAPTER 2

Story Seeds and the Inchoate

Michael Carrithers

■ ■ ■ ■ ■ ■

IN THIS CHAPTER I WANT to make two points. The first concerns an episode in contemporary German history when a new item of rhetoric appeared, and with it a new and, in a global perspective, unusual understanding of nationalist history. The term is *Vergangenheitsbewältigung,* 'overcoming the past', which came to be used routinely as a way of considering the Nazi period, with its aggressive war and genocide. The idea here was that the Nazis left a legacy of destructive, anti-democratic self-deception and willful ignorance behind, and that the only way to deal with that catastrophic legacy was to bring the deeds of the Nazis to consciousness and, in so doing, to cleanse the national conscience.

My second point concerns the nature of this rhetoric, but also of rhetoric as such. In an influential piece which has inspired much subsequent work on figurative thought in culture, James Fernandez wrote that 'however men may analyze their experiences within any domain, they inevitably know and understand them best by referring them to other domains for elucidation' (Fernandez 1986: 25). In so saying, Fernandez was putting forward a strong claim for metaphor as the key to understanding culture in general, but also to understanding culture as rhetorical, argumentative and persuasive. My argument here is that narrative is no less pervasive and important a feature of persuasive culture. It is not that narrative competes with metaphor, but rather that the two can work together to forge a compelling construal of people and events.

Overcoming the Past

Vergangenheitsbewältigung is a typical German compound word. The first component, *Vergangenheit*, translates easily into English as 'the past' – though what might be meant by 'the past' can be quite complex and sprawling. *Bewältigung* is a verbal substantive, referring to 'mastering' or 'overcoming' some difficult matter, as a surgeon might overcome the challenge of a particularly testing operation, or an engineer might master the problem of traffic on a congested road. The compound refers specifically to acts of recollection or reparation that might be done in public about a catastrophic past, and though now Germans use the word more widely, it was originally applied to the Nazi period, 1933–45. The concept sailed into public awareness slightly more than ten years after Hitler's immolation, in the mid and later 1950s, as a metaphorical and rhetorical description of what some 'engaged democrats' at the periphery of public life in West Germany thought Germans should do (Fröhlich and Kohlstruck 1999). Instead of forgetting the Nazi past, they should remember it; instead of repressing it, they should confront it plainly; instead of keeping it private, they should make it public, before themselves and the world.

When such opinion was first expressed, it was a minority view in West Germany: in the 1950s and through much of the 1960s public discourse was dominated by what Hermann Lübbe later famously called a 'communicative silencing' (*kommunikatives Beschweigen*) – a tactful reticence about the Nazi period, a reticence which was understood, on the kindest interpretation, to support social solidarity and the integration of all parties into the postwar democracy. The term Vergangenheitsbewältigung, and the ideas and practices that it came to describe, only gradually moved with the passage of generations from the periphery of public life to the centre. The rebellious generation of 1968 is often regarded as the pivotal group, the first to burst through the silence, though their effect was actually felt much more in the 1980s, when they had risen to positions of influence (Bude 2001; the slow change of public opinion may be followed in Fulbrook 1999: 142–78). Today, two generations after the end of the war, the seriousness with which Nazi crimes are taken lays over them an aura of what amounts very nearly to sacredness, focused particularly on the Holocaust. The commentator Christoph Dieckmann draws an analogy between the 'memory of the Jews' murder' and that of Christ's murder, both establishing a collective understanding of the event as a 'dreadful happening from which history [is] defined' (*Die Zeit*, 21 January 1999). This amounts to what is surely an extraordinary phenomenon, a sort of negative patriotism, people unifying in condemnation of a grim period in their recent national history (see Fulbrook 1999). Note, though, that the timing, form, expressed sentiment or significance of such acts are often fiercely debated, so the consensus lies less in an explicit schedule of ethical values than in the confirmation that these are topics central to Germans' conception of their political nation (see Fulbrook 1999; Assmann and Frevert 1999; and the essays in Herz and Schwab-Trapp 1997).

When the Berlin Wall fell in 1989, the notion that there was a dark past that needed to be brought to light was then transferred to the freshly finished history of the GDR (German Democratic Republic or East Germany) and to the deeds of the GDR government; though in this case the specific image of Vergangenheitsbewältigung was set aside in favour of other figures, ones less tarnished by the early reluctance of West Germans to face their past. Nowadays Vergangenheitsbewältigung and allied figures are mostly used – their charisma routinized, their metaphors nearly frozen – for a class of relatively frequent public practices which would include, among others, the publication of a revealing book about the Nazi period or the GDR, or pronouncements by politicians of regret for the deeds of the past, or the production of a probing television documentary about the origins of Nazism or the Stasi, or the building or preserving of monuments – a museum, a documentation centre, a public sculpture, a section of the Wall – or indeed the prosecution in court of some person thought culpable, such as a concentration camp guard or the former East German Politburo members. Such acts are set forth as public statements rejecting those dark times and confirming an anti-totalitarian consensus.

From an ethnographic and comparative perspective, all this suggests an intensity of concern with history, alongside a willingness to delve into the noisome recesses of a national past, that are unusual even on a history-obsessed continent. This basic attitude was shared across both the Federal Republic and the GDR, and perhaps the most striking example of it appeared among members of the citizens' movement of the GDR that went into Stasi headquarters across the country at the end of 1989 and the beginning 1990: many of them planned – and carried placards to this effect even before the outcome of events was clear – to 'museumize' (*musealisieren*) those grim offices and cells, to transform them into harmless but eloquent and instructive mementos for the historical awareness of subsequent generations.

Metaphor: an Unmastered Past

Vergangenheitsbewältigung, as an image in public discourse, was passed into currency by Erich Müller-Gangloff, a writer and journalist with a background in the disciplines of history and German literature. Müller-Gangloff, born in 1907, was drafted into the Wehrmacht and experienced a conversion to (Protestant German) Christianity while a prisoner of war in 1945. After the war he founded the Evangelische Akademie Berlin-Brandenburg, an institution devoted to the lay Christian life and Christian reflection on personal, social and public issues. Using the Akademie as a platform, he organized a series of yearly meetings on the topic of the failed officers' coup against Hitler, beginning on the tenth anniversary of that event on 20 July 1954. By commemorating this event, Müller-Gangloff was trying to establish a line of continuity through the Nazi tyranny to an older German tradition of Christian virtue.

Yet around that faint glimmer of decency, Müller-Gangloff discerned only darkness. This is the way he began his opening speech at the second yearly meeting on 20 July 1955 (cited in Hanusch 1999: 121):

> Die Schatten einer unbewältigten Vergangenheit zeigen sich mächtiger denn je.
> The shadows of an unmastered past show themselves [to be] more powerful than ever.

Let me start with the metaphors in this rich passage. Fernandez offers this definition (1986: 8): Metaphor is 'a strategic predication upon an inchoate pronoun (an I, a you, a we, a they) which makes a movement and leads to a performance'. The movement is one of mind or heart brought about by affecting speech, and so by rhetoric in its plainest sense: speech used to persuade or convince. In this case the desired movement has a collective character, a general change in public sensibilities. This change would – or so hoped Müller-Gangloff – lead to public recognition of Germany's deeds during the Hitler period. Such public acts would be Fernandez's performance, the manifestation of the rhetoric's effect.

Fernandez also invites us to consider that each culture comprises in part a 'quality space', a notional arrangement of attributes peculiar to that culture, through which the target of the metaphor, the 'inchoate pronoun', may be moved by the qualities of that to which it is compared (1986: 12–13). In the Müller-Gangloff citation the key word is 'shadows', whose role is to suggest the quality of darkness, a darkness that, in Müller-Gangloff's arresting statement, looms over the present, but which originates in a dark past. In German – and for that matter, Christian and European – quality space, the movement from light towards darkness suggests a corresponding movement towards other qualities linked to darkness, such as evil and ignorance, and away from opposing qualities such as goodness and knowledge.

The key question, then, is this: where do we find the 'inchoate pronoun' which receives the predication of darkness/evil/ignorance? Well, in the first place, there is certainly something animate, something partly agent- or pronoun-like, in the 'shadows', which 'show themselves' and which are 'more powerful than ever', and I think this gesture towards dark agencies is important for the intensity of this passage. For Müller-Gangloff the spirit of Hitler – envisaged as a mesmeric evil genius, a powerful spirit of evil modelled in a Christian fashion – hovered always close to his thoughts about the immediate past. When he died, he left behind the unfinished manuscript of a book to be titled *Adolf Hitler or the Fearsome in Person*. Yet Hitler is not named here, and whatever or whoever these forces are, they are the more threatening for being unnamed. And in fact the imagery is ambiguous: are these shadows in the past, now defunct but whose aftereffects are still echoing, or are they shadows/persons still extant and still active?

In either case, it is 'the past', *die Vergangenheit*, that needs explication. Nurit Bird-David (2004), in an article looking from the outside into our North Atlantic cultures of history, has invited us to see how slowly our ideas of an historical past developed, and how elaborate they now are. And indeed our notions of the past are massively supported by an infrastructure of practices, from the care and cultivation of archives through the historical profession, publication, and the teaching of history in schools, to the building of museums and monuments to historical figures and events. Certainly all of this is true of Germany, and even more so: there one can speak quite rightly of an obsession with history (Assmann and Frevert 1999). Indeed the especially fervent practice of *Zeitgeschichte*, 'contemporary history', in Germany seeks to lend vivid verisimilitude to the disasters of the mid-twentieth century, making present to the mind what is lost by decay and death to the other five senses. So in the first place – in keeping with Müller-Gangloff's own training and practice as an historian – we can witness in the phrase 'the past' a looming company of the dead which make the present what it is.

But note that there is more than just a powerfully realized metaphor in Müller-Gangloff's rhetoric, for the use of 'the past' also works as a hint, an innuendo, a whisper of a suggestion that goes beyond metaphor alone. In English (and the equivalent works for German) one can say that 'he is a man with a past', and that vague gesturing works as a powerful *prolepsis*, an indication that something more is to come, namely a back story, a narrative of shadowy deeds, a revealing account of events and characters. So I turn now to narrative.

Story Seeds

Let me start from first principles again. I do not want to lose the valuable notion of the 'inchoate', nor that of 'inchoate pronouns', so the definition of narrative I propose is patterned on Fernandez's definition of metaphor: 'A story is the strategic insertion of inchoate pronouns in an inchoate situation into a storyline which makes a move and leads to a performance.'

The basic assertion here is: A story is a strategic insertion [of the inchoate] into a storyline. The notion of a storyline or plot is meant to include (1) characters, with their feelings, memories, intentions and attitudes, (2) their actions, (3) the effects of those actions on others, and on those others' feelings, memories, intentions and attitudes, and (4) so on, as those others may respond to the actions of the first. Stories, in other words, are synthetic, linking characters to their thoughts, to their actions, to the consequences of those actions, to the further characters and reactions of those affected, and onward in potentially limitless chains. As Bruner puts it succinctly, narrative is, in the first instance, a form of thought which concerns 'intention and action and the vicissitudes and consequences that mark their course' (1986: 13).

There is an extra twist here in of speaking about narrative thought, rather than only about narratives as a verbal performance. The effect is to cast the net more widely, in that narrative thought can be understood as supporting not only storytelling, but also the ability to understand, as well as to act intelligibly within, complex skeins of persons, actions and motives. The key term is perhaps *accountability*, meaning that people act in such a way that they can give an account – an acceptable narrative – of their actions to others, who can understand and judge those actions. Of course, as Charlotte Linde (1993) points out, the account actually given of some one action may differ from setting to setting, depending on the interlocutor and the course of conversation; and as anthropologists can so richly attest, the morality and reasoning may differ greatly from one society to another; but nevertheless, narrative accountability permeates human actions. So through narrative thinking we can – as, say, onlookers or investigators or anthropologists – retrospectively determine the storyline that led to a movement of mind and a performance. Or we can – as, say, politicians or therapists – suggest or project a storyline to others, hoping that it will lead to the appropriate performance.

More elaborated epic or written narrative is capable of displaying a whole world of human characters, human attitudes, human acts and human consequences, even a world so complex as Hitler's Germany and its aftermath (see for example Burleigh 2000). But stories can also be compact, brief, allusive and, like metaphor, can gain force and suggestiveness through brevity, and these are the stories I am pursuing here. Take this example, offered by Gergen and Gergen (1984): 'I thought she was my friend.' Uttered at the right time in the right tone to the right audience with the appropriate experience of the situation, this carries a whole plotline, and nothing more need be said (though it probably would be). Caesar could say simply, 'Veni, vidi, vici', and in the circumstances, he spoke volumes. When Chamberlain stepped from the plane to wave his piece of paper to the cameras after meeting and apparently reaching agreement with Hitler at Munich in 1938, he spoke of 'peace in our time', a phrase which came soon enough to suggest in its four words the whole tragic story of failed appeasement of the Nazis and the subsequent catastrophe.

Moreover stories, like metaphors, are mind-expanding: just as metaphors bring in another domain of thought to a topic of speech, widening our understanding, story can bring in a broader context, a more richly populated setting, inviting us to consider that more, and different, events and persons are relevant to the matter in question than we might have thought. The stories I have in mind are not elaborate ones, not the epic, the novel, the narrative history, but rather 'minimal narratives' (Carrithers 1995), minute seeds of story which, in a way directly analogous to the condensed, affecting, effective work of metaphor, unfold to make a movement and lead to a performance. Such story seeds need not – indeed by being 'minimal', most likely do not – have a conversational or literary preface which would suggest that a story is to follow (Carrithers 1995; Streeck 1995). They may indeed be woven, unmarked, into everyday talk, as Cheryl Mattingly has shown so well (Mattingly 1998; see also Ochs and Capps 2001). Nor need we assume that minimal stories are dependent on some particular genre or genres of talk/writing: just as metaphors may pop up everywhere, so may minimal narratives. And when a minimal narrative finds resonance in listeners, it is because it calls up familiar information, familiar motives, familiar storylines – though it may nevertheless make unexpected connections, connections across gaps and against the grain.

As did the story seeds of Müller-Gangloff. His speeches and writing were rich in rhetorically intended narratives of 'the past'. I give a brief example from a later speech which sketches in some of the background to the menacing 'shadows' above (cited in Hanusch 1999: 122–23):

> We believe that the future has already begun, but we don't even stand in our own present, because we are not finished with our past, because we have not yet overcome it. ... The German *Volk* is today the least finished with its past. It is sick and degenerating despite glowing outward health. ... The twelve years of Hitler hegemony are ... repressed out of the consciousness of people in a cramped and sickly way. There is hardly any serious literature about the Nazi time, and those who had the most to do with it want least to know about it. It counts as tactless to speak of the hecatombs of murdered Jews and Russians.

Note, first, the markedly rhetorical style evinced in the lavish use of both metaphor and story seeds. The plainest – though in itself far from plain – example of minimal narrative in this passage lies in the sentence 'It counts as tactless to speak of the hecatombs of murdered Jews and Russians.' There are two seed stories here, one containing the other. The one contained is the phrase 'the hecatombs of murdered Jews and Russians', which can be expanded into the narrative declaration: '[Germans] murdered hecatombs of Jews and Russians.' The action is embodied in the word 'murdered', directing the audience's attention to a narrative prototype comprising an act of violence, a verdict on the act and a characterization of the two necessary participants to the act, a perpetrator and a victim. The perpetrator is implicit but unmistakable: the Germans. Those subjected to the murder, 'Jews' and 'Russians', take the listener to *those* people in *that* slice of history, encompassing not just what would later be called the Holocaust but also the wholesale slaughter of Russian civilians and prisoners of war. (Indeed, in the context of the then established Cold War and West Germany's enlistment on the side of NATO, it was perhaps the mention of murdered Russians that was the more 'tactless'.) In this passage the metaphor 'hecatombs' is secondary to the story seeds, but it does make a further movement, towards the sanctification of Jews and Russians as sacrificial victims, and giving colour to a number in a way not achievable by a number itself.

This tale, evoking the past, is enclosed in the second, 'it counts as tactless to speak of [murdered Jews etc.]', which depicts the then contemporary situation. The listener is invited to imagine what it might be like to mention the topic of murdered Jews and Russians in contemporary conversation, and the icy reception he would receive. For someone already in the flow of German society and conversation at the time, this barely sketched scene would call up a then frequently expressed opinion in West Germany, namely that Germans themselves were the chief or only victims – of Hitler's mesmerizing powers, of the brutal Russian assault in the east and the consequent expulsion or escape of Germans from those territories, of the Allied bombing, of the partition of Germany. But note, too, the achievement of the sentence as a whole: it covers in a nutshell both the relevant past of the Nazi period and the present period of denial, and delivers a moral judgement, not only in the word 'murdered', but also in the contrast between the murders and the 'tactlessness' of their mention in the present. More than a generation later, Ralph Giordano (1987) publicized the phrase 'the second guilt' (*die zweite Schuld*) to characterize this blameworthy German silence about the Nazi crimes: one crime compounded by the criminal denial of that crime.

Elsewhere metaphor and story work closely together. Earlier in the passage, where Müller-Gangloff asserts that 'The German *Volk* ... is sick and degenerating despite glowing outward health', he simultaneously moves the subject, *das Volk,* from health to sickness in quality space through metaphor, and inserts it into a narrative of spiritual disease. The skeleton of this narrative, modelled on a blend of Christian and Freudian thought, is familiar and can be taken in at a glance by those schooled in such ideas. But even though it can be told so briefly (and therefore effectively), note that this skeletal narrative is quite complex, bearing four stages and branching possibilities, namely (1) evil-doing, (2) unacknowledged guilt (repression), and then either (3) confession (self-awareness) and (4) salvation (a return to health), or continued affliction. In later discourse, the single word 'repression' (*Verdrängung*) – a concept borrowed from Freud's vocabulary to describe the forgetting of uncomfortable or inassimilable memories – was to become a powerful single story seed which would call up the whole narrative of Nazi crimes and 'the second guilt' of refusing to acknowledge them. Moreover, just as 'repression' in English carries an image of pressing against something to prevent its action, so does '*Verdrängung* in German; so this, too, is a metaphor as well as a story.

Some of the force of the sickness image/story derives from its shocking departure from a sheaf of other images and narrative seeds through which some Germans sought to distance postwar West Germany from its past (for a rich description of these, see Dubiel 1999). Narratives of progress and of the achievement of material modernity were in full flood, captured by Müller-Gangloff in the story kernel at the beginning of the passage, 'we believe that the future has begun'. Perhaps the most dominant among the public metaphors/stories of postwar West Germany was that of the West German 'economic miracle', the *Wirtschaftswunder*, the rapid postwar economic recovery. At the time Müller-Gangloff wrote, the recovery was well under way, as was the rhetoric of a 'miracle', suggesting not just the attainment of wealth, but also implicitly a moral or even spiritual success, a redemption by prosperity from the humiliation of defeat. Müller-Gangloff cuts right against the grain of such opinion by asserting that 'we don't even stand in our own present, because we are not finished with our past'.

But however contrary to accepted views this rhetoric machine of Müller-Gangloff's may have been, it was nevertheless made of well-worn, well-known, indeed mostly comfortable components lying ready to hand. In the vocabulary of ecological psychology his rhetoric *affords* agreement (see Costall and Leudar 1996 and other articles in that volume). The idea here is that, as a chair *affords* – that is, enables or invites – sitting, and stairs enable or invite climbing, and a hammer enables or invites holding and striking, so a well-formed rhetoric speech enables and invites understanding and assent. In this light we can think of Müller-Gangloff as creating with his rhetoric an artefact which is, so to speak, German-shaped and pre-moulded to the psychic body of his listeners, enabling their consent. He offers no new information and uses only images and stories already available, such as the image/story of sickness and the storyline of murder. This is true even where he forces the storyline against prevailing habit: the then dominant narrative connected the present back only as far as Germany's hour of utter defeat, *Stunde Null* or 'zero hour', thus making of the economic recovery a simple and heartening success story – from ruins at *Stunde Null* to riches a decade later. But Müller-Gangloff took listeners further back, to the evil days of the Nazis. He eased this narrative leap across a chasm in memory by suggesting the Christian/Freudian/Western story of sin and redemption, and by evoking undeniably known (if repressed) information, the mass slaughter of the Nazis' chosen foes across the continent. As a path affords or enables walking across rough ground, so Müller-Gangloff's narrative affords a psychic journey between a more comfortable present and a sickening, forbidding past.

A Handful of Heroes Standing against the Inchoate

The centre of Müller-Gangloff's concern, though, was not West German economic self-congratulation, but something altogether larger, the dangerous and incalculable situation then facing Germans and the rest of the world, a situation given at least some shape in one ominous metaphor/story seed: the Cold War. If we think of the inchoate as the very embodiment of uncertainty and fear, then the Cold War was certainly inchoate, an unaccountable situation in which unimaginable disaster was always present from one moment to the next.

Müller-Gangloff was especially concerned to remedy this fearful manifestation of the inchoate:

> Because we have not overcome the Hitler past, we are as a *Volk* still not at all mature enough to overcome inwardly the German partition [into East and West Germany], which is the latest monument to our already forgotten catastrophe. ... We must not crow about [*auftrumpfen*] our demands for justice [in respect of the now lost territories of the east as well as the partition], but must go the plainer and humbler way of witnessing [to our guilt]. ...We must therefore realize that the reunification of Germany ... could only result from the slow approach of positions in deadly opposition to one another. It [reunification] could be a contribution to the decontamination of the present propaganda of hate, that weighs presently upon the world in great measure because of the Hitler madness. (Quoted in Hanusch 1999: 123)

Müller-Gangloff's fundamental recommendation here is that Germany change its collective attitude toward the East, a recommendation captured in an image/story – 'we must ... go the plainer and humbler way of witnessing' – which suggests 'a company of journeying Christian penitents. This is opposed to those who 'crow' about their demands, a characterization realized in German in the word *auftrumpfen*, meaning not only to play the trump card but also to make confrontational claims with arrogant superiority. In so speaking, Müller-Gangloff opposed the – in his view – reactionary and morally pretentious anti-communist tendencies in the Adenauer government and the irredentist and populist claims of Germans 'driven from their homes' (*Heimatvertriebene*) in the East. Moreover, in naming sources for the present inchoate situation, he proposed that the wild and incalculable character of nuclear confrontation could be brought within the sphere of human moral judgement and control.

Yet if we look more closely at this passage, we can also discern a deeper rhetorical strategy and a wider field of the inchoate to which that strategy is addressed. Note that the passage is anchored by three 'inchoate pronouns' given narrative shape: Hitler, *das Volk*, and the "we" which includes Müller-Gangloff among *das Volk*. Let me begin with the matched pair, Hitler and *das Volk*.

Hitler is of course the antagonist throughout Müller-Gangloff's rhetoric, the inchoate 'he' made flesh, the incarnation of evil, the source not only of war and the murder of entire categories of people but also of the aftermath in mutual hatred and division. The protagonist playing against the antagonist Hitler was, for Müller-Gangloff, an inchoate plural pronoun given form as das Volk. As a piece of rhetoric, das Volk is a remnant left behind, not only by Nazism, its virulently simplifying cosmology and its propaganda machine, but also by previous generations of nationalist narrative (see especially Müller 2001). In effect, das Volk had become the vessel in which the acts of the powerful, the doings and sufferings of the nation-state in the world, and the vicissitudes of society within Germany all received persuasive form: whatever was done, whatever was undergone, was done or undergone by das Volk or for das Volk. The collective character of das Volk also requires other collective characters in the melodrama, such as the Bolsheviks and the Jews. For the Nazis, these national/race Others were joined in ceaseless struggle against das Volk, whereas for Müller-Gangloff, the Others suffered with das Volk in the tragedy of continuing hatred.

Now as Anne Müller (2001) has pointed out so well, this notion of das Volk as a character or person is part of a much wider pattern. In the first place, it is only one of many figurative plays on persons deployed to achieve clarifying and persuasive effect in political life in nineteenth- and twentieth-century Germany. One counterpart to das Volk is the figurative and narrative embodiment of the nation in the person of its leader: Bismarck, the Kaiser, the legendary Hermann/Arminius, and, of course, Hitler. The nature of the idealized leader changes with the flow of events; and such figures are found in many settings across the world, for populist (*völkisch*), monarchical, fascist or just plain typifying or stereotyping ideas were then, and are now, common and proliferating.

What all these have in common is the use of concrete, familiar and intimate ideas about the individual person and face-to-face relationships to achieve a narrative grasp of otherwise highly complex social events with an unknown and often distant origin. Writing early in the twentieth century, Walter Lippmann captured this personifying movement of mind thus:

In order to [understand complex events] we tend to personalize quantities, and to dramatize relations. As some sort of allegory, except in acutely sophisticated minds, the affairs of the world are represented. Social Movements, Economic Forces, National Interests, Public Opinion are treated as persons, or persons like the Pope, the President, Lenin, Morgan or the King become ideas and institutions. The deepest of all the stereotypes is the human stereotype which imputes human nature to inanimate or collective things. (Writing in 1922, quoted in Müller 2001).

Lippmann wrote in the social and political world that had just given us the First World War, and was soon to give us Nazism, the Second World War and the Cold War.

How can we characterize the inchoate to which these 'human stereotypes', these narrative seeds, were the answer? As I understand it, our inchoate world, seen without the stereotypes, is very nearly incalculable, and even 'acutely sophisticated minds' – historians perhaps? sociologists? anthropologists? – could only tame it, and that only provisionally, through enormous detail, fine nuance and the scholarly work of many hands and minds. It is a world full of what Max Weber called 'unintended consequences', full of opportunities but also of unexpected encounters, inexplicable others, poorly understood dangers, and threats from afar. It is a world of often sharply diverging interests, but also of an involuntary and often deleterious global connectedness which, as Eric Wolf has shown so clearly (1982), reaches far back into human history. In our times these connections lead to a threatening 'dark at the top of the stairs', as Fernandez called it, inhabited by opaque institutional forces, among them those of markets, of commercial and industrial corporations, of distant political negotiations and religious movements, and of the administrative machines of industrialized states whose powers to affect people's lives is matched by their impenetrability.

The Enacted Story

The third inchoate pronoun made flesh is the 'we' that runs through Müller-Gangloff's rhetoric. This 'we' is set as equivalent to das Volk, yes, but the provision of the first-person perspective alongside the third-person perspective of das Volk does a great deal more persuasive work as well. In the first place, the inclusion of himself among the guilty party marks a graceful Christian humility on Müller-Gangloff's part. It is easy to believe that this would enhance understanding and motivation in his original Christian audience (and readership). But, further, this 'we', insofar as it draws das Volk together with those actually present, establishes a clear relationship between the situation of speaking and the displaced topic of the conversation. Müller-Gangloff is not just pronouncing over some distant group and distant events, but, by including himself and his audience within his topic, he brings 'there' and 'then' into 'here' and 'now' and makes the Other into Oneself.

I have noted elsewhere (Carrithers 1992) the strong persuasive and involving effect that such indexicality can have. By including some marker referring to the situation of speaking – it may be a 'we', or a reference to the place or time of speaking, or a reference to the audience – the speaker gives guidance on how to take the talk. If, for example, Müller-Gangloff had instead occasionally thrown in an indexical 'dear reader' (or 'dear listener'), then we might have reason to take what he says ironically; or if he had added a parenthetical 'or at least that's what I think', we might take it with a grain of salt or regard his authority to speak in a different light. In the actual event, the effect is that of an exhortation to move as the characters of the minimal narrative do, from victims making 'demands for justice' to guilty penitents actively acknowledging the nature of what had happened. One way of putting this is to say that the use of the 'we' in apposition to 'das Volk' has the effect of placing both speaker and listener inside the narrative, as though they too were characters in the plot.

Yet the speaker is not part of the narrative in quite the same way as Hitler and das Volk are. And in fact there are two distinct narrative rhetorical movements here. One comprises the story seeds proper, which includes Hitler and das Volk, just as the earlier story seeds included the Jews and Russians. The minimal stories about these characters are displaced from the occasion of speaking and form the ostensible subject of the discourse: we could call them the actually narrated story seeds. The other rhetorical movement comprises the indexical and other markers which set the relationship between those participating in the discourse. From the present narrative point of view, these are played out by the speaker – and implicitly by the listeners/readers – rather than being an explicit topic of the text. Call these the *enacted* story seeds. This enacted rhetorical movement is formed in the taken-for-granted relationship created between speaker, listener and spoken-about (or the implied relationships of the writer, reader and written-about), and so lies just beyond the central attention of the parties to the discourse.

The enacted quality of Müller-Gangloff's authorial character was already set out in the first words of his introductory speech to the conference on 20 July 1955 – 'The shadows of an unmastered past show themselves [to be] more powerful than ever.' The nearly eschatological tone of this and later speeches, the sentential reference to fundamental goods and evils and the sweeping view across recent German history all establish Müller-Gangloff as taking a certain role. That role shares something of the politician addressing his constituency, but something more of the preacher addressing his flock. There is much in the style which is even grander, suggesting a prophet addressing his nation, the gravity of the matter bearing out the *gravitas* of the speaker. One great antimodel for such prophetic, hortatory speaking was of course Hitler himself, but in fact the German public had lived, especially since 1918, in a great reverberating iron chamber of contending world views and political prophesying, including that of the Communist Party. Still, these comparisons are to a degree invidious, since Müller-Gangloff himself spoke, not so much *ex cathedra*, at the head of his constituency, but rather from the midst of them.

Rhetoric 'zero', Reality 1

Nevertheless rhetoric – both in its narrated and enacted dimensions – represents an aspiration to convince, rather than a sure-fire recipe for convincing. Indeed the possibility of failure is already built into the aspiration. To speak as hopefully as Müller-Gangloff required vividness in image and story, but also a capaciousness in scope which carried its own difficulties. This sort of portentous political and moral talk must also, in its very nature, be broad in its reference, general, applicable to the whole category of people who are at once its target and topic. But that is also the problem, for such generality is almost certain to be deeply flawed by infidelity to the actual world. The contrast is between the clear, simple and unified world comprehended in the wide embrace of the rhetor and the messy mercurial divergence and contentiousness of actual experience.

Let me illustrate. In 1959, Müller-Gangloff and colleagues exhorted the nation to join in the 'Action Signal of Atonement' (*Aktion Sühnezeichen*), and in so doing they revealed what the qualifications might be to join this great German penitent 'we'. They would be, for example, 'whoever is frightened by the sinful and boundless self-assertion through horrific and systematic inhumanity that a *Volk*, our *Volk*, has practiced and allowed to happen', or 'whoever has understood that one must account for oneself and may not be dissuaded from such accounting by accusing others and their supposed lack of insight'. These people were to signal their atonement by 'the visible sign of an act' and in so doing, to 'step out of the zone of obstinate silence and irrelevant discussion' (Hanusch 1999: 128).

These adjurations were in fact felt, however, only among a small minority of Protestant Christians, and certainly not among the whole Volk. The problem is that, once one states some criterion about who should respond to the rhetoric ('whoever has understood that one must account for oneself'), the comprehensiveness assumed by such terms as das Volk falls away. The total of possible addressees of such pronouncements ('our Volk') must, in sober reality, embrace a hugely various populace with hugely various experiences and attitudes, many of whom will not understand 'that one must account for oneself'. Some Protestant Christians did feel at home in a 'we' with Müller-Gangloff, but many other Germans remained 'obstinately silent' because they still believed that 'our Volk' had been victimized in the war, or that Germany had been involved in a preventive strike against the inhuman Bolsheviks (an opinion reaffirmed by Cold War attitudes). And then there were those for whom the 'call' (*Aufruf*) was simply irrelevant in the struggle of their daily lives, or who rejected all political rhetoric after the excesses of the Nazis, or who may indeed have quietly resisted the Nazi cause anyway. This discrepancy, between the oversimplification of collective nouns and the variety of human life, accompanies all such rhetoric and not just Müller-Gangloff's or that of German nationalism. As German historians of everyday life have shown us so clearly – and as fieldworking anthropologists can confirm – we cannot and should not conflate the public sphere, and the representations of life found in the public sphere, with the actual experiences of people as seen through their unpredictably distinctive accounts of their own lives (see for example Niethammer 1987; Lüdtke 1993; and the superb treatment of the 'refugees and exiles' from the formerly German East by Hahn and Hahn 2001).

Anne Müller (2001) suggests that the attribution of the intentions and acts appropriate to individuals to a uniform collective such as das Volk is a metaphorical move, and certainly we have seen the plentiful application of metaphor in Müller-Gangloff's talk. But here I think it equally useful to start from the 'social bias' in human intelligence, the tendency to see everything, even the objects of the physical world, as acting in a person-like way, with intentions and feelings (Carrithers 1992; Goody 1995), and therefore fitting into at least a rudimentary narrative. The projection of person-like attributes from the small onto an ever larger scale no doubt strains such personifying, rendering it ever more approximate, as one goes from singular to plural ('Germans') and then to collective nouns (*Deutschland, das Volk*), and from face-to-face interactions to those of ever more complicated forms of social organization and confrontation. As the strain increases, so does the slippage between what is known and conceived on good grounds and what is conceived approximately, if vividly. This is the territory of Lippmann's stereotypes, or what Schütz called 'types': the social world seen at a distance and categorized through rules of thumb, rather than known as individuals, as one knows family and friends, through intimate experience (see Carrithers 2000, but also Friedrich 1989). For the practical rhetorician offering listeners/readers a guide to that larger world, all the irreducible variety of any assemblage of people, and the sheer complexity of any situation they may find themselves in, must be resolutely ignored, and a simplifying version found, in order to make that mental movement which leads to a performance.

Conclusion

Metaphor and narrative are not mutually inconsistent strategies, but rather can work together to achieve a persuasive effect, and indeed to create a more or less consistent interpretation of a whole landscape of events and their aftermath. On one hand, such rhetorical effort depends upon a general capacity of human beings to find connections between one realm and another. Donald Brenneis has referred to this as analogy (2005), and I have written here and elsewhere (1992) of 'slippage' from one concept to the next. It is such slippage that allows Müller-Gangloff to place Russians into the story template of 'murder', just as he could place Nazi figures and especially Hitler in the quality space of darkness and therefore evil. But on the other hand, this general capacity, call it 'figurative thought', always has a specific and pointed use in the flow of social life.

The language I have adopted – of difficult situations and of the bestowal of sense and policy on them – also suggests how another pair of concepts, sociality and culture, might be brought into a useful relationship. As I understand it, one of the chief features of our human sociality is its constant mutability and plasticity, its historicity, such that our social life is filled with one emergency after the next as we react constantly upon one another. Under these circumstances, culture is less a structure such as a sheltering house – an analogy I have often heard offered to summarize anthropologists' views on the matter – than a 'resource and repertoire', as Brenneis puts it (2005: 446). That repertoire is used to tame mentally the flood of events and to suggest possible paths of action. Among that repertoire are knowledge, images and narrative schemas, as I have set out here. One question that anthropologists have got quite good at answering is: What do these things mean? Indeed we have developed cogent generalizing answers this question, especially under the challenge of cognitivism (see Shore 1996; Strauss and Quinn 1997). But here I have asked a different question, that is: How are items of the repertoire used? This sets stories, images and schemas back among the emergencies and predicaments of ongoing social life. It is for that reason that I have insisted on seeing culture as having a rhetorical edge, as being used not just to find significance in events, but to move both oneself and others towards a relevant performance (see Carrithers 2005b).

Once we see the repertoire of culture in its living setting, we can also see that the repertoire itself is subject to constant reinterpretation and metamorphosis, as if social life were a hothouse in which figurative thought continually branches and mutates. Sometimes a story seed or metaphor comes to live only in darkness, in its richly fertile avoidance: thus to speak of das Volk with the unironic certainty displayed by Müller-Gangloff, or even to speak of it at all, now seems distasteful in German public discourse, because it is too redolent of Nazi ideas. And sometimes the sense of a trope can ramify into many further meanings. In Müller-Gangloff's hands, the phrase 'unmastered past' – *unbe-*

wältigte Vergangenheit – began life in the 1950s as a reproachful commentary on Germany's postwar silence on the Nazi past. It is a phrase that, at its most grimly optimistic, looks forward to something that has not yet happened at all, and leaves that 'past' as the main topic. But some time – and I suppose this must have happened largely during the 1980s, when acts of recollection and contrition about that past became nearly routine – this phrase was quietly replaced by the abstract substantive *Vergangenheitsbewältigung*, 'mastering the past', which is first attested in the authoritative Duden dictionary in the 1993 edition. Same image/story, different perspective: this is a phrase fitted to describe acts commonly committed. It makes the 'mastering' the main topic. The phrase can now be used routinely and with little or no moral weight to describe a certain genre of public acts. And indeed the original sense can be largely lost. I have heard a speaker on a television talk show remark in passing that '*Vergangenheitsbewältigung* must of course be done again and again'. This points to a sort of total routinization of the phrase: the original idea, that the past could be 'mastered' or 'overcome', as a difficult problem is mastered and solved, jars with the scheduled and ceremonial character of repeated public acts. What was once a struggle is now a habit.

And there are other interpretations as well. I want to leave the last word to Bernhard Schlink, writer and jurist, looking back at Germany's Vergangenheitsbewältigung from the 1990s. He writes with a moral seriousness which we can recognize as kin to that of Müller-Gangloff and other writers on this topic. So that at least remains a constant. But here we see Vergangenheitsbewältigung criticized and rejected. For what Schlink finds in the image/story is in fact its plainest sense, namely that one could overcome, master and vanquish Germany's Nazi past such that it disappears utterly. That seemed desirable to Müller-Gangloff and probably inspired his use of the figure. But the actual practice of 'overcoming the past' in this metaphorical, moral and spiritual sense turns out to embody an impossible aspiration, says Schlink. Whether we accept Müller-Gangloff's optimistic figurative use of the term, or Schlink's dourly literal interpretation, depends finally on where we place ourselves and others in the story. Here is Schlink:

> What is past cannot be overcome. It can be remembered, forgotten, or repressed. It can be revenged, punished, expiated, and regretted. It can happen again, consciously or unconsciously. It can be affected in its consequences, so that it does not act – or does not act in a certain way, or acts precisely in a certain way – upon the present or future. But what has happened has happened. What is past is unreachable and unchangeable. Overcoming in the proper sense, as one overcomes a task that first stands before one, and then is handled, and through the handling changes its shape and is finally done and disappears as a task – this does not exist for what is past. The fact that

the expression Vergangenheitsbewältigung, which finds no corresponding concept in English or French, has become current in Germany has revealed a yearning for the impossible: to bring the past into such an order that its recollection no longer weighs upon the present. (Schlink 1998: 433)

References

Assmann, Aleida and Ute Frevert. 1999. *Geschichtsvergessenheit,Geschichtsversessenheit: vom Umgang mit deutscher Vergangenheiten seit 1945*. Stuttgart: Deutsche Verlags-Anstalt.
Bird-David, Nurit. 2004. 'No Past No Present: a Critical-Nayaka Perspective on Cultural Remembering', *American Ethnologist* 13: 406–21.
Brenneis, Don. 2005. 'Comment', *Current Anthropology* 46: 446–47.
Bruner, Jerome. 1986. *Actual Minds, Possible Worlds*. Cambridge, MA: Harvard University Press.
Bude, Heinz. 2001. 'Achtundsechzig'. In *Deutsche Erinnerungsorte*, Vol. II, eds E. Francois and H. Schulze, pp. 122–36. Munich: C.H. Beck.
Burleigh, Michael. 2000. *The Third Reich: A New History*. London: Macmillan.
Carrithers, Michael. 1992. *Why Humans Have Cultures*. Oxford: Oxford University Press.
——— 1995. 'Stories in the Social and Mental Life of People'. *Social Intelligence and Interaction*, ed. Esther Goody. Cambridge: Cambridge University Press.
——— 2000. 'Hedgehogs, Foxes, and Persons: Resistance and Moral Creativity in East Germany and South India'. In *Being Human: Anthropological Universality and Particularity in Transdisciplinary Perspectives*, ed. Neil Roughley. New York: Walter de Gruyter.
——— 2005a. 'Anthropology as a Moral Science of Possibilities'. *Current Anthropology* 46: 433–46.
2005b. 'Why Anthropologists Should Study Rhetoric'. *Journal of the Royal Anthropological Institute* (n.s.) 11: 577–83.
——— 2006. '"Presenciando un naufragio": las figuraciones alemanas al afrontar el pasado para enfrentar el futuro' ['"Witnessing a shipwreck": German figurations in facing the past to face the future'], *Revista de Antropología Social*, 15: 193–230.
Costall, Alan and I. Leudar. 1996. 'Situating Action I: Truth in the Situation', *Ecological Psychology* 8: 101–10.
Dubiel, Helmut. 1999. *Niemand ist frei von der Geschichte: die nationalsozialistische Herrschaft in den Debatten des Deutschen Bundestages*. Vienna: Carl Hanser Verlag.
Fernandez, James. 1986. *Persuasions and Performances: The Play of Tropes in Culture*. Bloomington: University of Indiana Press.
——— ed. 1993. *Beyond Metaphor: The Theory of Tropes in Anthropology*. Palo Alto: Stanford University Press.
Frei, Norbert. 1996. *Vergangenheitspolitik: die Anfänge der Bundesrepublik und die NS-Vergangenheit*. Munich: C.H. Beck Verlag.
Friedrich, Paul. 1989. 'Language, Ideology, and Political Economy', *American Anthropologist* 91: 295–312.
Fröhlich, Claudia and M. Kohlstruck, eds. 1999. *Engagierte Demokraten: Vergangenheitspolitik in kritischer Absicht*. Münster: Westfälisches Dampfboot.
Fulbrook, Mary. 1999. *German National Identity after the Holocaust*. Cambridge: Polity Press.

Gergen, M. and K. Gergen. 1984. 'The Social Construction of Narrative Accounts'. In *Historical Social Psychology*, eds M. Gergen and K. Gergen. Hillsdale, NJ: Lawrence Erlbaum Associates.

Giordano, Ralph. 2000 [1987]. *Die zweite Schuld, oder von der Last, Deutscher zu sein*. Cologne: Kiepenheuer und Witsch.

Goody, Esther, ed. 1995. *Social Intelligence and Interaction: Expressions and Implications of the Social Bias in Human Intelligence*. Cambridge: Cambridge University Press.

Habermas, Jürgen. 1990 [1962]. *Strukturwandel der Öffentlichkeit*. Frankfurt am Main: Suhrkamp Verlag.

Hahn, Eva and Hans Henning Hahn. 2001. 'Flucht und Vertreibung'. In *Deutsche Erinnerungsorte*, Vol. I, eds Etienne Francois and Hagen Schulze. München: C.H. Beck Verlag.

Hanusch, Rolf. 1999. 'Erich Müller-Gangloff–ein Bürger auf der Grenze'. In *Engagierte Demokraten: Vergangenheitspolitik in kritischer Absicht*, eds. Claudia Fröhlich and M. Kohlstruck. Münster: Westfälisches Dampfboot.

Herz, Thomas and M. Schwab-Trapp, eds. 1997. *Umkämpfte Vergangenheit: Diskurse über den Nationalsozialismus seit 1945*. Opladen: Westdeutscher Verlag.

König, Helmut, M. Kohlstruck and A. Wöll, eds. 1998. *Vergangenheitsbewältigung am Ende des zwanzigsten Jahrhunderts*. Opladen: Westdeutscher Verlag.

Linde, Charlotte. 1993. *Life Stories: The Creation of Coherence*. Oxford: Oxford University Press.

Lüdtke, Alf. 1993. *Eigen-Sinn: Fabrikalltag, Arbeitererfahrungen und Politik vom Kaiserreich bis in den Faschismus*. Hamburg: Ergebnisse Verlag.

Mattingly, Cheryl. 1998. *Healing Dramas and Clinical Plots: The Narrative Structure of Experience*. Cambridge: Cambridge University Press.

Moeller, Robert G. 2001. 'Remembering the War in a Nation of Victims: West German Pasts in the 1950s'. In *The Miracle Years: A Cultural History of West Germany, 1949–1968*, ed. Hanna Schissler. Princeton, NJ: Princeton University Press.

Müller, Anne Friederike. 2001. '"Strength" and "Weakness" as Political Metaphors: an Ethnography of German Politics from 1871 to the Present'. Ph.D. Thesis, University of Cambridge.

Niethammer, Lutz. 1987. ' "Normalisierung" im Westen: Erinnerungsspuren in die 50er Jahren'. In *Ist der Nationalsozialismus Geschichte?: zu Historisierung und Historikerstreit*, ed. Dan Diner. Frankfurt am Main: Fischer Taschenbuch Verlag.

Ochs, Elinor and Lisa Capps. 2001. *Living Narrative: Creating Lives in Everyday Storytelling*. Cambridge, MA: Harvard University Press.

Schlink, Bernhard. 1998. 'Die Bewältigung der Vergangheit durch Recht'. In Vergangenheitsbewältigung am Ende des zwanzigsten Jahrhunderts, eds Helmut König, M. Kohlstruck and A. Wöll, pp. 433–51. Opladen: Westdesutscher Verlag.

Shore, Bradd. 1996. *Culture in Mind: Cognition, Culture, and the Problem of Meaning*. New York: Oxford University Press.

Strauss, Claudia, and Naomi Quinn. 1997. *A Cognitive Theory of Cultural Meaning*. New York: Cambridge University Press.

Streeck, Jürgen. 1995. 'On Projection'. In *Social Intelligence and Interaction*, ed. E. Goody. Cambridge: Cambridge University Press.

Wolf, Eric. 1982. *Europe and the People without History*. Berkeley: University of California Press.

CHAPTER 3

THE DIFFUSE IN TESTIMONIES

Stevan M. Weine

■ ■ ■ ■ ■ ■

TESTIMONY IS WHEN SURVIVORS OF traumas tell their story. This text considers several literary models for approaching how survivors of historical traumas may give their testimonies. Reading W.G. Sebald and rethinking his notion of the *diffuse* illuminates what historical traumas ask of the individual survivor giving testimony and of all those who seek to respond to survivors' traumas with a narrative. Applying Mikhail Bakhtin's theory of the dialogic narrative could assist survivors and those working with them in producing testimonies that engage the diffuse through better embodying the polyphonic, dialogic, unfinalizable nature of historical traumas. This text closes with an excerpt from a text concerning teenage Bosnian refugees in Chicago who are often reluctant to give their testimony. It shows the potential contribution of Sebald's and Bakhtin's approaches as embodied in a fictional narrative based on ethnographic evidence.

THE DIFFUSE

The author W.G. Sebald, who left Germany for England in 1956, wrote engrossing works of fictional prose concerning the experiences of mass historical traumas before his early death in a car crash in 2001. In *After Nature*, a book-length prose poem, Sebald wrote in German what may be translated as, 'Diffuse are the workings of violence' (2003: 105).

'Diffuse' applies to both the causes and the consequences of violence. It implies the constant interaction of causes and consequences, such that 'the one thing always / the other's beginning' (Sebald 2003: 105). Violence may beget trauma and trauma may beget violence.

'Diffuse' as in widespread and dispersed through many different realms of the living world, and entire networks of relationship and meaning. 'Diffuse' as in how violence may cast the natural order of things into a new and disturbed order that is often impossible to trace back to its origins. Rhetorically, we may say 'diffuse' as in vague and obscure when we try to put the experiences of violence into living words, either for ourselves and for others.

Once violence is in a system, it cannot be rooted out. Its presence may be felt in every sentence uttered, if only as a trace or an absence. That could not be more true of Sebald's published works of fictional prose, which offer a destabilizing literary testimony that corresponds to his proclamation on the diffuse. In Sebald's writings, there is no separation between the idea and its narrative elaboration. Thus, diffuse are the narratives of diffuseness. Sentences go on and on without paragraph breaks. To some readers, the writing, described as antiquated and dreamlike, is annoying. To others there is accuracy in its embodiment of the diffuse nature of historical trauma.

The link between the exposure to the traumatic event and the varying consequences is diffuse to the point of being obscure or impenetrable for the characters, the narrator and the reader. Nor is there much separation between the author and the protagonists. Some characters are historical and some are fictional, and the border between the fictional and the historical, including the border between the real author's and the fictional author's experience, is blurred or obscured. In a world beset by the diffuse, all are committed to wandering without maps, searching for lost souls, and starting unfinishable projects.

What is left for the survivors of these troubled histories is misery, fear, uncertainty, feverishness, tremor and numbness. Sometimes a dark humour sneaks in. Sometimes one figure finds another, and only rarely do they make some warm, meaningful contact with another, such as in *Austerlitz* when the narrator sits with Austerlitz and hears his incredible stories (Sebald 2001), or in *The Emigrants* (Sebald 1996) when a survivor's diary is surprisingly handed over to a seeker. Moments of recognition and insight come, but only through struggle amidst tremendous difficulties.

The diffuse saturates Sebald's world to such an extent that his vision is intensely melancholic. Excesses of violence, such as genocide and war, leads to broad and deep structural changes, in the social, cultural, political, historical, economic and psychological realms. Too diffuse are the sequelae for any clean or simple resolutions. That includes any simple resolutions that we may sometimes imagine coming from survivors giving their testimonies.

In the gloom what is always present is Sebald's masterful writing. A beautiful gloom it is. Yet what you first notice upon looking at a Sebald book is not the words but the curious photographs. You see railroad tracks from a lens sitting on one of the rails looking down the rail. You see clumsily assembled family portraits. Your see urban scenes of streets and buildings, a child's rucksack, maps of fortifications, library stacks. Much has been made by critics about the position of photographs in Sebald's books, many of which reflect if not heighten the sense of the diffuse. The photographs break into or out of the narrative as if to declare that words alone will not do here. They are suggestive in a way that generates emotions and ideas, some of which fit with the narrative, and some of which do not readily line up. They bring into the middle of the narrative a quality of the real. However, what they are not is some kind of explicit documentation of a trauma. The photographs extend, not resolve, the diffuse in the narrative.

Sebald's writing is empirical in the sense that his texts pay exquisite attention to social spaces, physical place and nature. He has a fascination with ruins and traces. In the wake of pain and loss, you try to decipher the relationships between what you now see before you, be it a town square or a moth or an aged building, and what you believe passed before. Your mind wanders even farther than your sight through loose networks of meaning into the broadest, but still stubbornly vague, patterns of associations, delving into architecture, biology, history and other realms of knowledge. In Sebald's books, such wanderings are not at all bound by chronological time. Past, present and future often coexist.

For example, Sebald wrote many pages on destitute resort hotels that he came across in Europe, such as the Grand Hotel des Roches Noires in Deauville, France. This 'gigantic brick palace' for 'American multimillionaires and English aristocrats' became a 'monumental monstrosity now sunk in the sand' (Sebald 1996: 118). Those places spoke to Sebald of a lost life of glamour that somehow resonated with the destruction and mass trauma associated with the Second World War and the Holocaust. But consistent with the diffuse, this is never named as such, but left open for the reader's consideration.

The artfulness of Sebald's writings have made him one of the leading literary voices concerning historical trauma. Yet some have asked whether the aesthetic perfection in Sebald achieves something more than beautification of desolation. I feel it does. To me it says that all those social, physical and natural spaces that have been touched by the processes of diffusion are potentially habitable and addressable. There is life, there is consciousness and there is meaning. They present at least the possibilities for growth of individuals, families, communities and cultures.

Testimony and Growth

To explore the relationship between traumas, testimonies and growth calls for further specification of what growth may mean, and for that I turn to the field of mental health and human rights, to consider what it has to say about these same matters that Sebald the novelist has explored in his writings.

I do so as a psychiatrist and scholar in the field of mental health and human rights. My work is providing community-based services for survivors and studying political violence in terms of its causes, consequences and responses. I have been doing testimony work since 1992 with many survivors, especially from Bosnia-Herzegovina and Kosovo (Weine 2006). I was first drawn to testimonies because of hope. Survivors give testimonies because they hope that their voices matter and that telling the story may lead to some good, for themselves or for others. The problem that I have is that testimonies often do not live up to this hope and I think this has to do with the limiting approaches of those who are in a position to manage the testimonies, such as mental health professionals, human rights workers, lawyers and journalists. I believe that following the objectifying approaches of profession and science, we have nearly managed to kill off the diffuse in testimony.

Testimony is an honest attempt to help, but it allows insufficient room for the diffuse. Let me give one illustration from early in the history of testimony. Two Chilean mental health professionals, Elizabeth Lira and Eugenia Weinstein, first introduced the 'testimony of political repression as a therapeutic instrument' in 1980 (Cienfuegos and Monelli 1983). This not only marked the start of the 'Latin American testimony school' but also defined the contemporary field of mental health and human rights. They were doctors associated with the Social Aid Foundation of the Christian Churches in Chile, who started doing a new kind of therapeutic work.

> You propose that the affected people record on a tape-recorder what has happened to them in order to make a documentary proof of the illegal acts and the violence which have been perpetrated against them. You point out to them that this detailed reconstruction can be painful but that it will permit them to understand the emotions, contradictions and ambivalence associated with this traumatic experience. (Agger and Jensen 1996: 106)

The doctors made the story less diffuse in several ways. One, they introduced quite a bit of structure into the storytelling to address their concerns about trauma. Two, through audiotaping and transcribing they fixed the story. Lira referred to the story as an 'instrument' that the survivors could reuse without having to tell it again, which could be painful. I appreciate what is gained when a story becomes an instrument. They documented improvements in the survivors' levels of distress. As a mental health intervention, this is important, but I also wonder what may be lost. I think what is lost can be measured in diffuseness, if diffuseness were measurable. Subsequent innovators of testimony work in Europe and America, including Inger Agger, Soren Jensen and Dori Laub, have created a literature on the clinical testimony that has contributed to extending the tendency to instrumentalize survivors' stories, as I have discussed extensively in *Testimony after Catastrophe* (2006). I too have done my part in neglecting the diffuse in trying to advance testimony work in mental health through relying upon psychiatric and scientific methods. For example, by standardizing Lira and Weinstein's method and using systematic assessments we were able to show that giving testimony decreases survivors' symptoms, but we could not explain how or why (Weine et al. 1998). The central problem with those and other mental health professionals' approach to testimonies is that they are overly dependent upon traumatic stress theory and cognitivist explanations which do not allow much room for consideration of stories, meanings, history and culture.

Testimony was everywhere in the Balkans in the 1990s, through the efforts of the United Nations War Crimes Tribunal, the mass media and different NGOs (nongovernmental organizations). The War Crimes Tribunal regarded testimony as legal evidence, with some modifications. The mass media often seemed to use testimonies to create a spectacle centred on atrocity so as to elicit what Hardt and Negri describe as a 'universal moral call' (Hardt and Negri 2000:103). Some NGOs attempted to use testimony to change or 'renarrativize' local attitudes regarding their own traumatic history, but ended up misunderstanding, reifying or judging local moral attitudes (Losi 2001). What these efforts have in common is an attempt to be more precise and more relevant to the stories' supposed purpose. But this practice of precision has taken us further away from testimony as a story bound with diffuseness.

The hope I find in Sebald's diffuse corresponds with the diffuse qualities of the stories that many survivors tell. Although most survivors are not novelists, often enough their testimonies have elements of the narrative power with respect to diffuseness that one finds in W.G. Sebald's novels. Or, as Hans Nossack wrote in *The End*, his account of Hamburg in 1943, 'And the one who told me his story did not know that with his imageless language he was creating an image such as no poet can create' (Nossack 2004: 63). I have seen many examples of testimonies of survivors of political violence naturally tending towards near artistic displays of storytelling. All testimonies are not like this. Everyone has moments that are tedious and boring. But very seldom do I feel that I want to skip a moment because every sentence brings the sense of possibility that something truly valuable may surprisingly appear. These are stories that live to be heard, and need to be heard and responded to in order to live.

Unlike the professionals and scientists, Sebald does not try to rein in diffuseness. Rather, he goes with it. Sebald says to me that part of the promise of testimony has less to do with discrete traumatic memories, which are few and far between, than with what kind of work the testimony is able to do with diffuseness, especially through rhetoric. Many passages within Sebald provide extraordinary descriptions of the challenges of the diffuse from within diffuseness. 'It seemed to him that his impressions had been erased by the very violence of their impact' (Sebald 1999: 6–7). As such, the diffuse presents challenges to remembering. 'Over the years I had puzzled out a good deal in my own mind, but in spite of that, far from becoming clearer, things now appeared to me more incomprehensible than ever' (Sebald 1999: 212). As such, the diffuse presents challenges of consciousness.

The diffuse is a hardship that may lead to mental collapse. Yet even in collapse, which is common in Sebald's characters, there is meaning, and there is the possibility for discovery and insight. Moments appear when through dialogue with another, or just with oneself, the strain is recognized not only as a strain in the self, but also as a strain in the world. There is the emergence of consciousness of and insight into personal and historical collapse as a condition of, but not necessarily an impediment to, life. Resolution and recovery, no. But truth and beauty, perhaps yes. Or if not truth and beauty then perhaps an exploration of landscapes of a peculiar beauty, however melancholy, beyond the trauma and, with that, some sense of expanded perspective and some restoration of self-worth and purpose.

As an established practice of storytelling, the mental health and human rights testimony believes enough in the power of stories to claim variously that stories can save a life, build peace and reconciliation, and document historical truth. Yet although the practitioner of testimony believes in survivors' stories, often he or she doesn't let testimony be the story that it wants to be or could be. Instead, he often treats testimonies instrumentally by narrowing the narratives to fit his aims, theory and method. This practice of testimony does not want to let survivors take a chance by keeping things open. Rather it says, we need to help them to adjust their voices in order to make the testimony more productive or to make the story into something more understandable or communicable. Some degree of structuring is probably necessary to have a testimony at all. Some degree of structuring may lead to specific achievements some of the time. But neither is a reason to accept always putting testimony into a box.

When we do, I worry that what we gain in terms of precision, we lose in terms of diffuseness and the life forces linked with it.

Trauma is diffuse, not a solitary thing that must be rooted out. To address trauma as a solitary thing, as the professions seem required to do, calls for a concerted restriction of language. To address trauma as diffuse requires an approach that in a way expects both much more and much less of testimony and of ourselves. Are you able to passionately search for the truth when you know so little? Can you talk about the time when you didn't know how things would turn out? When the world has turned upside down and the self hurts, can you keep the self and world from changing in relation to one another?

Diffusion involves the dispersal of persons and relationships and their meaning systems across geographical space, social space and time. Sometimes no answers are forthcoming. But that does not stop one from wondering and asking.

> Filled by a sense of having been abandoned, I remained standing for a while on the platform. The girl in the many-coloured jacket and the Franciscan nun had long since disappeared. What connection could there be, I then wondered and now wonder again, between those two beautiful female readers and this immense railway terminus which, when it was built in 1932, outdid all other train stations in Europe; and what relation was there between the so-called monuments of the past and the vague longing, propagated through our bodies, to people the dust-blown expanses and tidal plains of the future. (Sebald 1999: 106–7)

Attempts to try to answer passages like this are destined to fall flat. There is no possibility for explaining what individual searching is going on here, but I think you recognize that searching takes place in the broadest possible field of experience. Sebald characters are forever trying to reach the 'dust blown expanses and tidal plains of the future'.

We may be able to put that diffuseness to work. But how? After Sebald, how might we document and interpret historical traumas that have gone the way of the diffuse?

Bakhtin's Dialogic Theory of Testimony

What if, instead, we encouraged the limiting genre of testimonies to return to being living stories, with all their diffuseness? It is because of their status as stories, stories of living histories, that they are an energetic living thing. It is as stories that testimonies may make valuable contributions, for example, in the realm of culture where living stories are more widely accessible and engaging, whereas a legalistic or cognitive narrative is limited to a narrow context alone. On the other hand, I also recognize that letting testimonies be stories may mean letting the diffuse in and risk succumbing to despair, or worse, to hatreds. In order to consider how such stories may engage the diffuse in a productive way, I needed some help which I could not find in the literature on testimony in mental health and human rights. Instead, I found it in the works of the Russian literary philosopher Mikhail Bakhtin.

According to Ivo Strecker, rhetoric enables a new theory of culture because, 'culture emerges from and is sustained by rhetoric' (Strecker, Meyer, and Tyler 2003). This insight is not too far from Bakhtin, who believed that culture is sustained and changed by dialogism. Dialogism means that in speech, the voices speak and listen to one another openly and responsively. It also means that a word embodies 'within itself diverse, discriminating, often contradictory "talking" components' (Emerson 1997: 36). Dialogism offers a way not only to accept but to engage the diffuseness of words and stories that come from survivors.

I have tried to rethink how those who work with testimony could put dialogism to use to help individual survivors and their families, communities and societies, through living stories. I believe, but at this point cannot prove, that when testimony is approached as a dialogic narrative, it will be better able to serve those goals we want testimony to serve: diminishing suffering, building cultures of peace and reconciliation, and documenting historical truth. I believe that because I also believe that the power of testimonies lies in its being a dialogic narrative. Let me summarize the main principles of Bakhtin's dialogic theory and give some examples of how they may be applied to survivors giving testimony.

Dialogic theory could help to produce testimonies that better embody the polyphonic nature of survivors' experiences. Polyphony means that a multitude of voices interact with no predetermined result. Survivors' unedited testimonies often present a multitude of voices, including: who they were before the traumas, during the traumas, and in their aftermath; who survived and who perished. As active participants in living historical, social and cultural domains of experiences, survivors carry within them many different voices; these voices speak of themselves, of their journey, of those around them (friends and enemies, living and dead), of the eras in which they lived, and of their unique consciousnesses struggling over the odysseys of survival and witnessing. We need to hear and acknowledge all those different voices in order to represent truthfully the consciousness of those inside of traumas. This is so important because testimonies have great potential to enhance the consciousness of traumas and their meanings for both the survivors and for readers/listeners. Consciousness in this sense is a powerful and potentially transformative life force.

It is perhaps best conveyed in a story that gives a sense of what it was really like to pass through a historical trauma and to survive, with all its uncertainty and complexity. To realize that potential, survivors' stories must be told in such a way that there is an openness to the polyphonic.

Dialogic theory could also help to produce testimonies that facilitate multiple voices and positions speaking and listening to one another openly and responsibly. This is important because it may help to convey an ethical awareness with respect to traumas. By ethical awareness I am referring to the sense that the stories present us with voices and persons that are facing competing and conflicting obligations in the worlds of traumas. These stories ask us to question how we structure our own obligations; what we do or do not do; how we talk about or do not talk about traumas; what we hope for and what we stop hoping for when traumas enter our worlds. These stories are about the choices we make, or fail to make, or that others make for us. This of course includes the choices that are made when we ourselves are confronted by traumas. Traumas happen to people like us. We should see ourselves in their shoes, trying to do our best in an event that we did not ask for but must now accept. However, this does not mean that the stories present us with a closed system of ethical thinking. Many of the dilemmas remain open and unresolved, and are something to manage and to live with.

Dialogic theory could encourage us to produce testimonies that respect and convey the unfinalizability of traumas. Unfinalizability means that events are multi-potent and unfinished. This helps to find a position of hope after historical traumas. Finding hope after traumatization is one of the most important priorities. This is a hope that is rooted in an awareness of loss and violence, but which is still a force to be heard. No matter how forceful the troubles are, they still bear hope and show how life does its pushing back against injustice, suffering and death In the stories of traumas, sometimes the material realities of war, migration or terrorism are themselves enough to overwhelm the hope. In traumas, the position of hope is multifaceted and ambivalent. These stories ask, how do we live in a world in which our hopes and dreams are often not enough to effect meaningful change? How do we live and hope after hope?

In the face of the centrifugal pull of these voices and experiences of historical traumas, the survivor struggles for clarity, structure, purpose and meaning. Work is required, especially work involving dialogic interaction in the process of producing a testimony, in order for the survivor to tell a complete story that contains all these parts of the narrative and that retains a sense of openness. Giving testimony always presents the risk of succumbing to a monologizing proposition that would squelch the heterogeneity of voices and experiences and render a narrowed viewpoint and a single evaluation. Giving testimony is never guaranteed to produce any kind of helpful results.

The survivor has primary responsibility for producing a polyphonic and dialogic narrative. But the receiver who is listening and interacting has a special obligation to help the survivor to resist the tendencies towards monologism. The receiver must not regard the survivors as objects, but as 'subjects of their own directly signifying discourse' (Bakhtin 1984: 36). The receiver should not overwhelm the survivors' voices with his or her own 'surplus' of information or understanding, for example, coming from academic theory or political ideology (Bakhtin 1984: 73). The receiver is not to approach the giving of testimony as a 'system', but as an encounter which adheres to what Bakhtin found in the polyphonic novel: 'a concrete event made up of organized human orientations and voices'.

This may seem like too much. Sometimes it is. In Sebald's *Vertigo*, the narrator asks 'what is it that undoes a writer?' (Sebald 1999: 15). The diffusion of the workings of violence may be enough to undo both the giver and receiver of testimony. Testimony is not good for those like Uncle Ambros Adelwarth in *The Emigrants*, a man of many traumas and adventures, who stopped speaking, leading years later to his nephew's seeking out the traces of his uncle's past. He meets Dr Abramsky from the asylum where Ambros ended his days, who recalls 'your great-uncle's longing for an extinction as total and irreversible as possible of his capacity to think and remember' (Sebald 1996: 114). And yet, according to Sebald's book, years later, the desire to tell the story was fulfilled by Uncle Adelwarth's nephew. Sometimes the young help the old, and sometimes it's the other way around, as the strands of the diffuse are picked up by someone from an older generation.

Kulenovic's Walks

I want to share some writing from a book I am working on that is tentatively titled, *Our City of Refuge* (Weine n.d.). It is an ethnography of Bosnian teenage refugees in Chicago. Because I have been involved with this community for more than ten years, I have access to many stories and voices, far more than I could ever use. I got to a point in the writing where I believed that the problem I faced was my eyes, ears and voice. I felt that drawing upon my trauma professional voice, or even my social science voice, did not offer an adequate response to their experiences.

The problem was also that testimony is not necessarily a good fit with adolescent survivors. Many were too young to remember what happened. Or they are thinking not of the past, but about today and tomorrow. Besides, talking can be so boring. Yet it would also be inaccurate to say that the troubling past is out of their lives. So this was an instance that required a special kind of observer to see and to articulate something about their experiences. Some of that observation I could do, but only by creating a surrogate narrator who could condense many voices and stories, and make them available to the young survivors, laying them down, perhaps for the survivors at present, or perhaps for sometime later.

Picture Kulenovic sitting on a park bench at Foster Beach in November, before dark. He is bundled up in a worn brown leather coat, his hands stuffed in his pockets to keep them out of the cold and the wind. Kulenovic is out on one of his long walks. He has stopped to catch his breath. I call upon Kulenovic to help observe Bosnian teens in the city, but first, who is Kulenovic?

Kulenovic was a key member of the Sarajevo literary elite. He wrote novels and taught literature and theatre at the University of Sarajevo and was the President of Pen Bosnia-Herzegovina. Aleksander Hemon was once his student years before he became an international literary star. Kulenovic joined our university group in Chicago from 1995 to 1998, and years before, taught at the comparative literature faculty of the University of Sarajevo.

In Chicago, Kulenovic missed his writing friends and he missed his books. His small library was gone. He had to burn them for heat in the seige of Sarajevo in the winter of 1992, as was once shown on CNN. He lit a pile of books with a cigarette lighter, and kept tossing new ones in. After the flames died down he noticed that not all books, or all parts of all books, burned as well. At the end, in the pile there were bindings, covers, pages, perhaps even whole chapters, that did not turn to ash. A letter from Susan Sontag had helped him to get citizenship. She promised that he could stay with her in New York. After arrival he called her and was told, 'It was just a ruse to get you out of there.' He really thought he was going to bask in the bright lights of the New York literati. Instead, he came to Chicago, a place long more suited to the peasantry of immigrants who were employed in the factories. This much is true.

The Kulenovic in this book is part fiction. I did this to Kulenovic because of my friend Mirsad's suggestion. One afternoon over lunch at Noon O Kabab on Kedzie Street, my friend Mirsad asked, what if you saw on a park bench near Foster beach a middle aged German man, with a moustache, Khakis, and glasses, writing in his notebook. If W.G. Sebald had not died in a car accident in England at age 57, but was here in Chicago, looking at the life here, then what would he write about the Bosnians in Edgewater?

Kulenvoic went from being a celebrated novelist to being prematurely aged man on the dole. His colleagues, fellow travelers, and students were scattered all over the globe, trying to eke out livings and sustain their writing. Like the others, Kulenovic occasionally got invitations from American universities, such as the one I attended with him for a conference on exiled writers. It was a civilized affair, not so unlike what he was accustomed to in universities across Europe. At the moment he was being introduced by the organizer, Kulenovic realized that here he was now a dinosaur. He would never here write like the writer he was in Europe.

Kulenovic was growing fatter from too much inactivity. Walks by the lake were his only exercise. He took long walks guided by no map but by his own recorded sense of where he was and where he wanted to go, which day by day, walk by walk, was growing. On pleasant days, he went to Berger Park and read and smoked. He enjoyed the Bosnian books that were passed around in the community or he read in English what his wife brought him from the library. At least here he had time to read.

He did not fit here and never would in this busy country. He could not both understand himself and understand this new life. He felt the same about the children around him. Kulenovic loved children, of course. But now more than ever they confused and irritated him. He used to know them. But Bosnian youth were different here. They were taking on characteristics of this new life too quickly.

Even the kids say this about themselves. One kid said, they are all show offs. If they have anything to show off, that is the thing they now live for. They don't know what life is and how to live.

When he went to the high school to talk with the Bosnian class, he heard a lot of this. The girls didn't like what was happening to Bosnian guys. One told him, 'I hate Bosnian guys that think they are Ghetto. They think they are so hip-hop. It makes me sick. They dress and act like that and they are so rude but I know in my heart they are not like that. They just see this popular image and want to be like that.' Kulenovic nodded when they said hip-hop but he didn't know the first thing about it.

Another student said, 'I get very disturbed looking at some Bosnian teenagers because I think they lost their identity and are trying to live up to certain standards. If they are trying to be American they pick up the negative American side.'

'They are trying to be like American people, like some gang members. They came here one or two years ago and are buying cars for twenty thousand dollars are they are cool. You can't really talk to them. They are stupid. They are always acting.'

Whenever he heard about teens in trouble, Kulenovic heard their parents protest: 'For them! We came here for them! We came here so that they would not have to grow up in a war.' This is true, and many parents would do the same. But it was hard for Kulenovic to simply take the parents' side. They were actually fighting another war. The war against change. They signed up for refuge, not migration and culture change. They did not save their kids from war to lose them to America.

Kulenovic sees those kids, how they are acting, how they are struggling. He wants to help the kids, but how? If he truly loved children, Kulenovic asked himself, then why had he never written about childhood proper? The books he wrote were about adults rediscovering or reminiscing about their childhoods. Adults whose childhood was stolen from them and who were forever searching for it. Like A. whose adult life was occupied by an impossible project about the design of public buildings and who found out belatedly that he came to London on a Kindertransport from Prague, escaping the catastrophe that took his parents away.

It was too late now. He would never write novels anymore. At most he could see sketching a few fragments. Something to publish in Chicago's Bosnian magazine. America fascinated and repulsed him. But he did not recognize a story there. Walking on the path to Foster Beach he took notice of that big pink complex across the field where his fellow countrymen liked to play soccer and roast lambs. The building struck him because it looked old and he had discovered that nothing was allowed to look old in America for very long. It was a ruin from another era. The likelihood that it would soon be demolished made Kulenovic curious. So one day he went in and talked to the doorman. He was too embarrassed by his broken English to talk for too long, but he had to satisfy his curiosity about the big pink building. The doorman told about its former life as the Edgewater Beach Resort. The fancy guests, lavish parties, and splendid beachwalk where the rich people and celebrities played.

Kulenovic felt that this was the kind of place that would have interested him when he was writing novels. Now he preferred drinks over the daily discipline of writing. But still he could imagine. He might have written about a former high roller at the Edgewater, now aged and deteriorating in that aged and deteriorating faced pink building. Kulenovic had always liked characters that were driven to excess, but later lost the capacity to sustain it. Persons who had outlived their lives and came to suicide or the asylum, like Ambros Adelworth. He was fascinated by buildings that had ceased to function as designed, and had some new invented function or none at all and were dilapidated. Some parts had been cleared away to make room for the sleek new glass and steel towers. The part of the beach hotel that was still standing was now old stock apartments, filled with the elderly. Now the thought of writing about the outlived depressed him because he knew that he had outlived his Bosnian literary life. All the people of Bosnia-Herzegovina had outlived their Yugoslav life. They had outlived the state of Yugoslavia, the idea of a multi-ethnic Bosnia, and the month long vacations by the Dalmation Sea. There was no place for them expect in nostalgic dreams, or park benches and pink buildings in far away cities. Drinking was better.

One day by the beach he was struck by the coincidence of Bosnian teens finding a spot to hang out right near the former beach resort. When he walked down to Foster beach, he saw how much those kids enjoyed themselves. They gathered, *laughed, and bounced in ways that neither he, nor anyone of his generation was able to manage in Chicago. Naturally, this irritated him. At first, out of spite, he asked, of what do they know less: the history of their play spot in Chicago or the history of their home country? Home country? Their home country was America not Bosnia-Herzegovina. But Kulenovic knew himself as a writer well enough to know that he could not do anything with an image that just made him mad. Besides he sounded as bitter and pathetic as their parents. How could he ever make them come alive on the page?*

Kulenovic had liked to write in his novels about adult protagonists who looked back. That approach had worked well for him in Europe, decades after the Second World War. In America, there was no way for Kulenovic to get these teens to look back the way his adult protagonists would. Not at this moment in time. They did not know their own history. It was not their fault that they knew only a child's Bosnia-Herzegovina. Whose fault was it? It was his generation's fault that their life in Yugoslavia had come tumbling down. Kulenovic knew that he had to be more sympathetic with the teens. He should start with the places they know and love.

That would be the beach, where Kulenovic liked to watch them. Foster Beach was no sea, but it could not be completely severed from the Adriatic Sea that all Bosnians loved so much. The teens may not be able to return to Neum, Dubruvnik, Makarska, or their family's favorite vacation spot, but they bring a little bit of their desire with them each time they make their way out to Foster Beach.

And yet their spot by the beach and the parking lot was no family spot. It was strictly for teenagers. In America, they were asking for, or demanding a spot of their own, away from parents and grandparents, brothers and sisters. They needed a spot to be themselves, to be to themselves, and talk to each other. To listen to their music, to wear their clothes, tell their jokes, and to act however they wanted to act. To act silly, smart, sexy, cocky, risky, and stupid. Most Americans, when they go to the beach, they dressed down. Kulenovic noticed that the Bosnian kids dressed up. Their shirts were buttoned down or tucked in, their hair was combed, and their shoes were new. Foster Beach was the place, so you had better look your best.

If they were teens in Bosnia, then they would have had somewhere to go where parents wouldn't have to worry about them, like the city square or the soccerfield after a game. As teens in Chicago, they needed such a place even more than they once would have, but they had a far harder time finding it. Their parents so worried all the time. They worried that their teens were in danger, and they worried that they would be lost to the culture of American youth in the city, and they worried that as parents they had done the wrong thing by coming here.

What worried their parents so was intoxicating and liberating to the teens. Once away from home, being in America meant being away from the whole Bos-

nian way of life that had bound them. It was like permanent vacation, and coincidentally but appropriately enough, it was in a former vacation spot.

Kulenovic thought he was on to something when he picked up on the vacation vibes and resort sense submerged in Edgewater. The site of the Edgewater Beach Resort was a famous, pleasurable spot by the lake that resonated with the vacation spot of their youths. Because of who he was, and how he thought, and what he wrote, he picked up on another sense: There's a heaviness on this beach.

Edgewater spoke to Kulenovic of a resort that could not be sustained and good times that were extinguished. Time ran its course. When the expansion of Lake Shore Drive took its beach away in the late 1960s, the resort lost its life blood. Without the beachfront, there was no possibility for casting a spell upon the Midwestern gentlemen and ladies that came here to play. Now they'd drive to Wisconsin or Michigan, or they'd hop on a plane and fly to Florida, Mexico, California and get a real ocean. It wasn't so hard for them to find other places to play. They had money.

When Bosnia-Herzegovina declared independence, the Bosnian people lost their beaches. Yes, they still had Neum, an Ocean City like Bosnian settlement on the Dalmatian coast. But it was a far cry from the same as all the spots they loved in Croatia, now another country. Adding to this darkness was the fact that when many Bosnians became refugees of the Serbian ethnic cleansing, they became refugees in Croatia, and were sent to live in empty resort hotels by the sea. It was off season and the hotels were empty, so they filled them up with Bosnians and they became small refugee camps. It was never intended to be permanent but to this day Croatia has not been able to rehabilitate many of those resorts. Many of the same kids who played on Foster beach had spent months to years in Dalmatian beach resorts when their families fled the war in Bosnia-Herzegovina. Isn't it interesting, Kulenovic thought, that the site the teens chose for play contained not only the memory of vacation and release, but also that of ruin and destruction? Now he thought he was on to something.

And yet all this was lived as if written in a code. The teens did not know that code. They hadn't a key for unlocking the clue to links between this and that. Kulenovic did not think he could break that code either. His head was not sufficiently clear for as many hours as would be required. Besides, he doubted that anybody from his generation could. Did it even matter? These teens were so caught up in the new life in America, that they were not sure what to do with the old. They had all their lives to live with their memories. It was entirely possible to live without them, many seemed to believe. They could very well be right.

They found a cure for their dirty city blues, mused Kulenovic, and the words started to flow like that hadn't in a long time. Was it the water they stood near or the cars that they flew in that helped get them out of that hole? It could keep them for years and for years. It could take away all of their fears and their tears.

But there could come a day when they'll sit down and say it was not worth what they gave away.

'Edgewater, not Bosnia, will become the old country. That's how American Jews feel about New York's Lower East Side', I said to Kulenovic when he and I took a long walk together one grey day in January 1996. Even if they move to Skokie, Niles or Desplaines, they must pass through here again to get to the city. As they pass the light where Lake Shore begins, they may look over their right shoulder and see it staring back. That old pink stone, if it's still standing, could draw them in. It could make them dream of worlds left behind, of things that could not possibly linger, of the destruction of a way of life. Or it could make them point the finger at the lies they told them were true. Lies about buildings and countries that were supposedly built to last. Someday they'll turn the corner and see the building come down, and then think of shelling and snipers. Someday they'll happen upon a new building rising like they once imagined their brilliant futures.

References

Agger, I. and S. Jensen. 1996. *Trauma and Healing under State Terrorism*. London: Zed Books.
Bakhtin, M. 1984. *Problems of Dostoevsky's Poetics* trans. Caryl Emerson. Minneapolis: University of Minnesota Press.
Cienfuegos, A.J. and C. Monelli. 1983. 'The Testimony of Political Repression as a Therapeutic Instrument', *American Journal of Orthopsychiatry* 53: (1): 43–51.
Emerson, C. 1997. *The First Hundred Years of Mikhail Bakhtin*. Princeton: Princeton University Press.
Hardt, M. and A. Negri. 2000. *Empire*. Cambridge, MA and London: Harvard University Press.
Losi, N. 2001. 'Beyond the Archives of Memory', *Psychosocial Notebook* (October issue): 5–14.
Nossack, Hans Erich. 2004. *The End: Hamburg 1943*. Chicago: University of Chicago Press.
Sebald, W.B. 1996. *The Emigrants*. New York: New Directions.
——— 1999. *Vertigo*. New York: New Directions.
——— 2001. *Austerlitz*. New York: Random House.
——— 2003. *After Nature*. New York: Modern Library Paperbacks.
Strecker, I., C. Meyer and S. Tyler. 2003. 'Rhetoric Culture: Outline of a Project for the Study of the Interaction of Rhetoric and Culture'. Posted at http://www.rhetoricculture.org/outline.htm (accessed January 2003).
Weine, S.M. 1999. *When History Is a Nightmare: Lives and Memories of Ethnic Cleansing in Bosnia-Herzegovina*. New Brunswick, NJ: Rutgers University Press.
——— 2006. *Testimony after Catastrophe: Narrating the Traumas of Political Violence*. Evanston, IL: Northwestern University Press.
——— S.M. n.d. *Our City of Refuge: Teens, War and Freedom*. Unpublished Manuscript.
Weine, S.M. et al. 2006. 'Testimony Psychotherapy in Bosnian Refugees: A Pilot Study', *American Journal of Psychiatry* 155: 1720–26.

CHAPTER 4

MEDICAL RHETORIC IN THE U.S. AND AFRICA
THE ONCOLOGIST AS CHARON

Megan Biesele

■ ■ ■ ■ ■ ■

INTRODUCTION

A rhetorical subtitle for this paper might be 'The Ubiquity of Persuasion in Medicine'. As in most other areas of human life, it is difficult, in healing performance and discourse, to get away from the primacy of nuanced communication about socialized belief. Thinking back some twelve years after my original writing in light of both anthropological work on Ju/'hoan San texts of many kinds and the complex indigenous politics which increasingly inform their production and use, I feel that social anthropology is nothing if not combined with rhetorical awareness.

The heart of the paper is a contrast in rhetorical styles between a Ju/'hoan San psychic healer in Namibia and a big-city cancer doctor in Texas. Classical allusions to Charon and the Styx reinforce the ritual, performative and persuasion-centred nature of the analysis. The twist near the end, discovered late in the game by those keeping the chronicle, was that the cancer doctor was also a student of philosophy who viewed euthanasia positively.

Twelve years after first presenting a version of this essay I am ready to say now that the renamed eldest daughter who 'glares at the doctor' in this paper is myself. My then co-author anthropologist Robbie Davis-Floyd and I chose to distance ourselves at the time through the rhetorical trope of observation.

Though we allowed its participant nature to emerge somewhat, the reality was much closer and in fact excruciating. I will be eternally grateful to Robbie Davis-Floyd for insisting that I start writing this experience, using all the analytic and persuasive tools I could then muster, as soon as I possibly could after my mother died. It was the very best thing I could have done to heal – not only the grief from the loss but my anger at the social production of her death.

Ju/'hoan Medical Rhetoric

On first listening it is hard to hear any obvious rhetorical back-and-forth between patients and healers in the medical practice of Ju/'hoan San ('Bushmen') hunter-gatherers of the Kalahari Desert of Southern Africa. In the small, face-to-face, extended-family communities in which the Ju/'hoan generally pass their whole lives, by the time the healer comes to the patient s(he), like others in the community, has heard the litany of the patient's aches and pains many times. Never does s(he) have to say anything like, 'Now, what seems to be the trouble?' Instead, a healthy tradition of near-continuous 'complaint discourse' (Rosenberg 1990) flourishes among the Ju/'hoansi. Thus the aural world is felted together on a daily basis, for healers as well as others, with up-to-date information on the state of health and happiness of each individual in the community. Rhetorical 'exchange' between Ju/'hoan doctors and patients could thus be regarded sequentially, as discontinuous in time.

Important, more immediate exchanges do take place, however, between the healers and the spirits in the context of healing. These exchanges, occurring in 'real time', are heard by most onlookers, including the patient, as one-sided orations. The responses from the spirit world are audible only to those few others who are in a similar altered state. These orations take place in a matrix of clear assumptions and practices regarding the gods and the spirits of the departed and their ongoing interactions with the living. Ju/'hoan healing beliefs revolve around the concept of n/om, or healing energy, a supernatural potency residing in the bellies of human healers. This n/om is activated by strenuous all-night dancing until it boils up the spinal column to a spot at the top of the spine called the n//ao spot. From here it travels down the arms to the tips of the fingers, where it can be used for healing by laying on of hands. Both men and women, in fact large fractions of the population, at some time in their lives experience and cultivate the altered state, !aia, brought on by the boiling of the n/om. When in the altered state, the healers are able to see and converse with the spirits, who have been attracted by the music and by the beauty of the firelit dancing. Members of the community thus have regular access to the power of altered states through their n/om kxaosi, or 'owners of n/om' who function somewhat as do shamans in Siberian societies. People celebrate the bravery of these healers, who they say have dared death itself to bring them healing power and knowledge from the other world.

The circular form of the associated dance, with men dancing behind a ring of seated women and the fire in the middle, unites the different Ju/'hoan players in this drama, causing them to participate in the making of a single, dynamic and unifying form. Sometimes an unspoken tension in the community is voiced by the trancers and in this way its threat to harmonious relations is dispelled. Ancient as the dance form is, it often embodies, through contemporary artistry, new realizations germane to local conditions and new developments in society. This open-endedness is here, as in the Ju/'hoan storytelling tradition, key to its effectiveness and the continuation of its ability to galvanize belief.

Healing orations are also echoed in other, more everyday contexts, such as in 'self-delectative' playing of the thumb piano. In the following quotation from 'Song Texts from the Master of Tricks', which I published in 1975, the healer conveys a sense of humility, of ultimate vulnerability, but also of cunning agency in the face of death:

> Terrible God deceives, torments.
> God's arms descend into my fingers.
> Yesterday God said 'Be my child and listen.
> Take what I say to the people.'
> God's arms, God's arms.
> A young soul lives in the western sky
> And is still learning. ...
>
> Where will I hide from God's death?
> The day when God speaks where will I be?
> Where will I hide from terrible God who torments me?
> The year of my death is known.
> The day of my death is known.
> Owner of tricks, yes, am I.
> Master of lying, hoo!
> One who can fool you, that's me.
> Master of tricks, yes.
> Owner of lies!
>
> A young /ibi bird am I,
> A little bird living in its mother's house,
> Still learning. I am God's son,
> I am like the lightning bird

Who just flies on,
Doesn't know where he's going,
Even goes to strangers' homes
And is not afraid.

U.S. Oncological Rhetoric

In November 1990 a seventy-year-old woman, whom I will call Mrs Margaret Bell, entered the hospital suffering from severe dehydration following chemotherapy. She had been diagnosed with colon cancer with metastases to the liver in July. When she was admitted, she was convinced of her ability to recover. When she left the hospital, rehydrated and feeling better after a ten-day stay, she became determined to die. By her own report, the oncologist's words played a significant role in this transformation. As she explained her experience, his dramatically ritualized and repeated pronouncement of her terminal status, reinforced by other aspects of her hospital experience, eventually integrated itself in her mind as a primary 'failure' that added heavy symbolic weight to other 'system failures' she was experiencing. The terminal diagnosis quickly came to form one piece of a new reality matrix that held her death to be imminent and her task to prepare herself for death.

In a later interview, the oncologist shed light on this transformative moment: he called the task of announcing terminal status one of the central responsibilities of the cancer physician. He identified the doctor–patient interaction surrounding this announcement as a main determinant of 'a good death'. It was clear that the physician, 'Dr Henderson', had his most anxiety-laden communication with the patient during the three days it took him to get her to accept that she was going to die. This freighted communication stood in marked contrast to the kind but brief and distant contacts the doctor had previously had with Mrs Bell. The announcement of terminality seemed to be a key element in the oncologist's ritual role. This chapter addresses both the humane purpose behind communication of the terminal diagnosis – helping the patient to prepare herself spiritually and to make the best use of remaining time – and the rhetoric which reinforced the claim of the medical establishment to symbolic hegemony over the bodily processes of life and death.[1]

The Cancer Physician's Role in Technocratic Social Drama

In the popular view, oncologists as a class are alternately celebrated for their willingness to play the difficult part of the bearer of the tidings of death, and condemned for their reputed unwillingness to include the patient as part of the healing team (Henriques, Stadil and Baden 1980; Buckman 1984; GIVIO 1986). Some are further characterized as heartless technical automatons unable to relate humanely to patients and families or as intent on speeding the patient to an early death through self-fulfilling prophecies. Still others, however, have come, in the course of helping dying patients, to seem like compassionate and competent conductors to the world of death, performing the important role of lessening pain and fear (Good et al. 1990). Because death is so often not only the literal but also the symbolic – i.e., expected – outcome of cancer, oncologists inevitably take on roles that carry ritual as well as medical freight. A perception that Dr Henderson's performance encompassed aspects of the role of Charon, who ferried the souls of the dead across the River Styx, occurred ineluctably to me as a close observer.

This last comparison illustrates a critical point. Despite biomedicine's departure from shamanism, religious and medical practices align themselves again when an unknown such as cancer, and the fear of its outcome, is involved. Indeed, until AIDS came on the scene, cancer reigned as the most feared disease in America. I contend that this unity of medical and religious roles is operative for cancer doctors even where individual patients have histories of personal religious practice to help them through the period of dying. Mrs Bell's experience illustrates the ways in which these symbolic and ritual dimensions of the physician's role can both enable the transformative process of dying and reinforce powerful tenets of the American technocratic model.

As medical anthropologist Robbie Davis-Floyd has written, the technocratic model of life processes is an important part of the American core value system which conceptualizes the human body as a machine, giving primary responsibility for its repair and maintenance to medical technicians (Davis-Floyd 1987, 1992). The technocratic model expresses two key dualistic organizing principles of American culture: the Cartesian separation of mind from body, and the belief in the possibility and the benefits of human separation from and control over nature, including the body. The medical management of birth and death are key phases in the development and reinforcement of this model.

Likewise, a dramatic hospitalization experience focuses enormous socialization pressures on an ill, and thus receptive, individual. It is instructive, then, to observe the elements of performance used by the hospital team, as led by the oncologist, in inculcating the patient with the core values of technocracy and in aligning her own perceptions and models of her illness and its meaning with those of the hospital staff. These performance elements include time disruption, symbolic distancing of practitioner from patient in hospital practice (Konner 1987; Stein 1990), and the effective silencing of the patient as an independent voice (DiGiacomo 1987). Mrs Bell had simply not been able to discuss with Dr Henderson the holistic healing philosophy (Cousins 1979, 1989; Simonton et al. 1980; Siegel 1986) that had animated her struggle against her disease. She and her family were shaken by the realization that in the entire oncology profession of their large city they had been able to discover only this single young doctor willing to administer an experimental treatment combination, but that even he stopped short of enthusiasm for 'mind-made health'. They were uneasy with the split between home, where one could take a hand in one's own healing, and clinic, where one could not. It wasn't that their holistic views were overtly denigrated in the clinic, but rather that the atmosphere at the clinic allowed them no conversational room to even discuss them.

The fact that Mrs Bell, like most female patients, was treated by a male physician also had repercussions. The relatively higher status of men in American society reinforces the drama of the doctor's role for a woman patient in ways that are further disempowering. However, as a result of years of working for a well-known holistically oriented nutritionist, Mrs Bell had also developed strong respect for self-care, patient responsibility and the holistic approach to healing. Where the technocratic model is based on principles of separation and mechanicity, the holistic paradigm is based on principles of interconnectedness and organicity (Davis-Floyd 1992). This dichotomy set up a structural tension in Bell's own life – a tension that also structured the drama of her death. Yet in turn, this structural tension was ultimately resolved through the manner of her dying, for she partly chose, and was partly persuaded by her family, to live out her remaining weeks at home in ever-deepening connection with her family, and to die there. This resistance to the full application of the technocratic model to her illness and death (which might have resulted in the applying of 'heroic measures' in the hospital, and a lingering death hooked up to machines) led the patient and her family to feel that she had died 'a good death' in spite of the disappointments encountered in treatment – a judgement with which the physician too concurred. Although he did not see or interact with her in the last weeks of her life and was not present in person to 'ferry her across', Dr Henderson, in his role as Charon, was with her and with the family until the end.

Terminality: A Drama in Three Acts

One day while Mrs Bell was still in the hospital, Dr Henderson informed her that there would be no more treatment. After examining her and reading her charts, he told Mrs Bell without preamble that 'resistance had developed', that she couldn't handle the treatment, and that there was nothing else known that could help her.

This was Act I in a dramatic three-day attempt to get Mrs Bell to accept the 'fact', as Dr Henderson saw it, that she was going to die. On this first day, the stage was set as follows: the eldest daughter sat on the window ledge at her mother's bedside. The doctor sat slumped in a chair in the furthest corner of the room, his posture suggesting both earnestness and a lack of ease. Mrs Bell and her daughter became suddenly anxious, both because they had waited six tension-filled days for this particular doctor to answer some questions about acute problems that had developed in the hospital, and because this was the first time in their three-month association with him that they could remember him actually sitting down with them. (His earlier talks had been careful and calm, but he had conducted them on his feet, while examining Mrs Bell on a raised table, or passing by in the hall while his nurse administered chemotherapy.)

After briefly discussing her systemic problems, Dr Henderson said that Margaret Bell was 'in a terminal phase'. He said that she would be getting no more chemotherapy because of the resistance, as seen in a blood indicator of tumour activity and on the CT scan, which revealed no appreciable shrinkage of tumours. Mrs Bell drew herself up with what dignity she could muster, and said that she accepted the diagnosis but did not consider herself 'terminal'. She said that she was still fighting. The daughter by her own admission was 'glaring' at the doctor and silently applauding her mother's spirited answer. Mrs Bell then asked the doctor, with a sourness quite uncharacteristic of her, whether he thought nutrition could play a role in healing. The unwillingness of the medical profession to consider nutritional approaches had been a long-time sore topic with her both professionally and personally, so when Dr Henderson answered with the single word 'no' the atmosphere became very quiet – and very charged. Mrs Bell said, 'Then that's all I have to say to you for now', and Dr Henderson stood and went out of the door.

Early the following morning he returned for Act II. He seemed more rested than the previous day and quite energetic, like a person who knows he has a job to do and feels equal to the task. He said clearly that she was 'terminal, and that isn't necessarily bad. One can prepare oneself for death'. Mrs Bell's response surprised even her daughter, who (though she had long ago thrown in her lot with the self-healing philosophies and had been listening to the personal empowerment tapes right along with her mother) thought that by now the diagnosis of terminality was quite clear. 'What I want to know,' said Mrs Bell, 'is how are you and "Dr Abdul" going to build me up so I can continue chemotherapy?' Dr Henderson appeared to realize at that point that Mrs Bell and at least some of her family were still reacting with denial, and he just left it. Indeed, her daughter said that 'It was as if she had not heard what he said.' Before he left the room, Mrs Bell requested a look at the CT scan taken a few days earlier and the addition of a vitamin C infusion to her IV bottle. Dr Henderson quietly agreed to both requests and departed.

Later that day, when Dr James Bell was sitting with his wife, Dr Henderson returned with the CT scan of her abdomen. In technocratic diagnosis, the CT scan, as external, 'objective' evidence obtained by tests and machines, constitutes a defining source of authoritative knowledge: that is, knowledge that forms the basis for decisions made and actions taken. It was apparent that the liver was largely taken over by tumours. The nursing staff did add an ascorbic acid solution to the IV, though at a much lower percentage than that recommended by Mrs Bell's nutritional therapy colleagues. Mrs Bell spent a quiet afternoon listening to her husband read to her: her eyes were bothering her and reading was difficult, though it never had been before. She seemed untroubled by this annoyance.

Meanwhile, the family 'cheering squad' (as they called themselves) went into action and rallied around the telephone checking out every possible lead. Much of the activity centred around the question of whether 'Dr Abdul' in the neighbouring city concurred with Dr Henderson's assessment of 'resistance'. When at last it was ascertained that he did, and had in fact already told Dr Henderson that further treatment seemed counterindicated, Mrs Bell's daughters began to confront for the first time the probable reality that their mother was going to die. This is how the stage was set as Dr Henderson and Mrs Bell went into the last act in their joint drama – acceptance of terminal status by the patient.

Early on Wednesday morning, when Mrs Bell's middle daughter was with her, Dr Henderson came back a third time. Mrs Bell asked him what treatments she would be getting when she got out of the hospital. The question was in the context of possibly continuing vitamin C infusions via a periodic IV drip. He said, 'I'm not recommending any. It's important for you to not just keep trying quackery but to think about your death.' Margaret then said, 'Oh, so you're saying I'm really terminal?' Dr Henderson replied, 'You've been terminal since you got your diagnosis in July.'

Later the middle daughter encountered Dr Henderson in the hall, and said 'She's finally accepted it.' He said, 'I was beginning to get worried.' On the afternoon of the same day, when the eldest daughter was with her mother, Dr Henderson again came in and repeated for a fourth time that she was terminal. It was as if he needed to reassure himself that she had indeed accepted her status. And perhaps he also wanted to make sure that the eldest daughter, who had been the primary caregiver, had, like her sister, accepted it too. To this eldest daughter, it seemed as though her mother was behaving as if she were receiving the news for the first time. When the doctor left, Mrs Bell said, 'I wish he'd told me before, so I could have gotten my study in order.'

In the weeks that followed back home, there suddenly appeared the motif of acceptance of death in Mrs Bell's talk. Soon she had completed the process of cognitive restructuring that accompanies all major perceptual shifts (dAquili, Laughlin and McManus 1979): in other words, her cognitive system had re-constellated around the diagnosis of terminality. When asked in an interview what were the deciding factors in this process, she answered that it was the combination of seeing the CT scan and the many repetitions by the doctor that she was terminal. In the days following the interview, her behaviour consistently expressed the thoroughness of this process of cognitive restructuring. Her clear-eyed acceptance of death's inevitability enabled her family too to relax into the next phase. Said one family member, 'It was as if the whole house stopped fighting and gave a sigh of relief.'

A Contrapuntal Dialectic between Philosophy and Performance

A chance discovery that Dr Henderson was working towards a doctorate in philosophy in order to pursue a strong academic interest in the ethics of euthanasia led me to request a formal interview with him. The interview was conducted a week after Mrs Bell's death. Early on, Dr Henderson had remarked, 'Dying is not something that happens to you. It is still something you can participate in.' It quickly became clear that Dr Henderson was committed to the social support of the dying in a profound way, and that he found his own niche as a cancer doctor to be just there, defining the limits of science clearly so that patients could prepare themselves for their deaths by completing their connections with life. What galvanized him was practising 'medicine,' which for him included taking full responsibility for 'taking care of them until they die' as opposed to surgery, which he said was 'just slice-of-time oriented ... where you do not have to take care of the whole patient, where you are either successful or not in that limited slice of time. It does not seem to be as rewarding.'

He said that medicine, as opposed to surgery, 'should be good at knowing when the battle is lost and you need to change directions and provide some comfort... It is trying to do everything you can and still be the court of last resort for a lot of people.' A period of practice in a small Mennonite community had helped form his outlook in this regard: he characterized it as a community with 'no loss of connection... The diagnosis of cancer was a signal that someone needed to be taken care of and hardly anyone went out of this little community to be taken care of.' He went on to say that had he been in a big city he would have continued in academic medicine, doing haematologic cancer protocols, etc. 'But I don't think I would have been as satisfied as I could be now because academic communities are so disjointed from the community of the patient that you can't provide total care. All you can do is provide heroic care.'

He preferred, he said, that there be 'some look over the long term even if it's only a couple of weeks. I'm not here to say, "well, I have nothing to offer you and you need to go someplace else".' It was clear that the 'long-term look' and 'total care' had a great deal to do with mediation of the dying process once curative medicine had reached acknowledged limits. In Mrs Bell's case it was clear from the way Dr Henderson went into action at the time of his announcement of the diagnosis of terminality that his sense of his role was centred just there – an observation confirmed by his own words in the later interview:

> The greater likelihood a patient has of being cured the more adamant I am about trying to get them to take chemotherapy. But if there is no cure rate we are really just talking about quality.
>
> Dying is an event we all have to go through and it seems to me you are short-changed if you don't [have the chance to] do the things you would regret not doing if you didn't know about it... You look at what you have to leave people. And that is all you can do. You leave something. You leave whatever you do through your connections...
>
> So, I do believe a lot can be made of the death. It can be a good death. [But in our culture] it has been hidden. It has been suppressed by medicine. Medicine has held out a hope that has been unrealistic... People still die ... too often in the hospital, too often not aware of what has happened to them. And they are older, and separated from their families. It's partly medicine and it's partly society.

At almost every point in the interview the narrative arrows, returning, pointed towards death. As this was clearly a focal point in Dr Henderson's perception of his role, I asked how his medical school training had prepared him to handle it. He answered that in medical school 'it's not as intense since you are not the one who is primarily responsible... Now I find since I am primarily responsible for patients that it has become difficult, an emotional effort, to help people die'. Characteristic features of biomedicine as described by a number of social scientists include a hierarchical physician–patient relationship in which the physician contains his authoritative knowledge within the community of biomedical practitioners, doling out small pieces of information to the patient while maintaining a general unwillingness to share this knowledge and information (Klein 1979; Fisher and Todd 1983; Lyng 1990). Susan DiGiacomo (1987) poignantly describes her five-year struggle not only with Hodgkins disease but also with the resistance her physicians demonstrated towards keeping her fully informed. An anthropologist and Ph.D. candidate at the time of her initial diagnosis, she desired a collegial relationship with her physicians in which knowledge would be shared and treatment mutually decided, while they sought to enforce a strict hierarchy in which she would follow the treatments they prescribed without asking too many questions. So pervasive is this approach in biomedicine that Stephen Lyng, in envisioning an ideal 'countersystem', suggests that in such a system, 'the practitioner's primary role would be educational, while the patient would assume primary responsibility for selecting a diagnosis and treatment regimen from among the various alternatives presented' (1990: 61).

Like DiGiacomo, Mrs Bell keenly felt throughout the course of her illness the disjuncture between the technocratic approach to healing and her own. This sense of disjuncture was intensified by her lifelong commitment to the idea of nutritional support for the immune system. She had doubts throughout the course of chemotherapy about whether she could fruitfully discuss nutrition with either her doctor or her nurse, doubts that were finally confirmed in the hospital during the dramatic announcement of terminality. The question she blurted out, 'Do you believe that nutrition can play a role in healing?' was one she had been longing to ask for months, as the answer would precisely define the limits of their system of shared beliefs. Dr Henderson's flat 'No' cemented the disjuncture, making impossible any kind of conceptual reconciliation between Margaret Bell's own beliefs and those of the medical personnel treating her, ultimately augmenting her sense of hopelessness.

In other words, although Mrs Bell and her family continued to pay good attention to her diet, the dissonance created by the total devaluation of this practice by the medical profession intensified her alienation from a part of herself. In Kleinman's (1988) terms, this situation constitutes a failure of conversation, a failure of the healer to empathetically enter into the patient's own discourse concerning her lived experience:

> Of all the tradecraft of the physician, nothing more effectively empowers patients. The very act of negotiation, if it is genuine ... necessitates that at the very least the physician show respect for the patient's point of view. The real challenge is for the physician to engage in negotiation with the patient as colleagues involved in care as collaboration. The practitioner begins this phase of care by elaborating an explicit comparison between the lay model and the professional biomedical model. The physician can determine points of disagreement ... he must be prepared to hear out their criticisms ... he must expose his uncertainty and the limits of his understanding, as well as his critical reaction to relevant popular and commercial images... The negotiation may end up in a compromise closer to the patient's position, a compromise closer to the doctor's position, or a joint lesson in demystifying professional and public discourse. (Kleinman 1988: 243)

Such a joint lesson in demystification was precisely what Bell was longing for. The psychological trauma of her illness experience stemmed from the ultimate and total lack of this kind of mutual negotiation, which she experienced as an extreme philosophical tension and and ultimate putdown.

Kleinman's conversation-centred approach to healing points up the structural tension in Dr Henderson's own working philosophy – the same tension that structured Margaret Bell's experience of illness and death. In Henderson's own words, he values connectedness and seeks for patients to be connected with both their families and himself. Yet his orientation to diagnosis, treatment and interaction with patients is highly technocratic: his words express, and his behaviour enacts, a more deeply held valuation of distance and separation. The pure science of complex tests is, as he put it, 'fun', 'a relief' from the strain of human commitment. He does not engage patients in two-way explorations of the experience or meanings of their illnesses.

In this, he is not alone. As Arthur Kleinman notes in *The Illness Narratives*, at the heart of healing lies the potential for a powerful dialectic that can draw the practitioner into the patient's experience and so can make of illness and treatment a rare opportunity for moral education. But instead, the modern medical care system does just about everything to drive the practitioner's attention away from the experience of illness. The system thereby contributes importantly to the alienation of the chronically ill from their professional caregivers and, paradoxically, to the relinquishment by the practitioner of that aspect of the healer's art that is most ancient, most powerful, and most existentially rewarding. (1988: xiv).

The Oncologist as Charon: Ethnoconcepts as Cultural Containment

Anthropologists have identified the most destructive concomitant of illness as fear of the unknown. For example, drawing on the works of such earlier theorists as Lévi-Strauss and Turner, Edward Schieffelin (1985) describes Kaluli healing seances in Papua/New Guinea as emergent social constructions that draw upon and actualize group knowledge about the unknown. He emphasizes that removal of chaotic fear through such dramatic social ordering processes lies at the heart of shamanistic cures.

In official American ideology, religion and medicine, like religion and state, split off from each other long ago. However, in practice the physician, laden as he is not only with responsibility for the body but also with heavy ritual and symbolic weight, has enormous influence over the psyche as well – a shamanic function of which American doctors themselves are often aware, and whose potential they even consciously exploit. Correspondingly, one of the main services American doctors, especially oncologists, provide is a cognitive system in diagnosis and treatment (or lack thereof) that organizes and alleviates the chaos of fear. Perhaps they do this partly by taking into themselves as ritual figures all those unknowns of mysterious disease processes and of death, thereby relieving patients of that wondering that is beyond their capabilities. As they are themselves untrained in shamanic myth and mystery, the full alleviation of such wondering is beyond the oncologists' skills, as well. Nevertheless, the ritual function of these doctors in Western society is consolidated by their exclusive control of authoritative, highly specialized scientific information, despite its conceptual emptiness/inability to explain. Yet the function itself is as simple and as old as the Christian idea of carrying another man's burdens for him, an idea shared by many ancient religions and healing traditions.

'Man,' wrote Suzanne Langer, 'can adapt himself somehow to anything his imagination can cope with, but he cannot deal with chaos' (1974: 23). It was Malinowski who first made clear the roles of religion and magic in inducing socially-agreed-upon confidence in observances designed to keep chaos at bay. Expanding on Malinowski's insights, Turner (1974) and Geertz (1973) emphasized the processual nature of 'reality', showing that ritual performances are not only models of what humans believe, but models for ensuring that they will believe it. The physician/healer who can assume the load of chaos from their patients will demonstrate a capacity to heal which may have little or nothing to do with specific knowledge of treatment or cures.

Seen this way, the oncologist's role must finally be understood as having profoundly mystical dimensions. This doctor is Charon in no mechanistic sense: even were euthanasia not legally problematic, morphine is ultimately no way out of the ethical dilemmas of his mandate. His task remains as hard as the task of the mythic thaumaturge has always been. In effect, he does address the lived experience of illness as well as the mechanics of disease. As arbiter of both the potentials and the limitations of scientific medicine against a disease virtually synonymous with death, he holds the reins on what the unassisted patient and family both fear and dare to hope. The mystery they fear is clear; what they dare to hope for – new discoveries in the nick of time, the power of the mind to transcend statistics, the possibility that choosing the time and the manner of death may be an affirmation of life, the ultimate rightness of their hunch that death will be an opening-out rather than a closing-in – may be much more individual, a result of their histories as persons.

But all individualism must be culturally contained, and this is where the cancer doctor's role has what is perhaps its central defining power. If a central act for many oncologists is the announcement of terminality and getting the patient to accept that diagnosis in the interests of 'a good death', it is clear that defining 'a good death' – known by anthropologists to be a social and religious preoccupation of societies in general (Fox 1973; Needham 1973) – has become at least partly the province of these specialists. If one realizes further that under certain conditions medical euthanasia may be permitted by our society, that these conditions are most often met in cancer cases, and that providing the means for euthanasia under these conditions is defined by at least some oncologists as 'bringing about a good death,' the implications of a role far beyond the medical one as contemporarily conceived are inescapable.

In the end, in Mrs Bell's case, the question of who does Charon's actual ferrying, and to where, was left open. But some boatman figure standing ready to meet the dying passenger and carry her across seems just as necessary in our age as in ancient times. If dying has become medicalized in America, it has not done so without bringing elements of performance into the medical profession along with it. If the choice of euthanasia, which Dr Henderson in an interview himself described as 'exiting stage right', is not yet actually condoned medically in America as a good death, it is at least a ready metaphor for evoking the performative aspects of dying.

'Speaking the speech of the spirits'

Ideas about illness and healing are as precisely idiosyncratic to specific cultures as is verbal language. Ethnoconcepts form part of the cultural signature: though there may be variation within traditions, part of what holds the members of a culture together is the containment provided by such ideas. This containment holds true for people whether they live in traditional or in highly industrialized societies. As anthropologists often point out, a biomedicine that is trying to humanize itself could learn much from other conceptual systems and practices. The Ju/'hoansi have a long and trusted heritage of altered-state healing by laying on of hands. In this tradition, religion and healing are inextricably linked. Such high value is placed on n/om (an intangible potency or energy activated in the healers' bodies and through the social setting) that herbal medicine, though known, is relatively little elaborated. Faith is put instead in the transformative experience shared by patient, healer and local band.

In Ju/'hoan healers' ideas of death and fate lies an even more striking contrast to Western medicine. For them, the power to kill a person lies in the hands of !Xu or //Gauwa (God). A healer has no foreknowledge of what he can cure and what he cannot cure. He must try to the limit of his strength and if he is defeated, the patient will die. No fault accrues to him if this happens: instead he is socially rewarded for having tried his best. For Ju/'hoansi, the strength of n/om is not a thing that one can augment by wishing or trying. It is given to the healers through the whim of !Xu. It does not set its owners apart or above others in the society, and they do not receive material benefits for using it. They participate, as do all the people, in the dancing and singing which accompany healing, for the pleasure of participation in a beautiful social event. Next, n/om is conceived as a thing only multiplied, never divided, by being shared. Thus Ju/'hoan healers are not concerned that when someone dies they have not tried hard enough (as a physician who has not kept up with the latest medical journals might feel) since a certain equable fatalism releases them from personal responsibility.

These factors have important correlates in the realm of individual psychology and social structure. First, n/om is not jealously protected, because sharing it redounds to the good of all. Nor are there material rewards to be had for exclusive control of n/om or its secrets. So a priesthood doesn't form, and egotism in the defensive sense does not characterize the social interactions of the n/omkxaosi with the ill. Second, the ultimate responsibility for life and death is far removed from these practitioners. Unlike practitioners of biomedicine, with its stoutly defended turf, Ju/'hoan healers are not assailed by accusations of ill-preparedness, coming either from others or from within themselves. They do not have to know everything. They can help ease the fear of sickness or of death, just as some biomedical doctors do, but they do not have to perform expert prognoses.

For these reasons, their role, even when dealing with grave illnesses like the recently introduced tuberculosis, does not define itself around an announcement of terminality or urgings to the patient to order her affairs. It is life- and hope-affirming throughout, holding to one source of hope – the patient's will to keep trying – as the indicator that effort should still be expended.

It is here that Ju/'hoan traditional practices and newer holistic medical approaches in the U.S. most significantly converge. In both approaches the patient is an autonomous actor, her individuality valued, her inclusion on the healing team a given. But, contrary to the American holistic tradition's emphasis on acceptance as an important part of the dying process (Kubler-Ross 1975), in the Ju/'hoan tradition the sick are alive until proven dead, given the benefit of the doubt as long as they are still breathing (and sometimes even afterwards): they are culturally allowed the ability to make the miraculous recovery if it is in them – or if, as the Ju/'hoansi believe, it is in !Xu's (//Gauwa's) will.

■ ■ ■

Seeing the ease with which Ju/'hoan healers accepted that death was ultimately out of their hands, I was filled with compassion for doctors whose techno-scientific tradition forces them to incur so much personal responsibility. I remembered Dr Henderson's words: 'Since I have become primarily responsible

for patients … it has become difficult, an emotional effort, to help people die.'
I believe that what we can learn from non-'experts" ministrations to the ill,
through their spiritual or humane approaches to the whole person, is profound. The rhetorical dialogue involving healer and patient can profoundly determine, if not the outcome of the illness process, every motion of their entwined minds as they step together towards the shore.

Note

1. An increasing number of studies deal with issues of communication and empowerment in the relationships among patient, physician and supporting others: see Fisher and Todd 1983; Romanucci-Ross et al. 1983; Baer 1987; DiGiacomo 1987, 1992; Kleinman 1988; Good et al. 1990, 1993; Good 1991.

References

d'Aquili, Eugene G., Charles D. Laughlin and John McManus, eds. 1979. *The Spectrum of Ritual: A Bio-Genetic Structural Analysis*. New York: Columbia University Press.

Baer, Hans A., ed. 1987. *Encounters with Biomedicine: Case Studies in Medical Anthropology*. New York: Gordon and Breach Science Publishers.

Biesele, Megan. 1975. 'Song Texts by the Master of Tricks: Kalahari San Thumb Piano Music'. *Botswana Notes and Records*, Vol. 7. Gaborone, Botswana: The Botswana Society.

——— 1979. 'Old K"xau'. In *Shamanic Voices*, ed. J. Halifax. pp. 54–62 New York: Dutton.

——— 1990a. *Shaken Roots: Bushmen of Namibia Today*, with photographs by Paul Weinberg. Johannesburg: Environmental Development Agency.

——— 1990b. *Learning a 'New' Language of Democracy: Bushmen in an Independent Namibia*. Nyae Nyae Development Foundation of Namibia, Windhoek, Namibia.

——— 1992. *'Women Like Meat': Ju/'hoan Bushman Folklore and Foraging Ideology*. Johannesburg: Witwatersrand University Press.

Biesele, Megan, ed. with R. Gordon and R.B. Lee. 1987. *The Past and Future of !Kung Ethnography: Critical Reflections and Symbolic Perspectives*. Essays in Honor of Lorna Marshall. Hamburg: Helmut Buske Verlag.

Biesele, Megan and Robbie Davis-Floyd. 1994. 'Dying as Medical Performance: the Oncologist as Charon'. In *The Performance of Healing*, eds C. Laderman and M. Roseman. London: Routledge.

Biesele, Megan, and Richard Katz. 1986. '!Kung Healing: The Symbolism of Sex Roles and Culture Change'. In *The Past and Future of !Kung Ethnography*, eds M. Biesele, R. Gordon and R.B. Lee. Hamburg: Helmut Buske Verlag.

Buckman, Robert. 1984. 'Breaking Bad News: Why Is It Still So Difficult?' *British Medical Journal* 288: 1597–99.

Cousins, Norman. 1979. *Anatomy of an Illness*. New York: Bantam.

——— 1989. *Head First: The Biology of Hope*. New York: E.P. Dutton.

Davis-Floyd, Robbie E. 1982. 'Myth, Ritual, and Shamanism: A Symbolic Analysis of Cultural Vitality in Mexico'. Unpublished manuscript.

—— 1987. 'The Technological Model of Birth', *Journal of American Folklore* 100(398): 93–109.
—— 1988. 'Birth as an American Rite of Passage'. In *Childbirth in America: Anthropological Perspectives.* Karen Michaelson and contributors. Beacon Hill, MA: Bergin and Garvey Publishers.
—— 1992. *Birth as an American Rite of Passage.* Berkeley and London: University of California Press.
DiGiacomo, Susan. 1987. 'Biomedicine as a Cultural System: An Anthropologist in the Kingdom of the Sick'. In *Encounters with Biomedicine: Case Studies in Medical Anthropology.* ed. Hans A. Baer, pp. 315–46 New York: Gordon and Breach.
—— 1992. 'Metaphor as Illness: Postmodern Dilemmas in the Representation of Body, Mind, and Disorder.' *Medical Anthropology* 14: 109–37.
Ferguson, Marilyn. 1980. *The Aquarian Conspiracy.* Los Angeles: J.P. Tarcher.
Fisher, Sue and Alexandra Dumas Todd.1983. *The Social Organization of Doctor–Patient Communication.* Washington, DC: The Center for Applied Linguistics.
Fox, James J. 1973. 'On Bad Death and the Left Hand: A Study of Rotinese Symbolic Inversions'. In *Right and Left: Essays on Dual Symbolic Classification*, ed. Rodney Needham, pp. 342–68 Chicago: University of Chicago Press.
Geertz, Clifford. 1973 *The Interpretation of Cultures.* New York: Basic Books.
GIVIO (Interdisciplinary Group for Cancer Care Evaluation, Italy). 1986. 'What Doctors Tell Patients with Breast Cancer about Diagnosis and Treatment: Findings from a Study in General Hospitals', *British Journal of Cancer* 54: 319–26.
Good, Mary Jo Delvecchio. 1991. 'The Practice of Biomedicine and the Discourse on Hope: A Preliminary Investigation into the Culture of American Oncology.' In *Anthropologies of Medicine: A Colloquium on West European and North American Perspectives,* eds Beatrix Pfleiderer and Gilles Bibeau. Special Edition of *Curare* 7: 121-36.
Good, Mary Jo DelVecchio, Byron J. Good, Cynthia Schaffer and Stuart E. Lind. 1990. 'American Oncology and the Discourse on Hope', *Culture, Medicine and Psychiatry* 14: 59–79.
Good, Mary Jo Delvecchio, Linda Hunt, Tsunetsugu Munakata, Yasuki Kobayashi. 1993. 'A Comparative Analysis of the Culture of Biomedicine: Disclosure and the Consequences for Treatment in the Practice of Oncology'. In *Health and Health Care in Developing Societies,* eds P. Conrad and Eugene Gallagher. Philadelphia: Temple University Press.
Guenther, Mathias. 1999. *Tricksters and Trancers: Bushman Religion and Society.* Bloomington: Indiana University Press.
Harrington, Maureen. 1990. 'The Medieval and the Modern,' Sunday *Denver Post,* Contemporary Section, 23 September 1990, pp. 14–20.
Henriques B., F. Stadil and H. Baden 1980. 'Patient Information about Cancer: A Prospective Study of Patient's Opinion and Reaction to Information about Cancer Diagnosis', *Acta Chir. Scand.* 146: 309.
Hertz, Robert. 1960 [1909]. *Death and the Right Hand,* trans. Rodney and Claudia Needham. London: Cohen and West, New York: The Free Press.
Katz, Richard. 1982. *Boiling Energy: Community Healing among the Kalahari !Kung.* Cambridge, MA: Harvard University Press.
Katz, Richard, and Megan Biesele. 1980. *Male and Female Approaches to Healing among the Kalahari !Kung.* 2nd International Conference on Hunting and Gathering Societies. Deptartment of Anthropology, Laval University, Quebec.

——— 1987. '!Kung Healing: The Symbolism of Sex Roles and Culture Change'. In *The Past and Future of !Kung Ethnography: Critical Reflections and Symbolic Perspectives*, eds M. Biesele et al. Hamburg: Helmut Buske.

Katz, Richard, Megan Biesele and Verna St. Denis. 1997. *'Healing Makes Our Hearts Happy': Spirituality and Transformation among the Ju/'hoansi of the Kalahari*. Rochester, VT: Inner Traditions Press.

Klein, Norman. 1979. *Culture, Curers, and Contagion: Readings for Medical Social Science*. Novato, CA: Chandler and Sharp Publishers, Inc.

Kleinman, Arthur. 1988. *The Illness Narratives: Suffering, Healing, and the Human Condition*. New York: Basic Books.

Konner, Melvin. 1987. *Becoming a Doctor: A Journey of Initiation in Medical School*. New York: Viking.

Kubler-Ross, Elizabeth. 1975. *On Death and Dying*. New York: Harper and Row.

Langer, Suzanne K. 1974. *Mind: An Essay on Human Feeling*. Baltimore: Johns Hopkins University Press.

Long, Susan O. and Bruce D. Long. 1982 'Curable Cancers and Fatal Ulcers: Attitudes toward Cancer in Japan', *Social Science and Medicine* 16: 2101–8.

Lyng, Stephen. 1990. *Holistic Health and Biomedical Medicine*. Albany, NY: State University of New York Press.

Marshall, Lorna. 1999. *Nyae Nyae !Kung Beliefs and Rites*. Cambridge, MA: Peabody Museum Press.

Moerman, Daniel E. 1987. 'Physiology and Symbols: the Anthropological Implications of the Placebo Effect'. In *The Anthropology of Medicine*, ed. Lola Romanucci Ross, pp. 156–68. South Hadley: Bergin and Garvey.

Needham, Rodney, ed. 1973. *Right and Left: Essays on Dual Symbolic Classification*. Chicago and London: University of Chicago Press.

Romanucci-Ross, Lola, ed. 1983. *The Anthropology of Medicine: From Culture to Method*. South Hadley, MA: Bergin and Garvey.

Rosenberg, Harriet. 1990. 'Complaint Discourse Aging, and Caregiving Among the !Kung San of Botswana'. In *The Cultural Context of Aging*, ed. Jay Sokolovsky, pp. 19–41. New York: Bergin and Garvey.

Schieffelin, Edward L. 1985. 'Performance and the Cultural Construction of Reality', *American Ethnologist* 12 (4): 707–23.

Siegel, Bernie. 1986. *Love, Medicine, and Miracles*. New York: Harper and Row.

Simonton, O. Carl, Stephanie Matthews-Simonton and James Creighton 1980. *Getting Well Again*. New York: Bantam.

Stein, Howard F. 1990. *American Medicine as Culture*. Boulder, CO: Westview Press.

Todd, Alexandra and Sue Fisher, eds. 1983. *The Social Organization of Doctor–Patient Communication*. Washington DC: Center for Applied Linguistics.

Turner, Victor 1974. *Dramas, Fields, and Metaphors: Symbolic Action in Human Society*. Ithaca/London: Cornell University Press.

CHAPTER 5

'AS IF GOYA WAS ON HAND AS A MARKSMAN'[1]
FOOT AND MOUTH DISEASE AS A RHETORICAL AND CULTURAL PHENOMENON

Brigitte Nerlich

■ ■ ■ ■ ■ ■ ■

> Mary had a little lamb
> Its mouth was full of blisters
> And now it's lying in a ditch
> With all its brothers and sisters.
> Schoolyard rhyme, March 2001

INTRODUCTION

Foot and mouth disease (FMD), a highly infectious animal disease, broke out in the U.K. in the spring of 2001 and swept through the countryside for seven months. It attracted long and intensive coverage in the press, on television and on the web. From the start the government declared war on the disease and implemented a slaughter, culling or killing policy, combined with a policy of shutting down the countryside to prevent the spread of the virus. Although this war frame might initially have been useful in rallying support for the slaughter policy and to create a feeling of acceptance, solidarity and control, the metaphor later backfired when a metaphorical war turned into a literal and all too well documented holocaust. This might have made it almost impossible to argue for or to implement more environmentally friendly alternatives to slaughter, such as vaccination or a combination of vaccination and slaughter.

I will argue that both the metaphor of war and the slaughter policy tapped into a wide network of cultural narratives, metaphors and potent images. Only by looking at the cultural context in which the policy and the metaphors and images surrounding it interacted can one understand why politicians stuck to this policy throughout the epidemic and how farmers and the general public reacted to this policy (see Döring and Nerlich forthcoming). I will attempt to show how FMD as a cultural phenomenon became caught up between what some might argue was an effective way of managing risk and what many saw as an exceedingly crude and largely counterproductive exercise in risk communication (see Donaldson, Lowe and Ward 2002: 32).

This chapter was inspired by three research traditions: cognitive linguistics and the study of metaphor, which has become a popular area of linguistic research since the 1980s (Lakoff and Johnson 1980); cultural, social and symbolic anthropology, where the study of the social and ritual uses of metaphor has become popular since the 1970s (Turner 1974; Sapir and Crocker 1977); and the study of social representations in social psychology (Harré 1984; Moscovici 1984; Wagner 1994). I will examine how both the policy of slaughter, used to eradicate FMD, and the media reaction to the outbreak and to the policy, were framed by a repertoire of metaphors and images which draws on both universal and historically and culturally specific reservoirs of narratives and symbols.

Foot and Mouth Disease in the U.K. – a Short Summary of Events

The first case of FMD in the U.K. since the 'great epidemic' of 1967, and a smaller outbreak in 1981, was reported on 20 February 2001 on a pig farm in Northumberland. FMD is a highly contagious disease that affects mostly farm animals. Movement preventions were established and the old policy of slaughter, the so-called 'stamping-out' policy (see Woods 2004 for a history of this policy), was implemented to prevent the spreading of the virus to other (cloven-hoofed) animals. On 25 February cases were identified on farms as far away as Devon, in pigs, cattle and sheep. At the beginning of March cases of FMD increased rapidly in Cumbria, but ministers and officials from MAFF (the then Ministry of Agriculture, Farming and Fisheries) declared the situation 'under control'. At the end of March the Prime Minister Tony Blair took personal charge of the situation and brought in the army to control the disease. In April the epidemic reached its peak. In May the general election was postponed. In June it took place amid hopes that the epidemic was (yet again) under control, but it flared up again in certain 'hot spots', especially North Yorkshire (see Nerlich and Wright 2006). At the end of September 2001 there were more than 2,000 reported cases, but the epidemic was coming to a halt. By the end of the epidemic up to eight million (mostly healthy) animals had been slaughtered and disposed of (burned, rendered or buried), and in January 2002 Britain regained the coveted disease-free status, which means that it was free to export meat again.

'Superficially, the problem was one of a highly contagious disease – but FMD is not a threat to human health and it is not even normally fatal to animals. From a public policy point of view, foot and mouth is entirely an economic disease.' (Donaldson, Lowe and Ward, 2002: 32). The (indirect) impact of FMD on human health was therefore largely overlooked. However, Mort et al. (2005) have gathered data from diaries, interviews and group meetings which indicate that the epidemic gave rise to widespread individual and community trauma and has had lasting negative health, economic and social impacts on the people who live in those affected rural areas (see also Nerlich and Döring 2005). The severe social and psychological implications of FMD have also been highlighted in a report prepared by the European Parliament (European Parliament 2002). In this chapter I claim that the social impact of FMD can only be understood if we study FMD not only as a disease and not only as an economic phenomenon, but as a rhetorical and cultural one.

FMD: A Cultural Phenomenon

FMD is more than just a veterinary and scientific problem. For farmers the 'event' became a 'crisis', a 'plague', an 'epidemic' and a 'national disaster' because they feared, yet again, for their livelihood as well as for the welfare of their animals. For food consumers it became a 'crisis' because FMD came in the wake of a long list of other health and food scares, such as listeria in eggs, salmonella in chicken, BSE (or mad cow disease), E. coli in meat, swine fever, the panic over genetically modified food (GM food), a resurgence of AIDS, as well as other calamities, such as fuel protests, the breakdown of the rail system, devastating floods, and debates about global warming, industrialization, commercialization, and globalization (see Nerlich 2004b). This conjunction of negative social representations of food and health contributed to an immediate 'catastrophizing' of the FMD event by farmers, consumers and the media alike: 'In good times it would be a disaster, but in times like these it is a catastrophe'. (GU, 26/02/01).

From the tone of the media coverage, and the end-of-the-world warnings from farmers, most Britons probably reckon F&M is a killer disease, which, once it touches a herd, rapidly wipes out the lot. As for humans, it's surely a death sentence to eat meat infected with the bug: your foot probably falls off and your mouth seizes up forever. Why else would government rules insist that infected animals be slaughtered instantly and the disease be eradicated so absolutely? It must be a merciless plague. (GU, 28/02/01)

But most importantly, FMD became a 'crisis' and a 'tragedy' because of the *remedies* used to treat the disease, vividly depicted in newspapers, on television screens and on the web in the shape of burning pyres and smoking piles of carcasses. As George Bernard Shaw said in Man and Superman (Act 3): 'In the arts of life man invents nothing; but in the arts of death he outdoes nature herself, and produces by chemistry and machinery all the slaughter of plague, pestilence and famine' (quoted in Moodie 2001, online).

The potent and emotionally charged images of death and destruction resonated with a wide network of historical narratives, symbols and metaphors, which turned FMD from a clinical into a cultural (social, linguistic) phenomenon. They also resonated with a network of hidden conceptual metaphors (such as 'FMD is a journey') (see Nerlich, Hamilton and Rowe 2002), which are a part of everyday speech and affect the ways in which we perceive, think and act, but which normally go unnoticed (see Lakoff and Johnson 1980). The images and emotions triggered by the handling of FMD also generated a deeply cultural response in the form of narratives, poems (see Nerlich and Döring 2005), photo collages, artwork, video footage and even theatre plays, such as New Life and Silence of a Dale (Lawrence and Petch 2002; Bartlett, 2003) (see; http://www.littoral.org.uk/project_grassroots.htm).

Studying FMD as a cultural phenomenon will give us the opportunity to ask a number of questions. Answers to these questions should have relevance not only for understanding the public and the policy reaction to FMD in the U.K. in 2001, but also for an understanding of similar phenomena in the past, such as BSE, and in the future when other animal or human epidemics, such as avian influenza, will certainly happen (on the social understanding of epidemics, see also Rosenberg 1992; Rosenberg and Golden 1992).

- Which type of knowledge influences public thinking and acting when faced with an event like FMD?
- What is the power of images and metaphors in shaping the emotional bases of public fears about FMD?
- From which domains of public knowledge are these metaphors and images taken?

- Do these or other images and metaphors also inform 'rational' attempts at dealing with FMD?
- Does the use of certain images have implications for the policy adopted to deal with an event like FMD? And would the use of different images have had different effects?
- How do rhetoric, culture and politics interact?

This chapter can obviously not supply answers to all these questions. It will focus on the interaction between rhetoric, culture and politics. Using a conceptual framework pioneered by the social psychologist Wolfgang Wagner, it will first attempt to study FMD as an exercise in collective material and collective symbolic coping. This will be followed by an analysis of the metaphorical and symbolic repertoires exploited during the crisis, based mainly on a corpus of articles taken from the British broadsheet, *the Guardian*.

Dealing with FMD – between Collective Material and Collective Symbolic Coping

As already indicated, the outbreak of FMD followed in the wake of a series of health scares, food scares and other 'disasters'. The handling of the BSE crisis in particular had primed the public and the media to distrust officials and to panic. So-called 'experts' had said that BSE posed no risk to human health, but it did. So who was to say that FMD would not do the same? People felt that they had been misled in the past and that they would possibly be misled yet again (that the public was misled by the government was general headline news after the publication of the Phillips report on 27 October 2000).

When the first cases of FMD were reported, the government had two options to 'cope' with this outbreak. It could either see it as a (scientific) challenge, an opportunity to search for new remedies to an old problem and an opportunity to discuss openly the state of British agriculture and agricultural practices, to coordinate and direct new scientific research into the emergence and spread of the disease, and, finally, to reassure the public that dealing with FMD would not pose any health risks. Or else it could deal with FMD as it had dealt with it for the past century: by imposing a slaughter policy (also called: eradication policy, containment policy, culling policy, stamping-out policy).

As the campaign of reassurance had been a mistake in the BSE crisis (see the Philips report on the BSE crisis: Phillips report 2000), and as directing new scientific research into the emergence and spread of the disease (as recommended in the Phillips report) would not have pleased farmers faced with fears about economical survival, and would have looked like hesitation and wavering, the natural option was to implement the slaughter policy. It had worked in 1967. It had worked in 1981. So, why should it not work now? As North (2001b: 25) pointed out: 'But not only was the Ministry unable to factor these changes [in agriculture and the rural economy, BN] into its control plan, it was not even able to change the plan. That was set in stone. ...'

It also allowed them to use a metaphor that seems to be entirely natural in crises like FMD, namely the war metaphor, and to skilfully exploit its immense rhetorical potential.

The use of this metaphor created, at least initially, a certain solidarity between the government, the farmers and the public and ensured that a policy that some saw as outdated was regarded, at least for a time and at least by some, as time-honoured and solid, as a policy 'that works'. Declaring 'war' against the disease reinforced this solidarity. In the following I will first show how the concepts of 'natural attitude' (Orleans, n.d., online) and 'symbolic coping' (see Wagner, Kronberger and Seifert 2002) can be used to explain some aspects of the public and the policy reaction to FMD.

At a time of 'crisis' (or at least what was portrayed *as* a crisis) it is 'natural' to react almost 'instinctively', to do what is thought to be 'common sense', and to take refuge in well-rehearsed recipes for action, to implement well-known disease control policies. This natural attitude can be compared to what Wagner et al. call the 'collective material coping' with a disease or new scientific phenomenon (what government and public services actually *do* to avert potential harm posed by a technological innovation or threat to public health) (see Wagner et al. 2002: 324).

When FMD occurred the natural attitude towards this outbreak was primarily one of: 'let's kill the virus'. And if killing the virus meant slaughtering millions of animals then this is what one had to put up with. To use any other method, such as vaccination (which would also have 'killed' the virus, but in a much less visible and spectacular way), was seen in some way as 'unnatural' or was what some called 'unthinkable' (GU, 25/03/01). It just didn't resonate with the traditional images we have of killing 'something' and demonstrating control over something. Politicians could have declared 'war on viruses by inoculation' and sent in the 'soldiers of our fine veterinarians, combating the disease', but at a time when the same politicians were anticipating a battle for votes during a forthcoming election, this might not have appealed to the majority of U.K. citizens, only the more scientifically sophisticated minority.

To make this mass killing of animals more understandable, terms like *war, battle* and *combat* were immediately used to describe the 'fight' against the disease and FMD or the FMD virus became the common enemy. Falling back on the conceptual metaphor 'Handling FMD is a War', which underlies expressions such as 'the FMD frontline has moved', 'the war against FMD is not over yet', and so on, is almost unavoidable in these circumstances. In a report on a play based on FMD, the *Guardian* theatre critic Lyn Gardner wrote:

> The road from Hampsthwaite in North Yorkshire is picture-perfect. It takes us through rolling dales, past mile after mile of stone walling, into hamlets and villages. On a bright winter's afternoon, it looks *peaceful*. But two years ago a *battle* was *fought* here, as it was all over rural Britain. The *enemy* – the foot and mouth virus – was *vanquished* after months of *combat*, but for those who live in Nidderdale, the *scars* remain. (Gardner 2003: 14, italics added)

Making *war* against the virus and thus killing (culling!) animals was a policy that should be easy to understand and easy to visualize. Vaccination, by contrast, was much less easy to understand and much less easy to visualize. The war imagery sanctioned and sanctified the policy and vice versa. Warfare also exemplifies pure domination, and waging war against FMD could be seen as exerting domination and control of nature. In cases of war or warlike situations, patterns of understanding are immediately in place and can be used by the public to make sense of this warlike event and to feel in control. The government in turn can use these patterns of understanding and recipes for action to justify the use of certain policies.

The slaughter policy was intended to eradicate the virus by eradicating the carriers of the virus. It was accompanied by other measures intended to stop the virus from spreading. The virus became the deadly, invisible enemy that stalked the countryside, evoking images of past plagues, the Four Horsemen of the Apocalypse and the Grim Reaper. The measures to stop the virus from spreading were called 'biosecurity' measures and consisted mainly in movement control, isolation of infected farms (exclusion zones), and scrupulous disinfecting of farms, people and vehicles (see Nerlich and Wright, 2006). Just as the slaughter of animals can be regarded as a 'ritual', the use of disinfectant too can be seen as a symbolically charged purification ritual, a ritual that in some instances could get out of control. As Sue Wrennall, a farmer's wife and Ph.D. student, wrote: 'The physical activities involved in "cleansing and disinfection" maintained activity, but erased the material imprint of livestock farming, and the self identity inextricable from the "place" was fundamentally altered.' (Wrennall 2003). This is vividly described in the following extract from a fictional account of the impact of FMD:

> I've put disinfectant all around Little Josh's shippen like a sort of protective shield, and I never let them out now in case they breathe in the disease. (Morpurgo 2001: 47–48)

> Our fire may be out, but when I looked out of the window first thing this morning I could see the smoke from three fires drifting down the valley. It's

like the whole world is sick. And Dad is trying to wash it away. He's out there from dawn to dusk working like a madman. Ever since the ministry told him that every building on the farm has to be cleared out and disinfected, he hasn't stopped. He's out there now – and it's nearly nine o'clock at night – cleaning off the rafters in the lambing shed. He's been at it all day. Mum has tried to stop him, to slow him down. But he won't listen. (2001: 88–89)

In the end Dad is close to suicide and has to be hospitalized, but later recovers.

Evoking images of war and purification was supposed to rally the nation around the government, but there was a flip-side to this propaganda work, just as there was a flip-side to the actual work of slaughtering and disinfecting, as the images associated with this 'natural policy' were very negative: burning pyres; trenches full of carcasses; slaughtermen holding shotguns to the heads of animals; *keep out* signs everywhere, and so on. This was not the 'natural' and conventional image of the British countryside.

Initially shown to demonstrate just how deadly and dangerous the 'enemy' was and to justify the deadly weapons used in the war against FMD, these images soon turned the public's opinion against what began to be seen as a 'medieval policy'. As one writer said: the fight against FMD 'has finally found its rhythm of robotic kill, burn and bury, riding on a crest of angst, leaving in its wake bergs of death and ashes.' (Moodie 2001).

It is puzzling that despite a widespread public revulsion at the sight of such hellish pictures, and some demonstrations, this never led to a public revolution. One reason might be that the public, the press and the government were united to some extent by what some call 'collective symbolic coping' (Wagner et al. 2002).

Wagner et al. have studied public and media reactions in Europe following the release of genetically modified (GM) tomatoes. They tried to explain some of these reactions by using the concept of 'symbolic coping'. To paraphrase a part of the abstract of the article: symbolic coping occurs at times of increased policy activity and of media reporting which alerts the public. Wagner et al. suggest that at such times the 'public show a high proportion of beliefs in menacing images; that these beliefs are relatively independent of pre-existing popular science knowledge; and that they are functionally equivalent to scientific knowledge in providing judgemental confidence and reducing self-ascribed ignorance.' (2002: 323).

> In a modern society's division of labor, the government and public services are responsible for containing and averting the potential harm posed by a technological innovation. We shall call this *collective material coping*. The agents of material coping are scientific experts, bureaucrats and regulators in their institutional interplay. They, as well as lay people, develop an under-

standing, make sense of, or come to terms with the innovation. This will be referred to as *collective symbolic coping*. Experts usually draw in the symbolic resources of scientific understanding, such as theories and causal explanations. Lay people refer to the symbolic resources of everyday life and public communication. Both depend on symbolic coping to find a shared code for communication. (2002: 324)

Although the introduction of GM tomatoes was more startling than the occurrence of FMD, with which farmers have lived for centuries, the public reaction to this event was similar, as it was primed by the reporting of a long list of other food scares and disasters, including the GM controversy. These had set up a rather stable 'media template' (Kitzinger and Reilly 1997) or 'frame' (Conrad 1997) according to which FMD could be reported as yet another 'crisis', and 'symbolic coping' with this event could begin. As in the case of GM food, menacing images prevailed, especially those of war.

Let us look briefly at the similarities and differences between the types of symbolic coping involved when the public is faced with GM food or FMD.

In contrast to a GM tomato, FMD posed 'real' risks; it was not just an as yet hypothetical threat to human or animal health. However, although 'real risks' to animals and the economy were involved, FMD carried no direct risks for human health (only indirect ones emerging from the slaughter and disposal policy). And whereas people conceived of tomatoes as potential killers ('killer tomatoes') in their efforts at symbolic coping, a different type of symbolic coping was needed to deal with the reality of millions of animals being killed 'on screen' every day on the 'killing fields' of Britain.

Wagner et al. define symbolic coping 'as the activity of a collectivity which attempts to maintain the integrity of its worldview by making sense of any new phenomenon' (2002: 325). This was also the case with FMD, although a somewhat older phenomenon. The differences appear when we look at the stages of symbolic coping postulated by Wagner et al. (2002).

'First, for symbolic coping to occur, the new phenomenon must be communicated as being relevant and as challenging the taken for granted or desirable way of life' (2002: 325). FMD challenged the taken-for-granted view of a pastoral and idyllic countryside as a source of cheap food. As one *Guardian* writer pointed out: 'Farming ... is at the centre of who British people think they are. It has a heady, long-standing, romantic and sworn place in the cultural imagination' (GU, 26/03/01). FMD brought about a sudden clash between images of peacefully grazing cows on England's green and pleasant land and those of burning cows on giant pyres, between spring lambs gambolling across green meadows and soldiers 'slitting the throat of a spring lamb, or beating its brains out with a blunt instrument' (North 2001a: 12; see also North 2001b).

Clichés like 'the silence of the lambs' and 'silent spring' therefore abounded (see Nerlich 2003).

'Second, to accommodate the new phenomenon within the existing repertories of social knowledge, various interpretations, images and metaphors emerge in media and conversations which render it intelligible.' (Wagner et al. 2002: 325). This happened in the case of FMD as in the case of GM food. 'Gradually, the various interpretations tend to converge towards one or a few fairly widespread interpretations which define some essential attributes.' In the case of FMD a fairly stable and widespread interpretation based on a few core metaphors and images was in place almost from the start.

'Finally, the interpretations may consolidate or give way to a more scientifically accurate understanding in the long run' (Wagner et al. 2002: 325). This seems not to have happened in the case of FMD, although there was plenty of scientific evidence that could have made FMD more understandable and plenty of scientific arguments that could have been used to plead for the use of vaccination instead of slaughter. There was no real process of normalization, after which symbolic coping is supposed to be replaced by scientific understanding. At least there has been, up to now, an enormous resistance towards such normalization.

It is also notable that 'image-beliefs', which, according to Wagner et al., initially compensate for scientific knowledge and then fade, did indeed gradually fade, in the sense that they became less frequent in the media reporting, but were not really replaced by more scientific knowledge. Most of the image-beliefs persisted throughout the period we studied and became quite entrenched. What was initially a way of framing an issue (say, in terms of war or plague) became something of a symbolic blindfold, which prevented policy makers from envisaging any alternative means of dealing with FMD. The material coping by slaughtering resulted from a particular framing of (or coping with) the problem of FMD on the political level. This produced the symbolic material in the form of very negative images of pyres and burning carcasses, which, in turn, was used by the media as an illustration of the war going on in the countryside. These symbolically charged images made it easier for the public to initially accept the war metaphor as a menacing 'image-belief' of FMD, and for journalists to use them in their articles, where negatively charged metaphors and images are recognized and appreciated more easily than positively charged ones (see Steen 1994: chapter 9).

However, the accumulation and aggregation of these images later undermined this acceptance and led to a rejection of the policy – symbolic coping undermined material coping. As Wagner et al. write, 'collective coping is triggered by the media, which construe and communicate "some thing" as novel and as challenging an established way of life' (2002: 324). Let us now look more closely at the media response to the outbreak of FMD.

FMD and the Media

The media discourse was a major part of the process by which farmers and non-farmers constructed meaning of this new social situation and framed the issues surrounding FMD. So as to understand FMD as a cultural phenomenon it is therefore imperative to study the media discourse. In the case of FMD in particular the media were the main source of most people's knowledge of what went on out there 'in the countryside' and of the pictures of burning pyres and slaughtered animals, because the countryside itself had been shut down completely so as to prevent the virus from spreading. The media were also an outlet for farmers to talk about their plight and the plight of their animals and to vent their anger at the measures taken by the government and/or the delays in implementing them. The media were also the main tool politicians had to influence and steer the public mood and to try and create a climate of acceptance for the policies used to deal with FMD, an attempt that did not go unchallenged, though.

As FMD attracted large media attention over a very long time, I focused on one online archive of articles alone, established quite early on in the epidemic, by the *Guardian Unlimited*.[2] This special report received the European Online Journalism award 2001 as the best coverage of a news story.

I restricted the period of research to four months: from the end of February to the end of July, although outbreaks of FMD continued to occur and to be written about until the end of September. Out of 614 articles published during that time, we analysed 170 and extracted all metaphors, historical allusions and symbolic references from this material. Some supplementary matter was taken from the foot and mouth coverage in *The Times*, the *Daily Mail* and various online resources.

FMD Caught in a Network of Associations and Metaphors

In a paper following the bombing of the World Trade Center, the cognitive linguist George Lakoff has stressed that the 'images we see and recall interact with our system of metaphors. The results can be powerful' (Lakoff 2001). Although not as potent as the images and metaphors which interacted in people's minds after 11 September 2001, the images of burning pyres and heaps of carcasses broadcast and printed throughout the FMD crisis, which was just coming to an end when September 11 ended, interacted potently with other metaphors used to frame the issue, such as war and plague. During the last major FMD outbreak in 1967 the newspapers wrote: 'Silently, across the misty farmlands of Britain it advances, with all the remorselessness and stealth of a medieval plague ... It is foot-and-mouth, the disease that strikes fear into the heart of every farmer' (quoted by O'Neill 2001). In 2001 many farmers said things like: "'This is not a disease we have now. It is a plague. Cumbria is going to be wiped out.'" (GU, 23/03/01).

Studying the metaphors used during the outbreak of FMD might be useful if we want to achieve a clearer understanding of the whole sociocultural configuration built around FMD. Like Wolfram Aichinger, a literary scholar and historical anthropologist, I therefore see metaphors, and the narratives they are embedded in, as important and productive cultural forces in their relatedness to other social factors. To study the metaphors used during the FMD crisis is studying them 'at work' in 'real life', in their rich historical context, in their interaction with the whole fabric of culture and society (see Aichinger 2002). This approach resonates with anthropological research into the social and pragmatic uses of metaphor advocated since 1977 (see Sapir and Crocker 1977), an approach 'that seeks to probe into the cultural foundations behind metaphor' (Fernandez 1991: 7; see Holland and Quinn 1987). This research has gone on in parallel with the development of cognitive linguistics (Lakoff and Johnson 1980). However, the pathways taken by these research traditions only cross occasionally (see Fernandez, ed., 1991).

FMD provoked the reactions it did because it tapped into a network of sometimes clashing images about British farming and the British countryside. For farmers the countryside is a place of work and 'industry'; for 'townies' it is a rural or pastoral idyll, a place for relaxing walks and a provider of anonymous and cheap food. For both farmers and urban dwellers it was a relatively peaceful place. All this changed when the 'war' on FMD began, when the countryside was closed down, and when the images of mass killings were everywhere. In British cultural imagination the burning pyres clashed sharply with pictures of bucolic farming landscapes as painted by John Constable, for example, and reminded people of medieval funeral pyres. This clash between the ancient and the modern, the idyllic and the barbaric has also been explored in poems written during the crisis, poems that clashed with the standard pastoral poem by William Wordsworth (written 1804, published 1807; Wordsworth) that everybody knows:

> I wandered lonely as a cloud
> That floats on high o'er vales and hills,
> When all at once I saw a crowd,
> A host, of golden daffodils;
> Beside the lake, beneath the trees,
> Fluttering and dancing in the breeze.

Here are two of numerous poems written by poets, farmers, vets and children during the FMD outbreak, which overturn the image of the countryside evoked by Wordsworth (see Nerlich and Döring 2005, Döring and Nerlich in press).

Sad silent spring

Spring is a strange time to reap a harvest,
a harvest which tastes bitter in the mouth and catches at the throat.
Roadside daffodils are become roadside shrines – memorials to animals that
    are no more.
The empty fields stare back reproachfully, as if to say 'No life is here.
The flowers might bloom, the hedgerows may burst with buds and leaves
    and birds,
but the reasons we are here are gone.'
All reason is gone.

A panorama opens out of blank and bare fields, punctuated – by curtains of
smoke rising to dissipate into the atmosphere, like the unanswered questions,
    the reasons why.
At times smoke rolls across the fields, the hedges, the walls, and roads.
to go through is to smell and taste and sense what all Cumbria sees and hears:
Confusion, frustration, perplexity, anger, despair and grief.
And unanswered questions waft across the country.

At other times all human life and living was here
Fields full and frisking, spring full of life.
Soon enough there'll be another burgeoning, a colourful blossoming
of boards by the roadside – 'For sale' and 'Offers invited'
Children, men, women fells and fields weep the loss.
All things pass, but all things may not come again.

Mourn all the beasts and all the best of lives as lived at one with the land.
Night falls: 'Nor voice nor sound broke on the deep serene'
Voiceless certainly, but light against the dark the flames now seen.
Surely hell fire not lux eterna.
All things at rest, quietly whispering in the ear of night:
'Please let there be some life, some hope, or some God.'

(Allan 2001)

Farewell to Agriculture?

Each day another herd is rounded up,
Condemned to death, another rendezvous
At some disputed barricade, farmgates galvanised
Into action, padlocked, the chain of events

'D' notices and disinfectant,
Narrow lanes cowed into submission,
Animals held for questioning, shot like hostages
One by one as the invisible deadlines run out.

Obscure sheds thick with blood and urine,
Hedgerows rank with inquisitive film crews
Who take to the air and relay the drama,
Relentlessly as if it was the Blitz

Or Civil War creeping forward.
Armageddon on your doorstep,
Vietnam in North Devon and Cumbria,
Biological warfare in England's green and pleasant land,

Digital images broadcast every night into the safe,
Plush depths of suburban sitting rooms,
Contorted carcasses slung upside down
From outstretched digger arms,

The stench of funeral pyres,
Fuelling the night's curfew,
Long lines of flickering flames,
Anguish on a farmer's face.
(Crowden 2001)

During the FMD epidemic the media images of war, plagues, plague pits and burning pyres (plus other visual, olfactory and auditory associations, ritual enactments, anchorings of the present in the past, and so on) were combined, blended and integrated into a complex network of meaning, where they mutually supported and reinforced each other (see Aichinger 2002). These metaphors helped the public, the politicians, the scientists and the journalists to 'naturalise' a highly complex phenomenon and served at first as an anchor when they threatened to drown in the sea of medical, political, economic and social issues surrounding FMD. However, when the metaphors and images were repeated too often, both the public and the officials were found drifting in a sea of anxiety and revulsion.

Metaphors of war were used throughout the FMD outbreak. They were immediately adopted by politicians, such as the then Minister for Agriculture, Nick Brown. They were widely used in the newspapers, and also pervaded the talk of farmers, their wives and their children, some of which was recorded in various factual and fictional diaries, published in the press ('On the farm', GU, March 2001) and in book form (e.g. Morpurgo, *Out of the Ashes*, 2001, adapted and broadcast on CBBC, the BBC's children's channel in September 2001). Pictures of shotguns held to the heads of animals and the 'real' military moving in to slaughter animals and supervise their 'disposal' in mass graves, trenches and on mass pyres add symbolic weight to the metaphors. The sheer *mass* of slaughtered animals alone evoked images of killing fields and of mass killings during the First and Second World Wars (Bergen-Belsen), as well as Vietnam (especially after one minister had suggested the use of napalm as a way to make the fires burn more efficiently).

A more insidious, but still prevalent image was that of FMD as a criminal or as the perpetrator of a crime where the victims were the animals. However, in a curious twist of metaphorical framing FMD also took prisoners, as farmers became (virtual) prisoners on their farms and animals were imprisoned in their pens or on mud-locked fields. And, more curious still, the victims of FMD, the animals, became suspects and were traced, investigated, tracked by police, as if they were criminals, and later they were condemned to death and executed. In fact, the theme of crime and punishment went through the whole FMD episode like a (sometimes invisible) red thread, as FMD was seen as a punishment visited on farmers by 'nature' for either their squalid farm practices or their highly industrialized methods of farming – both regarded as 'sins' or 'crimes' against 'nature'.

FMD was often described as a raging fire and the fire metaphoric was also adopted in the fight *against* FMD ('firebreaks', etc.). The whole imagery surrounding fire was starkly highlighted by the real fires of the pyres burning all over the country. This then could elicit in people's minds further cognitive and cultural processing of terrifying and/or mysterious phenomena, especially pictures of hell and medieval funeral pyres (see Aichinger 2002).

From the start, FMD was also portrayed as a new type of plague or Black Death, with all the emotive and historical connotations this word carries with it. Plague metaphors were often linked to biblical references.

All metaphors used in the FMD discourse were embedded in a network of cultural, historical and religious narratives, on which they fed and which gave them heightened emotional power. This was especially evident when one calf, later called Phoenix, escaped slaughter after lying for five days beside the carcass of his shot mother. Phoenix 'rising from the ashes' became immediately a national icon of hope and recovery and helped to overcome the feelings of doom and fatalism that had started to become entrenched (see Hume 2001).

However, Phoenix can also be seen as a 'symbol of the government's obsession with and sensitivity to the front pages' (ibid.). Tony Blair's decision to have mercy on Phoenix and to save it from execution was certainly a good propaganda move. Despite all these positive connotations Phoenix also evoked counter-images of the worshipping of the 'Golden Calf', a symbol of the commercialization of farming, which was seen by some as lying at the root of the FMD crisis.

Finally, there were three types of more hidden but very pervasive fields of metaphoricity that ran through the whole FMD discourse: of FMD as engaged in a hand-to-hand combat with farmers and officials (FMD hits, strikes, deals a blow, a double whammy, and so on); of FMD being engaged on a long journey (FMD goes, marches, travels, reappears, etc.); of FMD being engaged in a contest or race with farmers and officials (FMD runs, speeds up, slows down, etc.), a race that officials constantly believed they were winning (we are on the home straight, we are stopping it in its tracks, etc.), whereas in fact they were overtaken by FMD at almost 'every turn'. These types of 'conceptual metaphors' normally go unnoticed but they structure and organize our thinking about crucial life events or, in this case, events of national importance.

It was remarkable that in the course of the FMD outbreak metaphors were gradually overtaken by reality; they were progressively literalized, one can say. This replaced to some extent the process of 'normalization' postulated by Wagner et al. Whereas at first fighting the disease was just a way of talking about the actions taken against FMD, a month into the outbreak the army was drafted in and 'war' was declared on the disease. What was *like* a military operation became a military operation. The use of metaphors reached a different level and officers engaged in the battle against FMD began to make direct comparisons with real wars, such as the Falklands, the Gulf war, Bosnia and so on. War also became more real as 'civil war' broke out between various factions, such as MAFF and farmers, government and MAFF, town and country, the pro-culling and the pro-vaccination lobby, and so on.

A similar turn of events and turn of metaphors can be observed in relation to FMD depicted as a criminal. The link between FMD and crime was from the start not only metaphorical, but literal: from suspicions that meat had been illegally imported, to illegal movements of sheep, to intentional spreading of disease, to criminal compensation claims, and so on. The metaphor and the reality of criminality were intertwined at almost every turn.

This literalization of the war and the crime metaphoric might partly explain why there was no popular revolution caused by popular revulsion. Initially war and crime had served as metaphors that created solidarity against a common enemy or perpetrator of a crime. But when civil war amongst those engaged in the war against FMD broke out and when criminal activities made people suspicious of each other, this solidarity was shattered. What little there was in terms of mutual trust was eroded. To create a new common bond in a fight against the government under these circumstances was almost impossible.

Conclusion

Waging war against FMD and killing thousands of animals was an old and tested policy of disease control. It has, however, not only clinical but also symbolic implications. It might have been used to show who was in control: man over nature and controlling FMD was implicitly seen as controlling 'the country', something especially important at a time of a general election. Had politicians adopted vaccination, they would have had much less opportunity for 'tough' speeches, headline-grabbing sound bites, and powerful photo shoots. Vaccination would have looked like 'giving in' to the disease, like 'backing down', like losing control and therefore losing face. So the only option was to try and capitalize on FMD, to exploit 'the political potential of catastrophes' (Beck 1992: 24). Using metaphors of war, plague, fire and hell helped to create what some call a 'moral panic'; it helped to instil fear in people and to encourage them to 'turn away from complexity and the visible social problems of everyday life and either to retreat into a "fortress mentality" – a feeling of helplessness, political powerlessness and paralysis – or to adopt a gung-ho "something must be done about" attitude' (McRobbie 1994: 199). Both attitudes were noticeable in the reactions to FMD, but especially the first, when farms came under siege from both the disease and governmental bureaucracy. However, the metaphors of war used to 'sell' the policy of slaughter to the public later backfired as the images of burning pyres and rotting carcasses showed that the eradication of FMD was more than just a metaphorical war. This eroded public trust in the policy and might potentially undermine the willingness of sections of the public to support a slaughter policy in future outbreaks.

In this chapter I have tried to examine how the culture in which we live contributed to framing the images of this epidemic and the reactions of journalists, politicians and the public. The public and the policy makers reacted in the way they did not because they had a deep scientific understanding of FMD but because the disease was embedded in a wide network of historical events, previous food and health scares, potent images, religious imagery, but most importantly metaphors of war and challenge. Only by understanding the language used in talking about FMD can we understand public (and that includes politicians') understanding of FMD. Policy makers should become aware of how profoundly metaphor affects us psychologically and emotionally and how vital language is for handling crises like FMD.

Acknowledgement

Research for this chapter was carried out as part of the work for a project financed by the Economic and Social Research Council studying the social and cultural impact of foot and mouth disease (award reference: L144 25 0050).

Notes

1. Line from the poem 'Please keep out – Please keep out', by James Crowden (2001). Used with the permission of the author.
2. GU= *Guardian Unlimited*. *Guardian Unlimited* archive (2001): Foot and mouth disease: http://www.guardian.co.uk/footandmouth/

References

Aichinger, W. 2002. 'St. Anthony Abbot, the Fire and the Pig: Metaphorisation of Disease and Extension of Meaning in the Middle Ages'. In *Metaphor, Cognition, and Culture*, ed. Z. Maalej. Frankfurt am Main: Peter Lang.

Allan, S. 2001. 'Sad Silent Spring'. [Online] Was available at: http://www.greenquarter.co.U.K./littoral/fmd/record/poems/# [now defunct].

Bartlett, A. 2003. *Silence of a Dale 2001: The Story of Foot and Mouth in the Words of Local People*. Play at Harrogate Theatre, February 2003, script.

Beck, U. 1992. *Risk Society: Towards a New Modernity*. London: Sage.

Conrad, P. 1997. 'Public Eyes and Private Genes: Historical Frames, News Constructions, and Social Problems', *Social Problems* 442: 139–54.

Crowden, J. 2001. 'The End of Agriculture?'. [Online] Available at: :http://www.jamescrowden.co.U.K./docs/foot_and_mouth_poetry.doc

Döring, M. and B. Nerlich in press, 'An Outbreak of Poetry: Mapping the Human Impact of the 2001 Foot and Mouth Disease Outbreak in the U.K. from a Cultural Point of View'. In *Sustaining Language*, eds A. Fill and H. Penz. Vienna: LIT Verlag.

—— Forthcoming. *From Mayhem to Meaning: Assessing the Social and Cultural Impact of Foot and Mouth Disease in the U.K. in 2001*. Manchester: Manchester University Press.

Donaldson, A., P. Lowe & N. Ward. 2002. 'Towards a Sustainable Rural Economy: Lessons from Foot and Mouth'. In *Sustainable Development and Social Inclusion*, ed. M. Eames with M. Adebowal. York: Joseph Rowntree Foundation.

European Parliament. 2002. Report by Temporary Committee on Foot and Mouth Disease [Online] Available at: http://www.europarl.europa.eu/sides/getDoc.do;jsessionid=51BDAC8887EF9201919559D8B5875929.node2?language=EN&pubRef=-//EP//NONSGML+REPORT+A5-2002-0405+0+DOC+PDF+V0//EN

Fernandez, J.W. 1991. 'Introduction: Confluents of an Inquiry'. In *Beyond Metaphor*, ed. Fernandez.

—— ed. 1991. *Beyond Metaphor*. Stanford: Stanford University Press.

Gardner, L. 2003. "After the Cull: Yorkshire Has Not Forgotten the Agony of Foot and

Mouth. Now a Play About the Crisis has Local Farmers Enthralled', *The Guardian*, 12 February, p. 14.
Guardian unlimited archive. 2001. Foot and mouth disease. [Online] Available at: http://www.guardian.co.U.K./footandmouth/
Harré, R. 1984. 'Some Reflections on the Concept of "Social Representation"', *Social Research* 51: 927–38.
Holland, D. and N. Quinn eds. 1987. *Cultural Models in Language and Thought.* Cambridge: Cambridge University Press.
Hume, M. 2001. 'A National Nervous Breakdown'. *Spiked-online*, 2 March. [Online] Available at: http://www.spiked-online.com
Kitzinger, J. and J. Reilly. 1997. 'The Rise and Fall of Risk Reporting: Media Coverage of Human Genetics Research, "False Memory Syndrome" and "Mad Cow Disease"', *European Journal of Communication* 123: 319–50.
Lakoff, G. 2001. 'September 11'. [Online] Available at: http://www.bilkent.edu.tr/~robin/lakoff.pdf
Lakoff, G. and M. Johnson. 1980. *Metaphors We Live By.* Chicago: Chicago University Press.
Lawrence, M. and H. Petch 2002, *New Life.* Play about foot and mouth disease that toured Yorkshire in October 2002.
McRobbie, A. 1994. *Post-Modernism and Popular Culture.* London: Routledge.
Moodie, M. 2001. 'The Full Oaklands'. 4 May 2001 [Online] Was available at: http://csf.colorado.edu/archive/2001/bdnow/msg01945.html. [Now defunct]
Morpurgo, M. 2001. *Out of the Ashes.* London: Macmillan Children's Books.
Mort, M., I. Convery, J. Baxter and C. Bailey. 2005. 'Psychosocial Effects of the 2001 U.K. Foot and Mouth Disease Epidemic in a Rural Population: Qualitative Diary-Based Study', *British Medical Journal* 331: 1234.
Moscovici, S. 1984. 'The Phenomenon of Social Representations', in *Social Representations,* ed. R.M. Farr and S. Moscovici. Cambridge: Cambridge University Press.
Nerlich, B. 2003. 'Silent Spring: Tracking the Fate of a Salient Metaphor in the British Media 1998–2002'. [Online] Available at http://www.metaphorik.de/04/nerlich.htm
——— 2004a. 'War on Foot and Mouth Disease in the U.K. in 2001: Towards a Cultural Understanding of Agriculture', *Agriculture and Human Values* 21 (1): 15–25.
——— 2004b. 'Risk, Blame and Culture: Foot and Mouth Disease and the Debate about Cheap Food'. In *The Politics of Food,* eds M. Lien and B. Nerlich, pp. 39–58. Oxford: Berg.
Nerlich, B., C. Hamilton and V. Rowe. 2002. 'Conceptualising Foot and Mouth Disease: The Socio-Cultural Role of Metaphors, Frames and Narratives'. [Online] Available at: *metaphorik.de*: http://www.metaphorik.de/02/nerlich.htm
Nerlich, B. and M. Döring. 2005. 'Poetic Justice? Rural Policy Clashes with Rural Poetry in the 2001 Outbreak of Foot and Mouth Disease in the U.K.', *Journal of Rural Studies* 21: 165–80.
Nerlich, B. and N. Wright. 2006. 'Biosecurity and Insecurity: The Interaction Between Policy and Ritual During the Foot and Mouth Crisis', *Environmental Values* 15 (4): 441–62.
North, R. 2001a. 'How Labour killed the countryside', *Daily Mail,* 9 September, p. 12.
——— 2001b. *The Death of British Agriculture.* London: Duckworth.
O'Neill, B. 2001. 'When foot-and-mouth didn't make the front page', *Spiked-Online,* 2 April. [Online] Available at: http://www.spiked-online.com
Orleans, M. n.d. 'Phenomenology'. *Encyclopedia of Sociology.* [Online] Available at: http://www.hss.fullerton.edu/sociology/orleans/phenomenology.htm

Phillips report: The BSE inquiry 2000. [Online] Available at: http://www.bse.org.U.K./
Rosenberg, C.E. 1992. *Explaining Epidemics and Other Studies in the History of Medicine.* Cambridge: Cambridge University Press.
Rosenberg, C.E. and J. Golden eds. 1992. *Framing Disease: Studies in Cultural History.* New Brunswick: Rutgers University Press.
Sapir, J. D. and J. Crocker eds. 1977. *The Social Use of Metaphor: Essays on the Anthropology of Rhetoric.* Philadelphia: University of Pennsylvania Press.
Shaw, G.B. 1903. *Man and Superman: A Comedy and a Philosophy.* Cambridge, MA: Harvard University Press.
Steen, G. 1994. *Understanding Metaphor in Literature: An Empirical Approach.* London: Longman.
Turner, V. 1974. *Dramas, Fields and Metaphors.* Ithaca, NY: Cornell University Press.
Wagner, W. 1994. *Alltagsdiskurs – Die Theorie sozialer Repräsentationen* (Everyday discourse – The theory of social representations). Göttingen: Hogrefe.
Wagner, W., N. Kronberger and F. Seifert. 2002. 'Collective Symbolic Coping with New Technology: Knowledge, Images and Public Discourse', *British Journal of Social Psychology* 41: 323–43.
Woods, A. 2004. *A Manufactured Plague: The History of Foot-and-Mouth Disease in Britain.* London: Earthscan.
Wordsworth, W. 1804/07. 'I wandered lonely as a cloud'. [Online] Available at: http://www.bartleby.com/145/ww260.html
Wrennall, S. 2003. 'The Cumbrian Farm Place: Methods of Disclosure after the 2001 Foot and Mouth Outbreak'. Paper for the Annual Meeting of the Association of American Geographers. [Online] Available at: http://convention.allacademic.com/aag2003/view_paper_info.html?pub_id=1859&part_id1=23665 [Now defunct]

CHAPTER 6

THE PALAESTRAL ASPECT OF RHETORIC

F.G. Bailey

■ ■ ■ ■ ■ ■

All rhetoric is palaestral. The metaphor of the wrestling-school is a vehicle for the rhetorical struggle to pin down another person and make him or her accept a definition of the situation. This essay examines the tactics used to do that and the sociocultural context that makes it possible.

THE LINTEL

In the late 1960s in Losa, a community of about 800 inhabitants in the Maritime Alps of northern Italy, I heard a tale – an anecdote – about a lintel. I will tell it and then ask a catch-all question: 'What does one need to know in order to understand what was going on?'

The storyteller was Roberto, a wealthy corporate executive who drove down from his office in Milan to spend weekends in his substantial house in the centre of Losa. He came in his chauffeured car. Roberto was an eager collector of local memorabilia. Hiking in the mountains, when he was passing a *baita* (a shack built in the upland pastures, occupied only when cattle were taken up the mountain to graze – virtually every baita, including this one, was by then derelict) he noticed that the stone lintel over the doorway had a date carved on it, the numbers spaced across its length. He worked out that it came from Losa's old *municipio* (town hall), which had been destroyed in the Napoleonic wars, and he decided that he must have it for his collection. He knew which family owned the baita (everyone knew at least the basics about everyone else in Losa and its environs) and the following weekend he sought out its head, offering both to buy the lintel and to have it replaced with a concrete beam. The owner, identified in the municipal register as *contadino*, a peasant, refused. He did so respectfully, explaining with great politeness and some eloquence that for his part he would be happy to *give* the stone to the gentleman (*signore*), but unfortunately this could not be done because the baita was jointly owned with his three brothers. It would be wrong to give it away or sell it without first asking their permission. He would have been more than glad to do that, but it was impossible because one brother was in the Argentine, one was in the U.S., and the third was in Nice, and he had been out of touch with all of them for many years. In the circumstances, the best he could do would be to cut off his portion of the stone, one-fourth, and give it to the gentleman.

Roberto, telling the story, said the man was a fool for passing up the chance to make a bit of money without having to do anything to earn it. Then he added that he himself had not been very smart. 'If I'd sent Vincenzo to ask for it as a favour – to prop up a gutter or something – he'd have got it without any fuss'. (Roberto was a modern-day seigneur in Losa; Vincenzo, a construction-crew foreman, was one of his henchmen.)

There are two obvious questions: (1) Why did the peasant refuse to sell? (2) Why did Roberto think that Vincenzo could have had the lintel for nothing? You can easily – and correctly – deduce the lintel owner's motives: he intended to cock a snook at Roberto. Nor – the second question – is it difficult to work out that, at least in Roberto's mind, the lintel owner had some kind of affinity with Vincenzo. You can also guess that both the refusal and the presumed link with Vincenzo had something to do with class. Roberto was a wealthy man and a *signore* (a gentleman) and the lintel owner was a peasant who worked with his hands, as did Vincenzo.

The motives are clear enough; and so also – in broad outline – is the context of class antagonism. What is less clear is why the peasant chose to deliver his refusal in that elaborately indirect fashion. What could have been a plain 'no' expanded into a parable about the alternative structures available to define morality in Losa.

A Plurality of Structures

I will use a simple interactionist and (qualified) intentionalist model of the part rhetoric plays in the working of social systems (where 'qualified' means that the model concerns purposive action but does not assume that what comes to pass is explained by the actor's intentions). The model is constructed out of two elements: one is a repertoire of alternative ideas both about how a system should work (a morality) and about how it actually works (a presumed reality). The other is a repertoire of persuasive techniques.

No structure and, more generally, no idea (including, I suppose, itself) could be an eternal verity. All structures and all theories, in varying degrees, are fallible insofar as they can be displaced by another structure, which the performers hope will better suit their purposes. Structures are constructs of the mind; they are not entities that exist outside the world of thought. None can be *true* in the clear and simple correspondence-sense of that word. As Christopher Fry put it in his play, *A Yard of Sun*, 'There may always be another reality / To make fiction of the truth we think we've arrived at.' To structure something is to give it an identity (a name) and impart to it, *imaginatively*, a stillness, a concreteness, a wholeness and an exclusivity that are not the reality. We have the poet's pen:

> And, as imagination bodies forth
> The forms of things unknown, the poet's pen
> Turns them into shapes, and gives to airy nothing
> A local habitation and a name.
>
> (Shakespeare, *A Midsummer Night's Dream*, V.i.)

Structures are imagined things. It follows that one and the same reality – which, unstructured, is Shakespeare's 'things unknown' – can be identified in different ways. When people interact this divergence is an ever-present possibility. There is then a competition to define the situation by the use of techniques that 'increase the mind's adherence to the theses presented for its assent' (Perelman and Olbrechts-Tyteca 1971: 4).

What 'theses' were being presented for 'assent'? Roberto, at the outset, clearly intended to structure their encounter on the principle of expected utility – of a market economy. He was a buyer; the peasant was a seller; they would negotiate and agree on a price. The lintel would be replaced with a concrete beam; the peasant would get money; and Roberto's collection of memorabilia would be enriched. The interaction would be strictly a business transaction, each party acting, as neoclassical economists assume is the norm in every interaction, 'rationally' – that is, each would act in what he believed to be his own best interests.

There is a marvellous univocality about the neoclassical economists' one-size-fits-all expected-utility definition of any exchange situation that interests them professionally: no status is of any relevance in understanding what is taking place except that of the rational, self-interested, calculating, economic person. Expected utility is (purportedly) a universal language; it presumes common ground, is neutral, and is without cultural entanglements; it is the extreme of abstraction.

But it is clearly too abstract. Roberto belonged to the upper class and the lintel-owner was a peasant; they both lived in the same community and therefore shared certain moral standards; they both spoke the three languages of the region (Italian, Piedmontese, and the local dialect, Niçois); and their families had lived there for generations and carried with them the baggage of a long history of past encounters. These facts, however, in the expected-utility frame were no more relevant to understanding the encounter than was the length of their hair or the colour of their eyes. In economic transactions all such contexts count for nothing.

In that light Roberto's opening move – suggesting a deal – is a reasonable (and economic) way to initiate an interaction; it assumes a motivational structure in the other person that is uncomplicated because it transcends culture and is part of a universal human nature: whoever they are, all they want is a good bargain. That assumption of universality makes transactionalism, on the principle of least effort, a suitable opening gambit in an exchange when one hopes to keep the matter uncomplicated.

Roberto failed to impose a simple market definition on their encounter. The peasant (but not saying so directly) did not agree that the language of transactions, used to make the offer, was unencumbered; rather it entailed, even if it did not voice, class antagonism and, in addition, it thus offended a different morality which the peasant claimed – disingenuously – was his guide. Tacitly rejecting the definition of himself and of Roberto as one-dimensional profit-minded bargainers, he responded with a prestational claim that appears to be simple and unambiguous but is in fact a layered complexity composed of two contradictory structures.

On the surface the peasant's redefinition of their encounter as a prestation is no less univocal than Roberto's 'economic man' transactional definition. The invocation of his brothers and their rights appears to be an unambiguous statement about the peasant himself and his moral community: he was the kind of person who is guided by the obligations of brotherhood. But there is also a hint in his words that Roberto, by offering him money as an inducement to betray brotherly obligations, was not behaving properly. In this there is an implied assumption that he and Roberto shared – or should have shared – the same moral standards. They were *paesani* – people who belonged to the same moral community, who define right and wrong in the same way, and who share a relationship of solidarity and mutual consideration. In conformity with this ethos the peasant spoke of his readiness to *give*, not sell, the lintel. The remark about brotherly obligation, therefore, could be construed as a reproach. It implied that poor people like himself upheld *paesano* morality and lived by its standards, while the rich used their money to get what they wanted, even when it meant subverting moral proprieties. None of this was openly stated;

it was insinuated. The peasant's finely polite manner indicated that Roberto's crass market attitude, and his disregard for traditional family values, should cause him to feel a touch of shame.

Roberto, telling the story, did not feel any shame that I could see. He recounted the peasant's sentiments about his obligations to his brothers without comment (other than a slightly rueful grin). I think he took it for granted that his audience (myself and others) would realize that what the peasant said was not all that the peasant was talking about. No one bothered to remark on the discrepancy between the claim of a strongly felt obligation and admitting to having been out of touch for many years. The message, in other words, had nothing to do with his obligation to his three brothers; it meant something else. It was deliberately, although not avowedly, multivocal.

Roberto did understand what was going on: he was being mocked. The peasant's elaborate protestations that he would dearly like to make a present of the lintel if only he were free to do so fell into the same category as his sermonizing about brotherly obligation: the words said one thing, they meant something different and contrary. That second meaning is coded in the shape-shifting noun, *signore* (gentleman), which the peasant used to refer to Roberto.

In Losa at that time the word 'signore' had three distinct meanings depending on the roles attributed to a signore and the structures in which they were said to operate. Two of these meanings provide a context for the story of the lintel. In the first, a signore was a person of wealth and standing who served the community, taking on the obligations of leadership, helping those less well off, and in return receiving the respect and admiration of ordinary people. Structured in this way, *signorilità* presupposed not only a stratified population – 'The rich man in his castle / The poor man at his gate / God made them high and lowly / And ordered their estate' – but also a relatively closed community. This was indeed the case in Losa, even down to the beginning of the Second World War. Ordinary folk had little to do with the world beyond their village and their valley, and when they needed to deal with the higher levels of the administration or the Church – to get a place in hospital, to avoid or defer conscription and the like – they sought the help of the gentry, because the gentry had *le braccia lunghe,* long arms that could reach out into world of the Church and the state. When the occasion called for it, people in Losa in the 1960s still treated that definition of signorilità as operative. Roberto, for example, had a considerable clientele of people obliged to him for the favours he had conferred on them using his wealth and his long arms.

The lintel owner's use of the word 'signore' in the process of rejecting Roberto's offer permits this *noblesse oblige* definition of the term to drift ironically into their encounter via the insinuation that Roberto was overlooking not only his obligations as a paesano, but also the special obligations that attached to those paesani who were also signori. The irony is there because a second and contradictory definition of 'signore', along with a correspondingly different social structure, is drawn into the situation. The peasant used this second definition to typecast Roberto and so to define their situation. Once again, however, the case was not made propositionally; it was implied.

The exemplar of this second type of signore was another man in the community whose status was slightly uncertain. He had useful outside connections (mainly with church dignitaries and in the world of commerce) and he was fairly rich, but his identity in the municipal register was not at Roberto's level, *benestante* (independently wealthy), but *commerciante* (businessman). Several years earlier he had bought a stretch of rock-strewn mountainside from three peasant brothers, who, they themselves boasted, had exploited his ignorance by inflating the price of land that they knew was absolutely unfit for agriculture of any kind. (He had told them he wanted to use it to develop thorn-stock on which to graft roses.) He held the land for a couple of years and then sold it, at a huge profit, to a cement company that needed to have access to the cliff behind it. He must have known all along of the company's plans. The three brothers felt themselves cheated. Word got about and he became the boilerplate case of the bad signore, the person who uses long arms not to benefit ordinary people but to do them down.

The lintel owner made no direct reference to class conflict. His entire discourse was overtly framed in only one part of the traditional paesano morality (brotherhood). It was left to Roberto to fill in for himself not only the signorilità part of that morality but also to make explicit, in his remark that Vincenzo could have had the stone for free, the unvoiced class antagonism. Thus the peasant managed both to disoblige a rich man and at the same time to claim, implicitly, a moral high ground. That morality, however, was an instrument, not a directive; the values of signorilità and brotherly-cum-community solidarity were used to convey their precise negation. By saying one thing the peasant insinuated its opposite.

That raises two questions. First, what motivated this indirectness? Discourse on the class struggle was certainly not without its own ample vocabulary to mark approval and disapproval. Second, how is it possible to do that? How does a message, which *surreptitiously* contains its own contradiction, invalidate itself and authenticate the contradicted meaning?

Motives and Tactics

In the discussion of motivation and tactics that follows I am not suggesting that the peasant systematically rehearsed in his mind all the alternative ways in which he might score off Roberto. Reading what is in another's mind is chancy. My target, however, is not other people's minds but the sociocultural setting in which they live. For that it is necessary to survey whatever courses of rational action were available in that culture and in that particular context. To do that one examines the costs and benefits of various alternative responses that were culturally available to the peasant. Whether or not in fact he made these calculations is at present beside the point.

It is conceivable (barely – I will say why in a moment) that the peasant was acting straightforwardly as a true believer in paesano values and signorilità, that he was genuinely upset by the amorality implicit in the money offer, and was trying, so to speak, to save Roberto from his baser self. Roberto did not think so; neither do I. Mockery, not soul-saving, was the motive. There are some oblique but quite unambiguous signs, to which I will come in a moment, that make the disrespect obvious.

When Roberto first made his bid to define their encounter as a transaction, the peasant might simply have accepted the offer. Or he might – Roberto would surely not have been surprised – have asked to be paid more. But to do that would be to accept Roberto's initial definition of their situation and to forego the chance to play the game of moral one-upmanship.

The peasant might, alternatively, have deliberately driven up the price to make Roberto baulk. That would have provided a left-wing soap-box from which to deploy themes of capitalist greed and thus occupy a different kind of moral high ground. For that there might have been some costs.

First, at that time and in that place Marxist rhetoric associated with 'The Revolution' had become something of a joke. One old man, who had been imprisoned in Mussolini's time as a Communist, used to drive a small flock of sheep past the elevated verandah where Roberto's aged mother sat in a wheelchair, sunning herself. He would stop and chat, looking up from the street, and on each occasion he would end the conversation with a warning: '*Viene la rivoluzione* ... Come the revolution and I will be sitting up there, Signora, and you will be driving the sheep to pasture.' They saw it – everyone saw it – as an ironic joke between paesani, not merely mitigating but for the moment altogether eliding the difference in wealth and class between them. The lintel owner had no place for that kind of irony. He was not sharing a joke with Roberto. (He did introduce an element of farce, but in a different way and with a different effect. I will come to that shortly.)

Second, the idiom of straight rentier-bashing might have been rhetorically ineffective because it addressed a theme that was situationally ambiguous. In Losa at that time the left/right political division was complicated. Losa had no more than a handful of Communists. The dominant cleavage lay between Christian Democrats (slightly in the majority) and Socialists. The Socialists were led by Roberto and some other well-to-do people, whose ideological convictions had less to do with socialist dogma than with their wartime experience, when, in 1943, they fought in the Partisan wars against Mussolini's Fascists and the German occupying forces. To have openly invoked the idiom of class warfare against Roberto, the leader of the principal left-wing group in the village, might, given the ironic contradictions of the situation, have been confusing. Effective rhetoric cannot rest on assertions that are merely confusing.

Third, to have played the class-antagonism card directly and openly would have deprived the lintel owner of the pleasure afforded by a winning game of indirectness. More on the joy of rhetoric later.

Paesano values, in contrast, preserved that gratification. They also had an immediate pay-off, because they were a *topos*, a rhetorical commonplace that could be presented, in apparent innocence, as the one and only and obviously 'true' definition of their situation, one that was instantly compelling on Roberto who was himself a signore and a paesano. The peasant deployed paesano values as if they were beyond contention, normatively imperative, despite the fact that everyone knew that in practice contradictory definitions of signore existed and that not everyone who claimed the title behaved in accordance with its traditional values. Family values in America have the same commonplace standing; there are dreadful families, and all families have problems, but to condemn the family roundly as an institution generally meets with disapproval, even outrage. Signorilità and paesano values had exactly that status. Roberto, having accepted them (by default of not contesting them), was thus logically constrained to accept the moral reasoning that supposedly prevented the peasant from handing over the lintel. In that way the lintel owner both defined and occupied a moral high ground.

That moral high ground, as I said, was an ironic fabrication. To use irony with the intention of hurting or embarrassing a victim is to walk the edge of a precipice, a fall being irony that goes unperceived and is accepted as sincere. Certainly there are occasions on which ironists prefer to entertain themselves and never let the victims know that they are victims. The lintel encounter was not of that kind. Therefore the peasant had to frame the message in such a way that it would be difficult for Roberto not to realize that what the message ostensibly conveyed was not the authentic message. In particular, he needed to make clear that his deference was in fact mockery. Roberto said nothing about the peasant's demeanour, other than what is implied in the elaborately polite words and phrases of the refusal. But even without a confirming visual image of the peasant's self-presentation, the words alone indicate the kind of gamesmanship that is played in Italian *complimenti*: praise is bestowed with such vigour and extravagance that the victim is embarrassed and the complimenter's lack of sincerity is made very obvious. The mildly idiotic concern for the interests of long-absent brothers in a baita that was already derelict, the very respectful forms of address, the anxious protestations to be of service, and the use of signore as a term of reference all signal humbuggery. So, above all, does the peasant's absurd offer to have his one-fourth of the stone cut off and given to 'the gentleman'.

The offer was absurd because the stone's value to Roberto was the date carved along its length. It was also absurd because to cut the lintel would cause the doorway to collapse and thus deprive the other brothers of their share of the baita, which itself was absurd because the baita was already a wreck. There is a Monty Python quality about the scene that makes the peasant, if one were to assume that the offer was sincerely made, look like an idiot. I am sure the offer was made with a straight face; but it was hardly sincere. It was ironic. (I like to imagine the peasant reinforcing his declaration about the obligations of brotherhood with what in Losa is taken to be the ultimate signal of heartfelt sincerity – the right hand placed across the heart.)

What else could one read into the suggestion except mockery? When Henry Ford told his customers they could have their new car in any colour they wished so long as it was black, the irony is at their expense because the offer that appears to cater to their preferences instantly repudiates itself. The peasant's offer is in the same category, a form of disrespect paid from behind a posture of deference. But his performance is more complicated than that; it contained yet another level of mockery. The peasant was clowning, ironically self-disparaging, mimicking the Boeotian half-witted creature that the gentry were supposed to see in a typical peasant. In doing so he sent two messages. First, he caricatured himself in order to caricature Roberto by insinuating that this was how Roberto, being crass, saw peasants. Second – the counter-punch – by invoking, with apparent sincerity, the framework of signorilità and at the same time putting on an idiot mask he enacted the idea that only idiots take signorilità seriously.

There was little that was hit-or-miss about the peasant's performance; he neutralized 'the aleatory characteristic of attributions of intent' (Herzfeld 2001: 67) in the use of irony, over which many scholars have exercised themselves (see Muecke 1969; Booth 1974; Hutcheon 1994). Roberto, the victim, was left under no illusions about what was the intended message. The peasant, hyperbolizing his own imbecility, had effectively extracted the substance of ambiguity from their encounter while leaving its outer form intact.

Combative Irony and the Joy of Rhetoric

The irony in this case is more than simple dissembling; it is dissembling in such a way that what is outwardly hidden from the victims is at the same time made obvious to them. This is an irony of ridicule akin to Socratic irony but by no means identical; I will call it 'combative'.

There are many kinds of irony (see Muecke 1969; Booth 1974; Hutcheon 1994). Combative irony is enacted and contrived for a purpose; it is not spectator irony, neither the mean-spirited judgemental variety of Hamlet's 'For 'tis the sport to have the engineer hoist with his own petard' nor the gentler kind that would see irony in the wealthy Roberto's confident and well-intentioned ploy so promptly negatived by an ungrateful not-at-all-wealthy peasant. A fortiori this is not an instance of dramatic irony. No tragedy is involved; no inexorable fate, known to the audience but not to the players, strikes down their hopes and ambitions. The victim, Roberto, is not left unaware; he is made to be an audience for the spectacle of his own entrapment. Irony that is merely observed is, for the observers, self-distancing; they are not engaged. Those who use combative irony are on the field, committed to action.

Combative irony differs from Goffman's 'subversive' irony, which is not combative. Subversive irony is collusive, deployed to protect a 'focused encounter' by taking the bite out of contexts (his 'properties') that, if presented directly, would disturb the regnant definition of a situation (1961: 76). The peasant was not protecting a defined situation. There was no prior agreement about what might be allowed to penetrate the 'membrane', because there was, as yet, no membrane. Goffman, as I noted earlier, is concerned less with how inchoate situations get defined than with how those already defined are protected from contexts (alternative structures) that would put them in peril.

Nor is combative irony like that other variety of apotropaic (or procataleptic) irony – also enacted and benevolently intended – that anticipates and prevents changes in a situation already defined to the speaker's liking. Rosa, an elderly woman (in another community in the Italian Alps) was terminally ill. A neighbour-woman dropped by to see if Rosa needed anything from the shop. Rosa handed her a letter to post, giving her 100 lire to pay for the required 100 lire stamp, and saying, 'With the change, buy yourself a coffee!' The coffee would have cost at least 150 lire. They both laughed and the woman went on her way. Rosa was making an ironic joke by indirectly voicing the idea (the opposite of what she hoped was the truth) that her friend might gossip about Rosa's failure to return favours. The irony was deployed to safeguard their friendship. That was not the peasant's irony; he used irony precisely to deny mutual regard.

Combative irony, by definition, presupposes antagonism. Liddel and Scott gloss *eironeia* as 'ignorance purposely affected to provoke or confound an antagonist' (a near enough description of the peasant's intentions) and add that it was a device used by Socrates against the Sophists. Socratic irony is a weapon; it is not the kind of constructive argumentative exchange envisaged in Gandhi's *satyagraha* (struggle to find truth) in which the debaters are not seen as contestants but as mutual critics, partners in a cooperative endeavour to find *the* truth that is waiting there to be discovered. Socratic irony is bare-knuckle stuff, rhetorical assault and battery, intended to wear opponents down, to exhaust their capacity for logical combat, to knock all the ideas out of their heads, and thus render them unable to resist an implantation of 'the truth' that Socrates, all the time protesting his own perplexity (and patently dissembling), professes not to know. In these circumstances the word 'persuade', with its etymology of sweetness, would, as in the case of the handgun, itself be an irony.

Socratic irony pays lip service to the protocols of logic and is purportedly deployed in the service of truth. The victims are reduced to silence because they cannot show that their conclusions follow from the premises that they have been manoeuvred into accepting. Combative irony is different; it is not a demonstration of correct logic but rather a pre-emptive assertion of the rightness of a premise – in the present case, paesano values. At the same time it is a demonstration of superiority – of superior cunning and superior agonistic skills: the peasant, from a posture of humility and self-disparaging half-wittedness, shows himself to be smarter than Roberto. Combative irony challenges the victims to look at what is being done to them and to acknowledge that they are helpless. It is the *complimenti* situation. To protest against complimenti with a feeble and embarrassed murmur of 'Shucks!' is to throw in the towel. To challenge irony with anything but a counter-irony is exactly that – an admission of defeat.

Roberto came out of the encounter partly amused, partly bemused, seeing himself not so much mugged as outmanoeuvred by an agile shape-shifter, and regretting that he had not used Vincenzo as his cat's paw in the first place and so spared himself the hassle. He did not tell the story in the manner of someone brainwashed, Socratic fashion, and on his way to believing that class antagonism was the dominant structure in Losa. He understood very clearly how the peasant saw (or implied he saw) life in Losa, but there was no sign that he himself, Roberto, as a result of the encounter, was moved to see it in the same way. He was not persuaded. Nor, I think, was the peasant trying to foist on Roberto – 'induce or increase the mind's adherence', to – the thesis that Losa was structured by class-antagonism. Certainly he enacted his own hostility towards Roberto and other rentiers. But that is not the same as promoting Roberto's 'adherence' to the class-antagonism definition.

In the end the encounter did not have much to do with persuasion. This was not Mark Anthony's rhetoric deployed to turn the Roman mob against Caesar's assassins. Mark Anthony shifted the foundations; the peasant had no such agenda. Nor was he trying to put across his ideas as 'truth'. Rather he intended to 'provoke or confound an antagonist', to put Roberto into the position of having no words to argue back. Essentially he was defining their *immediate* situation by defining himself as smarter and therefore superior. The complex deployment of paesano and signorilità values, to be 'unfolded' by Roberto into class antagonism, was a convenient vehicle for a display of rhetorical skill.

The ideas conveyed by paesano and signorilità entered the situation not as definienda but as contextual resources – weapons – that allowed the peasant to get the better of Roberto. The reward for winning was not a convert, but the winning itself – having the satisfaction of contemplating his victim knocked off balance, subtly but indisputably insulted, and quite unable to do anything about it. A bumpkin lookalike, a moralizing innocent apparently so anxious to please, reveals himself to be an artful and punishing strategist, happy to spike Roberto, not just because Roberto belongs to the rentier class, but also because spiking is a manifestation of palaestral skill, which can be an end in itself.

A game played for its own sake may or may not have an effect on its context (on structures). But even if it has no effect, structures remain an integral part of the model, not as explananda but as resources. Structures are like cards in a card game; without them the game could not be played at all.

Postscript: Morality

An interest in agency and strategies (and by entailment in rhetoric) often goes along with a Machiavellian turn of mind and Machiavelli generally has a bad press. 'A handbook for gangsters' was Bertrand Russell's verdict on *The Prince*. Machiavelli justified his attention to the techniques of winning on perfectly moral grounds: only those who knew how to win could put an end to the disorder that afflicted the Italy of his day. That aspect of his work, however, has not commanded popular attention.

What does the palaestral model have to say about right and wrong? To found the inquiry on the question 'What must be done in order to win?' would place it with the positivists – neoclassical economists and other rational-choice theorists – and so model rhetoric as something close to a natural system and therefore blind to moral issues. But my question is different: 'What *do people think* they must do in order to win?' We are looking for patterns in beliefs about social behaviour, not the laws that govern it. These patterns, obviously, can include what people think about good and evil. No less obviously, they do not include *our own* judgements about good and evil. Nor do I think they should.

Not everyone agrees; my own view, I suspect, will be considered pseudo-scientific and outdated. Fernandez and Huber, in their introduction and again in a coda to the essays in *Irony in Action,* anticipate the chill wind of disapproval that blows around many (but not all) forms of irony. An ironic view of life may also be a cynical view that ends in nihilism; it may both misrepresent the 'moral imagination' of the people studied and excise the moral sensitivities of those who study them. Irony points the scholar towards a 'detour from rather than a route to responsibility' (2001: 262–63). It indicates a 'suspension of commitment' and so undercuts moral standards and moral responsibility (2001: 15). That is not true of all forms of irony; certainly not of combative irony.

What is to be done about irresponsible forms of irony? Their answer, which has an appropriate whiff of manifesto, is this:

> While the moral imagination may not be much easier to define than irony itself, we would like to suggest a simple enough definition relevant to those who work in the human sciences: the creating of as clear an image, or set of images, as possible of existing social conditions in their positive and negative aspects, along with an image or set of images of one's own obligations for achieving through practical action better conditions for all concerned. In other words, scholars, like professionals more generally, have a set of responsibilities in the world, not just to their own fields. (2001: 263)

I would buy that more readily if they had also told me (a) why knowledge must be followed by good works, (b) how to determine 'better', and (c) how to keep our knowledge from being skewed by our 'moral imaginations'. My position is simpler. Rhetoric (including irony) is a communicative culturally prescribed activity, about which we are seeking knowledge. That, in itself, is enough: rhetoric is a tool. What use is made of it, or any other tool – 'achieving better conditions for all concerned' (a Pareto optimum shifted from economics into utilitarianism and every bit as impractical) – is an important but also an entirely separate issue. Evans-Pritchard got it right: 'Knowledge of man and of society is an end in itself and its pursuit a moral exercise that gains nothing and loses nothing by any practical use to which it can, or may, be put (1948: 14–15).

Acknowledgements

For comments and suggestions I thank Andrew Brown, Susan Brown, Dan Doyle, Felix Gierke, Joel Robbins, Lisa Rosen, Jeff Snodgrass and Don Tuzin. A substantial part of this essay is drawn from Chapter 8 of *The Saving Lie* (University of Pennsylvania Press, 2003) and is reproduced here with permission.

References

Barzini, Luigi. 1966. *The Italians*. London: Hamish Hamilton.
Berlin, Isaiah. 1980. *Against the Current*. New York: Viking.
Booth, Wayne C. 1974. *A Rhetoric of Irony*. Chicago: University of Chicago Press.
Evans-Pritchard, E.E. 1948. *Social Anthropology: An Inaugural Lecture*. Oxford: Clarendon Press.
Fernandez, James W. and Mary Taylor Huber, eds. 2001. *Irony in Action: Anthropology, Practice, and the Moral Imagination*. Chicago: University of Chicago Press.
Goffman, Erving. 1961. *Encounters*. Indianapolis: Bobbs-Merrill.
Herzfeld, Michael. 2001. 'Irony and Power: Toward a Politics of Mockery in Greece'. In *Irony in Action*, eds James W. Fernandez and Mary Taylor Huber. Chicago: University of Chicago Press.
Hutcheon, Linda. 1994. *Irony's Edge*. New York: Routledge.
Leach, E.R. 1954. *Political Systems of Highland Burma*. London: Bell.
Liddell, Henry George and Robert Scott. 1890. *A Greek–English Lexicon*, 7th ed. Oxford: Clarendon Press.
Muecke, D.C. 1969. *The Compass of Irony*. London: Methuen.
Perelman, Ch. and L. Olbrechts-Tyteca. 1971 [1958]. *The New Rhetoric: A Treatise on Argumentation*. Notre Dame, IN: University of Notre Dame Press.
Russell, Bertrand. 1946. *A History of Western Philosophy*. London: George Allen and Unwin.

CHAPTER 7

Ordeals of Language

Ellen B. Basso

■ ■ ■ ■ ■ ■

I

There is a kind of rhetorical functioning in the disorderly zones of human life, which sustains and transforms the persons involved. Linguistic operations at the edges of disorder appear as we engage our human deceptive and imaginative abilities, our abilities to produce alternatives, to resist what we learn is expected of us. In these zones, discomfort with the limits of our own cultures motivates tropological experiments, 'the sleight of hand at the limit of a text', as Voloshinov wrote. Here especially, the rhetorics of emotion work to transform socioemotional reality, having a critical and often unwitting impact on social life. Disordered by the hypocrisies of racism, when someone turns away from the groups to which allegiances are owed, disordered by tricksters and their deceptions, social life becomes subject to special discursive manoeuvrings.

Anthropological interest in the continuous and active interpersonal doing or making involves links between how learning becomes embodied in practice, and how this 'habitus' is shaped by what people say to and about one another. This is not to say we neglect the less conscious and deliberate processes such as memory, anticipation, repression, the sense of connection or belonging, and anxieties about acceptance. But within this complicated interpersonal realm of activity, there has been a turn from thinking about 'feelings', 'emotions' or 'attitudes' as private or 'subjective', a psychological realm distinguishable from other such realms, to an emphasis on the public, intersubjective and embodied (what is now called 'stance') (Kockleman 2004: 131). Also, the old anthropological notion of culture as shared sets of ideas or social behaviours, that occur in essentially homogenous communities, emerges as a socially plural construct in which our own speech is never entirely and exclusively our own, but always heteroglossic and polyvocal, formed always in relation to the speech of others. The historical fact of cultural heterogeneity is implicit in all social interaction, and of course often subverted by ideologies that assert the superiority of purity and single-voicedness or monologicality. Ideological rhetoric in the face of such difference contributes to the formation of particular sensitivities to certain interpersonal contexts. What may result in these contexts is self-suppression of voicing, a kind of repression of the self that allows the anxiety-producing event to be experienced as somewhat more manageable than would otherwise occur. As Takeo Doi in *The Anatomy of Dependence* (1981) discussed with regard to the rich *amae* vocabulary in Japan, what may result is the development of Whorfian-like patterns. This semiotic hegemony works together with ideologies of feeling and the particular discursive and grammatical features of specific languages, to produce what I call 'ordeals of language'. To underscore the role of rhetoric (including language ideology) in this ordeal, I begin by quoting a portion of a poem by the contemporary Native American writer Wendy Rose (Hopi-Miwok):

> It's not that your songs
> Are so much stronger or your feet more deeply
> Rooted, but that
> There are
> so many of you
> shouting in a single voice
> like a giant child.
> (Cited in Krupat, 1992: 247)

Ordeals of language are experienced when understanding the inherent contradictions in the 'texts of self' one is required to perform (Rebel 1989a: 126) we permit our own voices to be powerfully affected by the language of the dominant. 'Texts of self' are typically narrated or sequenced events involving voicing (in the most abstract sense to include speech/silence/gesture/gaze). Suppressed voices result from self-censorship, the idea that what others think of one is more important than what one thinks of oneself. In these situations we are willing accomplices in the domination that suppresses our voices, as we 'invoke a unity of desire in which opposing voices sing in complicitous harmony as a single voice.' (Tyler 1990: 297). Perhaps this is what Phillip Rieff meant when he wrote famously of the 'smile of sociability', that false but demanding sociability which has nothing to do with fraternity and everything to do with surface politeness and the unremitting demand for reciprocity. Rhetoric is complicitous in this voice suppression, contributing to what may be called an 'ordeal' in the sense of a severely difficult or painful experience that tests a person's character or endurance. Rhetorical patterns in the form of ritualized communication (affinal avoidance talk, joking relations, elaborate politeness forms, honorifics, and greeting and departure speech are some examples) overlie the 'ordeal' of suppressed voicing. This overlay assists in the repression of alternative voices out of commitment to an order that calls for it and threatens sanctions if not followed. A question emerges: what happens when people repeatedly experience differences between what they are taught to know and to feel (the dominant rhetorics of self and society) and what actually happens to them as they engage others, particularly through these ritualized communications?

One significant consequence of self-suppression of voicing is shame, a topic of considerable interest to anthropologists for some time. Most are familiar with Ruth Benedict's contrast between Japanese 'shame culture' and American 'guilt culture' proposed in her *Chrysanthemum and the Sword,* published at the end of Second World War, but the interest goes back to the beginnings of the twentieth century and the compilations of taboo beliefs and practices in the writings of Wilhelm Wundt and James G. Frazer. Frazer's compilation of data on 'shame' in his second volume of *The Golden Bough,* 'Taboo and the Perils of the Soul', was of course one of the foundations of Freud's *Totem and Taboo,* and we see in both these volumes how strong was late nineteenth-century European interest in the strange body techniques described by colonial-era travellers, missionaries and bureaucrats bent on describing the differences between local 'savages' and 'civilized' people. The manner of nursing and weaning infants, toilet training, in fact everything from childbirth to the treatment of the dead and beyond became the object of speculation as to evolutionary causality and function, with a noticeable emphasis on the psychological elements of such practices. It is from these early reports that we get the first modernist descriptions of 'shame' and 'shaming' relations, and these looked very strange indeed to a European observer, while at the same time the feelings these relations evoked were surprisingly familiar.

As we learn from even the earliest attempts at understanding, shame is substantially shaped by rhetoric, through ideologies of emotion and of language. Here, I will examine several examples of the events and situations ethnographers have characterized as 'shameful', exploring in what follows rhetorics of shame in three sets of very different examples: Japan, Euro-American modernity, and Amazonian Carib-speakers called Kalapalo. How 'ordeals of language' involving shame emerge depends upon locally relevant features of semiotic ideologies; ideologies of emotion and the 'pathology' of shame; and specific linguistic and generic factors. Rather than claiming semantic commensurability, I start not with words but with certain kinds of events or situations involving the suppression of voices. It is here that we see some interesting parallels.

The topic of Japanese shame (*haji*), has long been of interest in the study of Japanese culture by both Anglophone and Japanese anthropologists and psychologists. The Japanese sociologist Hamaguchi describes shame as the force channelling human beings towards 'elevation', a means of guidance in life. Shame is a 'consciousness [*ishiki*] acting as a type of morality'. Another sociologist, Sakuta, distinguished between public shame (corresponding to the fear of losing face before others), private shame (involving the internalization of this code) and another form of internal shame which he called *shuchi*, which is said to arise in circumstances when people cause harm to a group member or to others they have relied on. To an American, this might seem like a kind of guilt. In fact, the contrast between Ruth Benedict's 'shame' and 'guilt' turned out not to be particularly sustainable when examined more closely (Creighton 1990).

In 1917, the psychiatrist and contemporary of Freud, Professor Shooma Morita of the Jikei University School of Medicine, wrote of the syndrome of disconnectivity he called *shinkeishitsu*, 'neurasthenia' (now known as *nikokomori*, or 'shut-in syndrome'), in which young people shut themselves up in their rooms for weeks or years at a time. Morita's form of psychotherapy was designed to treat this neurosis found commonly among the Japanese and characterized by interpersonally oriented symptoms such as obsessive shyness, oversensitivity and feelings of inferiority (Reynolds 1976: 4). Morita identified this with a 'fear of outsiders' (*taijinkyofusho*). Reynolds suggests that this neurosis was in part a consequence of the strong emphasis in Japan on the *uchi/soto* (inside/outside) contrast, and the experiencing of 'shame' (*haji*) in the context of any activities that would reveal one's own, or one's group's 'concealed inside' (*ura*). Taijinkyofusho was actually an expression used to talk about the reactions of very small children to the presence of outsiders, but it came to be used as well to describe the peculiar reluctance of older persons, particularly teenagers, to confront the 'outside' for fear, most often of 'offending' people the person would come in contact with, usually with bodily functions. The Japanese tropic contrast between 'public' or 'revealed' (on the one hand) and 'concealed' (on the other), between 'outer' and 'inner' space (different from 'inner' and 'outer' in a European psychological sense) led to the formation of this neurosis. With regard to this tropic contrast, Takeo Doi claims that Japanese must come to terms with the contrast so as to be able to hold two 'mutually contradictory modes of perception' at the same time. The Japanese 'concealed'/'revealed' contrast, and the 'fact' that what others think of them is more important than what they think of themselves together contribute to the emphasis on performing 'external' or 'public' haji in a great variety of contexts.

I'll turn now to the specific linguistic features involved. Many authors have commented upon the Japanese sensitivity to all kinds of social communications. David Reynolds, for example, argues that skill at projecting a social image through language is an important technique for manoeuvring in Japanese society. Reynolds observes that the use of 'qualifying' sentence endings and conversational replies – *keredomo* ('however') or *ga* ('but'), the provisional *desho* ('probably'), and the cautious – *so desu* ('it seems') – may signal careful attention to the listener's response and soften speakers' commitments to their own communication, just in case they may have said something potentially disruptive to the social relationship (1976: 106). The famous Japanese levels of politeness consist of elaborate forms at all linguistic levels corresponding to hierarchic and 'self–other' distinctions. One speaks politely (to one or another degree) to another by humbling oneself, and honouring the other. Appropriate use of these levels is a marker of the haji one feels for the other. Closely connected to this are the elaborate apologies Japanese use not only where, to a modernist, 'apologies' would be due (some fault had been committed), but apologies that assert consciousness of intrusion on the other's privacy and inconveniencing the other simply through the interaction itself. Thus, failure to use the correct levels not only implies a disrespect for the hierarchic differences between speaker and other, and thus, failure to acknowledge one's place in society; it is also treated as a kind of selfishness, meaning, in the Japanese context, undue emphasis and revelation of one's own personal wishes and needs. In this particular way, Japanese people have occasion to understand their voices to be suppressed by convention.

A manga example illustrates these themes vividly. In 'Torishimaryaku Hira Namijrio' a short and unobtrusive person (his name Hira actually means 'grunt' – that is, a lower-level worker), has been recently selected to serve in an important position in the company. Hira arrives in his typically modest manner. He enters on foot, rather than having his driver take him to the underground executive parking area, where he is awaited by his superiors. Hira's modest demeanour elicits curiosity from some, arrogance from others, particularly Shimomura, a man who is to serve under him. Shimomura, not knowing who this 'grunt' really is when he arrives at the office where they are to work together, treats him most disrespectfully. When the high company official who has hired Hira arrives, Hira's real identity is revealed. The other man, deeply shamed, grovels in abject apology before him. A final scene shows Hira remarking to Shimomura about the 'benefits' of his pain, a devastating assertion of the power he wields over his subordinate. (This story follows a traditional model – a story of a superior leader who disguises himself before travelling throughout his realm to test his subjects' loyalty.)

II

Understanding the complicated economics of human satisfaction is also of course even more characteristic of Western-style modernities. Here, though, while the sides are often not clearly drawn, the emergence of identity cultures within democratic pluralism effect conflicting allegiances that are perhaps very different from the kinds of conflicts (or at least contentions) described in Japan between personal and group needs, perhaps because, unlike the two-sidedness of Japanese rhetorics of self, we insist on there being only one true self.

An important consequence of the close anthropological attention paid to the language and politics of emotion since the late 1980s, is that we are far more aware now of the place of our own categorical judgements in general and often ancient theories about the relationship between affect and expression: ideas about 'inner' and 'outer' (including the psychological concept of 'internationalization'), words and contrasts such as 'intention and expression', 'real feelings' as opposed to 'voiced sentiments', about superficial statements that conceal 'real and inner' emotional states (Appadurai 1990: 92), the very notion of 'conflict' itself, 'measured' versus 'insatiable' selves, and so forth. The modernist rhetorics of emotion coupled with aspects of our own language ideologies contribute very strongly to our own language ordeals, particularly regarding judgements of sincerity and truth.

While surely far less complex than Japanese levels of politeness, Western languages have also developed complex ways of marking status differences. Western pronominal differences, naming practices, honorifics, and the various civilities we are accustomed to use, are closely linked (as Brown and Gilman wrote so long ago) to formality, status and rank differences. In the many contexts of shared programmes and agendas, 'civilities' are one kind of our own ritualized communications. Persons who exchange these locutions allude to an ideology of equality and the sharing of 'sincerity' and 'truth'. Yet where social and personal differences are strongly marked by racialist rhetorics and equalities clearly do not exist, civilities may do little more than reinforce humiliating feelings of shameful marginality. The 'self-infliction' of voice suppression we see in so many novelistic and memoirist accounts occur precisely at the moments when civilities are exchanged, hence the idea of an 'ordeal of civility', an expression perhaps first used by the sociologist John Murray Cuddihy when writing of Jewish experiences of modernity (1974). This preference to submit may be connected to fears of a loss of self, a loss of identity coming from disconnection from a group, and this fear itself the result of day-to-day awareness of slights that suggest the connection is itself very tenuous and merely tolerated by a majority or by a tradition one hopes to enter. The linguistic cover-ups that are such an important feature of politeness or civility standards can thus be part of a highly conflicted doing or making of one's personhood throughout a lifetime.

The language ordeal that is an 'ordeal of civility' involves acquiescence to a tradition of politeness, and often results in a consciousness of participating in one's own subjugation and even abnegation. From the extreme conflict this arouses emerges a rhetorical performance that is a 'masking' performance, as a kind of survival strategy. This is not entirely satisfactory since one is conscious of its 'surface' character; this is a consciousness that only exists because of the ideologically accepted contrast between external and internal truth and sincerity, and may result in deep feelings of shame for abandoning one's own group identity.

Here's an example cited by Cuddihy from the correspondence of the well-known early German-Jewish feminist, Bertha Pappenheim (1859–1936), who considered herself an 'emancipated' (though Orthodox) Jewish woman. Writing during a period of rising anti-Semitism, Pappenheim was the leader in forming around 1904 a Jewish welfare association (*Jüdischer Frauenbund*) that dealt with the serious problems of women and families associated with industrialized capitalism and, for Jews, the escape from Eastern European pogroms to Western cities. Pappenheim writes of the difficulties she had persuading Jewish leaders (of a variety of political persuasions) to work on the problems that feminist movements throughout Europe were particularly concerned with: prostitution and venereal disease, the situation of impoverished women, and illegitimate children.

Cuddihy writes, 'On a trip to St. Petersburg to visit a group of Christian patrician ladies who had also organized themselves against prostitution and the "white slave trade", Pappenheim writes of the experience of having the fact of her own Jewishness, in the presence of these ladies, become an "unmentionable"'(all citations from Cuddihy 1974: 44–45):

> Of course, the unquestioning way with which the white slave dealers, procurers, and so on, are called "JEWS" is truly shocking. It would help very little if the Russian committee and some other people would get acquainted with me as with a Jewish woman who feels the shame and tries to work against it. The Jews are supposed to suffer quietly this kind of concealing. I want to vary the expression that everybody who is not against the meanness of our community is for it. One should not imagine that our enemies do not know what demoralization exists in the broad masses of the Jewish people. The (Jewish)

> leaders do not want to look, and speak only about sham ethics and solidarity. I would have liked it if the noble members of our Jewish people [i.e., both rabbinical and Zionist leaders] had been at the tea table of the Russian Princess yesterday and had noticed under the smooth, well-educated forms what I was feeling.

In a later letter Pappenheim writes from Moscow of a countess who turns out to be anti-Semitic. 'Our contact would have been different had we not been restrained by education and civilization, had we met ... a Christian and a Jewish woman, in a wilderness, a desert.' As Cuddihy observes, 'Shortly after, the Russian countess and the Viennese Jewess place around their substantive differences the brackets of bourgeois civility: they perform the social rites, the offering of thanks, handshakes, and "goodbyes".' The countess, Pappenheim writes, 'was kind enough to take me to my hotel... I thanked her. I said that I owed her thanks, for she had given me most important experiences and impressions. She said she would be happy if she had been useful to me.' To this, Pappenheim adds, 'My thanks were sincere, though I knew that, conventionally and politely, I shook hands with an enemy.' Having been brought up to be polite to people, Cuddihy concludes, 'Berta Pappenheim had been carefully taught to live secretly with certain feelings she had not expressed because she felt them to be impolite.' (Cuddihy 1974: 46).

From a more recent time in the United States comes another example of such an ordeal. The poet Toi Derricotte (1997) writes of her experiences as a very light-skinned African-American in a racially divided world.

> All my life I have passed invisibly into the white world, and all my life I have felt that sudden and alarming moment of consciousness there, of remembering I am black...sometimes in conversation with a white person who doesn't know I'm black, suddenly a feeling comes over me, a precursor–though nothing at all has been said about race – and I either wait helplessly for the other shoe to drop, try desperately to veer the conversation in another direction, or prepare myself for painful distinctions. My desire to escape is indistinguishable from my desire to escape from my 'blackness', my race, and I am filled with shame and fury. I think the first time I became conscious of this internal state was when I was 15, on my way cross-country on a train....

> The first day out, a young white man sat in the seat beside me. We had had a very pleasant conversation, but at night, when I grew tired, I asked him if he would go back to his seat so that I could stretch out. He said, 'If you saw what's sitting in the seat beside me, you'd know why I can't go back.' Of course I knew without looking back what he meant, and as I stood up and turned around to see, I felt that now familiar combination of sickening emotions:

hope that my sense of the situation was incorrect – in effect preferring to distrust my own perceptions–and fear that it wasn't, that my tender feelings for this man, and his feelings for me, were in mortal danger. If I spoke, I would make myself vulnerable. At the very least, he might categorize me in the same way he had categorized the other black person. If I didn't, I would be a coward, a betrayer of my people. ... I turned around and, sure enough, there was a young black man, a soldier, sitting in the seat. I said, very softly, 'If you don't want to sit next to him, you don't want to sit next to me.' I had hoped he'd be too stupid or deaf to understand. But he grew very quiet and said, after a few minutes, in an even softer voice than mine, 'you're kidding'. (Derricotte 1997: 25–27)

In both these modernist examples, the writer, trapped in an ordeal of civility, saw that it was impossible to know herself vis-à-vis the other in any other way than in a moment of vulnerability. Each writer had a choice: to remain silent, or to 'speak out'. Whatever the choice, the gulf between her feelings and the civility forms that were required would have remained.

III

In the Amazon communities of Kalapalo, conflicting allegiances also exist to be sure, and there are specific kinds of voice suppression or rather transformation that take place and are commented upon. Here, though, semiotic ideology is very different, for regarding language, it is thought to be in favour of deceit. Kalapalo rhetorics of deception don't invariably lead to distrust or scepticism, but may glorify linguistic creativity, costuming, trickery of all kinds (the creator being is a trickster). Kalapalo rhetorical strategies often involve what is called *augunda* or deceptive discourse, such as the performance of alternative 'selves' or allegiances. Kalapalo speakers are adept at a number of genres of ritualized communication including several chiefly 'oratorical' genres, and affinal discourse (associated with avoidance and semiotic 'inversions' of normal speech). Furthermore, code choice does not index 'sincerity' but an interpersonal strategy that involves acknowledging the otherness of the other.

Kalapalo communities are characterized by intense, and often almost continuous interaction. There, one's commitment to a certain 'social truth' (commitment to the perspectives of certain others) is suggested by an almost ritualized validation or ratification, and verification process in conversation. Validation and verification forms (stereotyped utterances, expletives, and the use of certain epistemological modalities) are the specifically linguistic features – within conversational dialogue at least – that stand as tropes for this 'social truth' – or its absence in the case of witchcraft disputes. In addition, in these communities a rhetorical ritualization of speech generally emerges as an iconic marker of commitment to a collective project; sincerity and truth in a modernist sense are irrelevant here as is the Japanese 'inner' and 'outer' contrast. Here we are talking about a multifaceted reality, parts of which may only partially and gradually be revealed.

The 'inverted' speech characteristic of Kalapalo affinal civility (see examples 1 and 2 below), for example, seems to develop a different interpersonal tenor than the 'civility' of Western languages where code choice is supposed to directly index feeling. It is even less like Japanese where choice of 'politeness' level is indexical not of feeling but of the specific hierarchic character of the interpersonal context. What is interesting in this context is that a mutually reflexive setting of deference is created within an informal, egalitarian situation of community that is the basis for marriage in the first place.

Kalapalo use a variety of linguistic strategies to speak to and about affines. These strategies can be arranged into a series based on degree of formality or deference. Most formal, perhaps, are teknonyms and other forms to emphasize the presence, absence or deceased status of offspring of unions when speaking about an affine to a close relative. Also important are descriptive expressions that substitute for words for husband (*iño*) and wife (*fitsu*) when uttered by a senior affine to a junior. Examples include 'the one who grooms that person' (*isahatofo*); or as in *eitogu ugiñi*, 'the one who fans your fire' (because the young wife sleeps beneath her husband and tends the hearth that warms them at night). I have also heard Kalapalo men speak formally of wives as *wimbatofo*, 'the one who makes what I drink'; *eytafûgiñi*, 'the one who joins up with you'; and (in the speech of a woman), *ukwitofo*, 'my speech partner'. Additionally important is the practice of using a vocabulary that expands the boundaries of the speaker's close family by including the other as a 'sister', 'younger brother', 'uncle' or 'aunt' (see Basso 1973). Even more formal is the practice of using deprecatory expressions to express esteem for an object one offers to an affine (I call these 'false devaluations'; the Kalapalo say this is one kind of 'deceptive speech', *augunda*). For the Kalapalo, these forms and body techniques are, collectively in affinal contexts, indications of the *ifutisunda ekugu*, 'notable respect', that such relatives should show one another. Finally, there are honorific-like deictic demonstratives used between family members; ketsaŋe with expository speech, fetsaŋe with imperatives or directives given through third parties when avoidance must be followed. Considered as a whole, the entire set of affinal forms allows a Kalapalo to deferentially characterize subtle differences in the relationships between relatives by marriage, despite the inappropriateness of comparing *ifutisu ekugu* and despite the fact that attributes marked by these relationship terms are not always made explicit by Kalapalo themselves.

My examples are taken from narrated representations of conversations occurring within people's houses, involving fathers-in-law, daughters, and/or their sons-in-law. These are very intimate, domestic contexts. We can see in these examples how, when affines do speak to each other, they are using not only special address/reference forms, but also characteristic grammatical features of affinal civility: (a) the use of the deictic demonstrative postpositions *fetsaŋe* ('what is wanted') and *aketsaŋe* ('what is decided'); (b) the epistemological markers *wãke*, 'assertions about distant past evidence that may no longer exist but was first hand', *nifa*, 'confirming another's deduction', and the contra-spective *muk^we* ('to hope, almost in vain'; (c) the agreement taxis form *apa* ('as you want me to do'). While none of these forms are exclusive to affinal discourse, in combination they are quite characteristic of how parents- and children-in-law talk to and about each other and to contribute to affinal 'registration'.

The conversation in example 1 took place after a young man had just moved into his father-in-law's house. The older man has already instructed his daughter (the new wife) to make her husband some freshly made manioc drink, which he then offered to the young man. This may have actually been the first 'conversation', if we can even call it that, which took place between the two, because young people do not address their parents-in-law directly. In offering the young man the drink, the older man used the odd expression, 'Here, drink this stuff your sister just washed her hands in'.

Example 1

ande timbake	'Here, drink'.
eh he, nïgifeke	'All right', he said.
untsi, ah iñandsu etiñatitsïgï ingambake	'My young relative, your sister is accustomed to wash her hands in this stuff so go ahead and drink it
iñandsu etiñatitsïgï.	What your sister is accustomed to wash her hands in.'
Eh he, nïgifeke.	'All right,' he said.

In this dialogue, the father-in-law honours his son-in-law by deprecating, or humbling, a finely prepared gift from his daughter. This kind of deprecation of one's gift is heard on other occasions, so we shouldn't consider it affinal speech per se, but, in the context, it is certainly an appropriate thing for a father-in-law to say and it is a 'formality'. In other words, we wouldn't hear someone say this to a casual visitor when she is offered food. The son-in-law's response is the characteristic '*eh he*'; he is confirming the meaning of the deprecation by validating the father-in-law's valuation of his daughter's food. This deprecation aspect of affinal civility humbles the speaker. Insofar as the father-in-law is by virtue of age and leadership of the household clearly dominant over the subordinate younger man, who must practise a variety of special avoidance and 'bride service' techniques, deprecation elevates the youth as important, worthy of respect, but more importantly helps him to realize when he is actually receiving respect.

Example 2 is a dialogue between a father-in-law and a new husband leaving with his wife for his own community. Here, affinal civility is shaped by responses that suggest a shared set of goals and values about marriage practices. The great precision and formality of these dialogues are important (though somewhat strange) examples for the listeners, both younger Kalapalo who are yet to marry, and older men and women who can readily appreciate the quality of the interpersonal tie by what is being said. Each of these perspectives makes the characters seem uniquely real to listeners, almost as if they are people living among them. In example 2, as the young couple leave for the man's settlement, he is instructed by her father to formally release her from seclusion by cutting her bangs, which have been allowed to grow over her face. The suggestion to cut her bangs is an acknowledgement on the father's part that sex has already or will shortly take place between them, and therefore that he has formally released her from puberty seclusion.

Example 2

Inkemuketsïfa añagïpa,	*When you're walking on your own path,*
iñandsu inïkenïmingo efeke, efeke.	*I hope you will think of the customary thing to do, you'll cut your sister's bangs, you yourself.*
Eh he.	*'I'll do that.'*
(Fengi tunïgï ifeke, agiketofo.	*(He gave him a pair of scissors, a cutting tool.*
Agikipitsigofoingo)	*He was going to use them to make her bangs.)*
eh he nïgifeke.	*'I'll do that.' he said.*

Kalapalo semiotic ideology also implicates the complex imagery surrounding tricksters. Trickster discourse is an openly revelatory discourse, closely connected to shamanism. Jim Cheney describes the 'trickster' character of Native American philosophy in the following way: 'Whereas for postmodernism "truth" is a matter of social construction and negotiation, for indigenous peoples truth (or the multifaceted faces of reality) is *revealed*. The world from time to time reveals yet another of its many dimensions' (n.d.: 10). Kalapalo tricksters and their shamanic languages are characterized in narratives by the absence of evidence or epistemological modalities: tricksterish polyphonic voicing and fully embodied participations in the worlds of powerful beings (sharing food, listening to and understanding their utterances, having sex and marrying them, etc.) is metaphorized through musicality, an icon of this full participation that crosses seemingly 'uncrossable' boundaries. Put somewhat differently, this is an opening up to the 'other' by deeply acknowledging the 'otherness' of Trickster's interlocutors. This 'opening up' is then coupled with validation/verification by human others, in the shamanic 'revelation' of ceremony (described in Basso 1985).

During ceremonial masking in particular an interested public of 'ordinary' people come to participate in the images of the shaman's dreaming and his relations with powerful beings. Personal projects become closely connected with the public and cultural at these times.

Whereas in the modernist examples described earlier, the underlying association of speech with sincerity leads to anxiety felt when connections are disturbed, in trickster societies creatively new connections are made, e.g., masks become revelations, not concealments (as with us). Modernist shame, an 'inner feeling', is something to be kept concealed or denied. In trickster societies it is rhetorically marked by ritual communication and ritualized deixis where certain spaces (like seclusion chambers, menstrual huts, and special paths and bathing areas) within the settlement are available for use when people feel themselves to be in this condition.

This discussion leads me to the ordeals of language in this society. For people who are unable to successfully play the game of social trickstership (following the rules of ritual communication and multiple personhood) the consequence is a certain kind of silence that goes along with physical transformation: that is, not a person's decision to discursively remain silent (as Keith Basso has described for Apaches) but removal or ostracism by the community, the end of conversation (this is what happens to witches or people who have gotten into public fights). A person's own decisive separation from social life itself is the strongest consequence of this process, the subject of many mythological and personal narratives. Anxieties and open difficulties with marriage are rarely discussed in ordinary speech, but they appear very often in narrative art that constitutes something close to a mythological genre of divorce.

One such traditional story concerns a man named Kusimefu, whose silencing ordeal of transformation is the consequence of his (apparently) inadvertent violation of ritual communication. In this story, Kusimefu walks along the path to a fishing place, not realizing his mother-in-law has been following close behind. Thinking she is his wife, he makes some clearly erotic remarks about their sex life. Startled, the older woman lets him know who he's been speaking to, and, feeling himself deeply shamed, he runs away and leaps into the water, turning himself into a catfish.

Discussion

I have not tried here to establish semantic commensurability between Japanese *haji*, English *shame*, German *Schande* and Kalapalo *ifutisu*. Rather, I have drawn attention to certain kinds of similar-looking events or situations where people are seen to suppress their own voices. One important result that we see in each set of examples are culturally and linguistically shaped 'sensitivities' or 'anticipations', expected, perhaps inevitable kinds of interpersonal situations in which the gulf between feelings and civilities become particularly foregrounded. During such ordeals of language, self-inflicted suppression of voices may not necessarily have to do directly with fear of the power of another. We might say, for example, that I have 'chosen to silence my own voice' when I have inadvertently violated some form of coded sociality. And the suppression of a voice is often one consequence of mutually perceived inequalities of power. But for most, this is an important choice that goes along with values about appropriate interaction. One important consequence of inadvertent violations or dramatic and sudden changes in the performance of coded sociality (particularly in domestic situations involving the body, such as opening the door on naked hosts) is a kind of deep embarrassment and withdrawal. In our own modernist Euro-American societies this experience is linked to our rhetoric of 'privacy', where spaces (physical and otherwise) are set aside for the practice of acts themselves defined as 'private' or 'personal' or even 'shameful'. In Kalapalo, 'shame' is not necessarily regarded as something the person should try to avoid, quite to the contrary. What is called *ifutisu* is associated with persons in withdrawn or secluded situations: women after childbirth, people in mourning, boys and girls undergoing puberty training, shamans learning their practice. These kinds of shame are all demanded of the participants, and there are body techniques that help induce it. For example, in Kalapalo (as elsewhere), where and how people move around in space can directly index their state of 'ifutisu' and let others know to preserve silence and thereby help the 'ashamed' person persist in that project. In Japan, the rhetorical contrast between *omote* (outer, revealed, expressed/verbal) and *ura* (inner, hidden, mind) is a lexical contrast but one that emphasizes not mutual exclusivity (as in the United States) but rather unity in the 'double-sidedness of things' (Doi 1989: 30). An example similar to the Kalapalo one is the social restraint of people in communal baths, where people don't greet one another during the initial cleansing process, but do so once they are actually in the bath itself. Here we have an inherent rhetorical emphasis not only on perpetual occurrence of the unsaid but on context or perspective. Pertinent here are allusions to the more spatialized contrast pertaining to human affairs: the contrast between *soto* (outside) and *uchi* (inside). What makes these culturally different one from another is how the individual interprets locally relevant epistemologies of personhood, emotional styles, and how shame is experienced as a kind of intersubjective, public and embodied affective regulator of interpersonal conduct in these places.

This 'unceasing necessary experience of inner conflict' is how we connect with others (Rebel 1989a: 127), surely an inevitable and constant fact of human life. Local ideas about language and how it is to be used are particularly interesting in this regard for how they reference the interpersonal dimensions of power and of epistemology, contributing to how particular ordeals of language are shaped and very precise ideas about what 'power' might mean in very specific contexts. Thus a language ideology that speaks of deception as something positive and creative is different from another ideology that understands deception as the opposite of 'truth' or 'honesty'. Anthropologists working in New Guinea describe initiation rituals during which taboo objects, purportedly the voices of dangerous forest spirits, are revealed to young male initiates to be musical instruments played by adult men. They suggest that this leads to initiates' distrust of the external conventions of speech in opposition to internal 'feelings' and 'sincerity'. Looking at Kalapalo materials, I've given you some idea of what can happen where the 'internal' versus 'external' contrast does not exist, where concern with 'sincerity' or 'truth' does not in any sense correspond to an objective reality.

To summarize the differences between these three sets of examples: I would say that 'shame' of modernity is understood to be an emotionalized inner feeling; what is 'inside' is truer than one's 'outer performance', a mask or 'cover' for reality. In Japan, such a contrast would be understood as an illness or neurosis where one is expected to be able to hold two different, even contradictory self-representations at the same time. The more diffuse range of haji is also desirable as a socially contextualized demeanour: one is expected to 'perform' and to 'embody' shame even if one is not feeling shame. In Kalapalo, ifutisu is similarly regarded as a somaticized and embodied index of a certain kind of interpersonal situation – a situation in which the complex ritualized rhetoric of avoidance and respect wards off accusations of witchcraft and asserts commensality. To come full circle, the multivocality of the trickster's 'scattered self' (Basso 1999) seems crazy to the modernist.

Because the realm of our social relationships is speech centred, generated in and through conversations, we learn about one another and thereby acquire strategic information about the conduct of subsequent action through speech. But one must consider also the actual conditions of fear and loathing that dictate the degree and magnitude of sacrifice that one person may have to make in order to achieve some level of equivalence or commensurability with the other. This sacrifice means that the person becomes responsible for her own abnegation due to the necessity of viewing the world as existing through experiences of inequalities, of which she is the repeated target. At best, uncertainties of feeling result; at most, alienating, isolating events arise that challenge trust, that make both participants feel worse than before – in short, that diminish the feeling of a successful interaction. Then, participants come away feeling that they have not been understood or 'known' in some essential way. Rhetoric appears here too, for these uncertainties do not prevent us from later retelling the story of our lives, 'honestly' or deceptively, as do European confidence men and Native American tricksters.

Acknowledgements

The current version of this paper was begun during my tenure as 2002 Fellow of the John Simon Guggenheim Foundation. My Kalapalo research has been supported by grants from the National Science Foundation, the Wenner-Gren Foundation for Anthropological Research, Inc., National Endowment for the Humanities, and the University of Arizona. I am grateful to many people for their encouragement and interest in this project. My Brazilian colleague and friend Dr. Bruna Francetto of the Universidade de Guanabara, Rio de Janeiro, invited me to return to the Alto Xingu with her in 1998 and graciously acted as my research sponsor. I owe special thanks to Professor Ivo Strecker of Johannes Gutenberg University, Mainz, who invited me to the conference on Rhetoric Culture and Language where I first presented the ideas in this chapter. Judith Irvine, Susan Phillips and Takeshi Inomata generously took the time to make important comments and suggestions on a later draft prepared for the Society for Psychological Anthropology meetings in San Diego, 2003. Thanks finally to the Southwest Psychoanalytic Society for inviting me to present yet another version to their membership in 2005.

References

Appadurai, Arjun. 1990. 'Topographies of the Self: Praise and Emotion in Hindu India'. In *Language and the Politics of Emotion,* eds Catherine Lutz and Lila Abu-Lughod. Cambridge: Cambridge University Press.
Basso, Ellen B. 1973. *The Kalapalo Indians of Central Brazil*. New York: Holt Rinehart Winston.
——— 1985. *A Musical View of the Universe: Kalapalo Myth and Ritual Performances*. Philadelphia: University of Pennsylvania Press.
——— 1999. 'The Trickster's Scattered Self'. In *Discourse and Conflict,* ed. Charles Briggs. Oxford: Oxford University Press.
——— 2007. 'The Kalapalo Affinal Civility Register', *Journal of Linguistic Anthropology,* forthcoming.

Cheney, Jim. n.d. 'Tricksters (in the Shadow of Civilization)'. In *Wilderness and Storytelling: Indigenous Epic as North American Culture,* eds Joe Sheridan and Darlene Clover.
Creighton, Millie R. 1990. 'Revisiting Shame and Guilt Cultures: A 40-Year Pilgrimage', *Ethos* 18 (3).
Cuddihy, John Murray. 1974. *The Ordeal of Civility: Freud, Marx, Lévi-Strauss and the Jewish Struggle with Modernity.* New York: Basic Books.
Derricotte, Toi. 1997. *The Black Notebooks.* New York: W.W. Norton
Doi, Takeo. 1981. *The Anatomy of Dependence.* Tokyo: Kodansha.
―――― 1989. *The Anatomy of Self: The Individual versus Society.* Tokyo: Kodansha.
Kockleman, Paul. 2004. 'Stance and Subjectivity', *Journal of Linguistic Anthropology* 14(2): 127–50.
Krupat, Arnold. 1992. *Ethnocriticism.* Berkeley: University of California Press.
Rebel, Hermann. 1989a. 'Cultural Hegemony and Class Experience: A Critical Reading of Recent Ethnological-Historical Approaches. (Part One)', *American Ethnologist* 16 (1): 117–36.
―――― 1989b. 'Cultural Hegemony and Class Experience: A Critical Reading of Recent Ethnological-Historical Approaches. (Part Two)', *American Ethnologist* 16 (2): 350–65.
Reynolds, David. 1976. *Morita Psychotherapy.* Berkeley: University of California Press.
Turner, Victor. 1974. *Dramas, Fields, and Metaphors: Symbolic Action in Human Society.* Ithaca and London: Cornell University Press
Tyler, Stephen A. 1987. *The Unspeakable: Discourse, Dialogue and Rhetoric in the Postmodern World.* Madison: University of Wisconsin Press.
―――― 1990. 'Ode to Dialog on the Occasion of the Un-for-Seen'. In *The Interpretation of Dialogue,* ed. Maranhão Tullio. Chicago: University of Chicago Press.

CHAPTER 8

INVENTIONS OF HYPERBOLIC CULTURE

Ralph Cintron

■ ■ ■ ■ ■ ■

If there is a theorist who worked both anthropologically and rhetorically and deserves to be called a major theorist of rhetoric culture, it is Michel de Certeau. Given that this paper is about 9/11 and the dialectics of modernity, a particular passage of his seems clairvoyant. At some point in his career he stood atop the World Trade Center and later wrote:

> On this stage of concrete, steel, and glass ... the tallest letters in the world compose a gigantic rhetoric of excess in both expenditure and production ... Unlike Rome, New York has never learned the art of growing old by playing on all its pasts. Its present invents itself, from hour to hour, in the act of throwing away its previous accomplishments and challenging the future. A city composed of paroxysmal places in monumental reliefs. The spectator can read in it a universe that is constantly exploding. (de Certeau 1988: 91)

There is a distinctive *enargia* and *energia* in de Certeau's writing: *enargia* in the sense of vivid 'ocular demonstration' and *energia* 'as a more general term for vigor and verve ... in expression' (Lanham 1991: 65). His method is not so much rigorously systematic or analytic but rather a piling up of images and ideas, each one a suggestive thesis. The result is a vast poesis, more impressionistic than realistic; brilliantly imaginative, to be sure, but not necessarily convincing for the empirically inclined.

If there is some truth to my characterization, then one might read de Certeau's text almost ironically, for New York City itself, in this account, represents another kind of *enargia/energia*, a material one linked to de Certeau's textual one. It is as if his textual sensibility, an inventive piling up, had found its material correlate – a city of piled-up inventions. (Or, those more cynically inclined might argue that de Certeau projected his distinctive subjectivity onto the city – a shortsighted argument, I believe.) At any rate, New York City here appears as a containment field, but barely so, of an excess of invention – the Brooklyn Bridge (opened in 1883), the Empire State Building (built in 1930), the World Trade Center (WTC, opened in 1973), each an architectural 'wonder' succeeding and outdoing the other. Indeed, they are material placeholders for a planetary mythic that has made New York City the symbol, like no other, of the hyperbolic hypermodern.

Some readers may respond to the term 'hyperbolic hypermodern' as another example of academe's overproduction of modernity terms. Maybe so, but it may also evoke de Certeau's notion of the present inventing itself at a kind of fast-forward speed. At any rate, de Certeau's account of invention and the accelerated present is widely shared by many thinkers on modernity (Berman 1982; Bauman 1993; Augé 1995; Casey 1998; Dear 2000; Koolhaas et al. 2000, to name a few). In sum, the claim is that modernity, in keeping with Marx's analysis of the Enlightenment and industrialization, has unleashed unparalleled productive capacities. It has harnessed labour power and machine power to produce successive waves of machines whose own potency outstrips the power of the very machines that produced them. Consider the well-worn example of television compressing space/time by delivering images almost at the moment of their occurrence and how this ability represents a technical 'advance' over prior technologies. It is through this sense of power steadily overcoming prior limits, as when the first manned spacecraft broke through the limits of the earthly and drifted into the unearthly, that we begin specifying the coordinates of modernity. The hyperbolic hypermodern, then, occurs where and when the limits of modernity confront their rupture, and this is a source of exuberance and optimism.

But, in a more negative vein, the notion of modernity as an accelerated present captures an underlying disquiet: has late capitalism or late modernity rushed too fast and too far, leaving behind all former moorings including codes of decency and social justice? Has the very notion of limit been discarded so that modernity continues to absorb even more of the world's *energia* without guidance? From this perspective, as so many have argued, the promised utopia of modernity has devolved into dystopia, and the vision of an enlightened, rationalized social order has become global disorder. If these are the conditions that our times have hurtled into (and not all would agree, particularly the keepers of wealth and power who profit from modernity), it is understandable that we would convert events into signs and read the experiences of the last century – the world wars, the various forms of holocausts and ethnic cleansings, the large-scale environmental stresses, the endless threats of different kinds of mass destruction, the vast and unequal distribution of global capital – as brilliant spectacles of a bankrupt modernity playing itself out with increasing rapidity on the largest stage possible, the entire planet. It seems reasonable to say, then, that hyperbolic material productivity has generated hyperbolic omens, or at least hyperbolic interpretations of insignificant signs. For hyperbole, in the sense being described here, is not so much a figure of speech, or a rhetorical descriptor of a particular kind of verbal act. Rather, it names the danger that was always there in the teachings and ethos of modernity – that is, that the wide-scale realization of human and material capacity[1] might distort the communal bond. Hyperbole, then, as the naming of excess and the making of astonishment points to and produces the large gap between actions that revel in their assertion of power as opposed to more mundane actions that sustain the communal and the ecological.

Of course, hyperbole also occurs in more conservative contexts and communities, and this too must be delineated in order to deliver a capacious understanding of the operations of hyperbole. Often it names a kind of comic buffoonery performed with exaggeration and excess that satirizes the pretension of an individual as a way of calling such a person back to community. Fairly clear in these instances is the difference between what is being hyperbolically satirized and the restraining norm that is being reinforced. Hyperbole here, then, serves normative values that someone's excess threatens. Part of the difficulty of modernity, however, is the extent to which innovation, originality, individuality, creativity and dynamism, which sanction rupturing, become heralded values; they cultivate an aspiration to go beyond. In this sense, excess becomes part of the structure of modernity. It erodes the force of the normative by labelling it, as postmoderns do, 'arbitrary'. What might once have been considered unseemly is now released. In the simplest of terms, a conversion of energy occurs: the pent-up potential of the unseemly, which had been under restraint, is now sanctioned, hence, released; or a change of place occurs: what was peripheral (unseemly) is ready to move to the centre. To repeat, in late modernity and late capitalism, hyperbole ceases to be a figure of speech marking the boundary of the probable and the improbable or a critical judgement determining the unseemly as against the proper; rather, it becomes part of the motor of what it means to be. 'Out with the old, in with the new', goes the American saying – and given what I have been arguing thus far, I can't help but note its strange exuberance and innocence.

De Certeau, then, for my purposes offers an appealing sensibility, one that straddles a somewhat standard critique of modernity with a certain ambiguous enthusiasm for the speed and irreverence by which intellectual and material monuments give way to the next round. He may criticize modernity's 'rhetoric of excess', but his own rhetoric is an enthusiastic excess. Are we not all caught in a similar double whammy? A plenitude of invention and an ever-accelerating present (both of which mark our era) may represent both our catastrophe and our exuberant liberation. I suspect that our social scene will never reveal one without the other.

The Prevalence of Invention

I want to argue next that the *topos* of invention, understood now as a key ingredient of accelerating modernity, is extraordinarily prevalent in the modern collective psyche. In a sense it saturates modern life as a deep value – indeed, an ideology or *doxa* (common opinion or, more broadly, state of mind). This has been recognized in rhetorical theory by Bender and Wellbery, when they claim that rhetoric, formerly a matter of distinct skills and techniques including *inventio* (a method of finding better and more effective arguments), has been replaced in today's world by 'rhetoricality'. Rhetoricality 'manifests the groundless, infinitely ramifying character of discourse in the modern world. ... Rhetoric is no longer the title of a doctrine and a practice, nor a form of cultural memory; it becomes instead something like the condition of our existence' (Bender and Wellbery 1990: 25). So *inventio* becomes invention, a pervasive newness, and rhetoric becomes rhetoricality, the pervasive and constantly produced force of language aimed to create newness in our world. Such rhetoricality appears in a number of everyday sites and practices. Consider, for instance, these idiomatic expressions from American English: 'the cutting edge', 'maintaining one's edge', 'edginess', 'thinking outside the box', 'staying ahead of the curve', and 'colouring outside the lines'. Idiomatic expressions (and proverbs in more traditional communities) are crystallizations of the reigning *topoi* or commonplaces of a community. As a result, they are excellent distillers of the structural and ideational contradictions of a people. The above examples solidify one of modernity's elemental semantic fields or *doxa*, namely, the value of challenging convention: 'testing your limits' and 'daring to be different'. Of course, there is no denying that these inducements to strive, overcome, or become original are tied to economic forces, namely, the commodification of the self-realized individual – hardworking, successful, and bearer of unlimited potential. (And in our current ideological moment it is this self-realized individual that is most heralded as the source of invention/innovation.) Nor can it be denied that innovation itself has become commodified insofar as its pursuit of the new is key to granting a 'competitive edge' to manufacturer, artist or intellectual. Commodification, then, helps to solidify invention/innovation as a deep value in the collective psyche, and the following verbal logos and statements derived from the webpages of a few Fortune 500 companies tell us how deeply saturated and even clichéd the commonplace of invention/innovation has become:

> Verizon Communications: Make progress every day.
>
> Motorola: Intelligence everywhere. Making things smarter and life better.
>
> General Electric: We bring good things to life. A community of ideas and solutions that work for you.
>
> American International Group: The freedom to dare.
>
> IBM: At IBM, we strive to lead in the creation, development, and manufacture of the industry's most advanced information technologies.
>
> Boeing: Forever new frontiers.
>
> J.P. Morgan Chase: Insights based on strategic research.
>
> Cardinal Health: Shortening the distance between innovation and the patient.
>
> Duke Energy: We generate what's next.
>
> El Paso Corporation: We will conduct our business in a bold, imaginative manner.
>
> Merck: Merck discovers, develops, manufactures, and markets a broad range of innovative products to improve human and animal health.
>
> Reliant Energy: We will be the one people choose for energy, innovation, opportunity, and investment.

We are witnessing here the self-promotions or *mythoi* of major corporations; or, if you prefer, some of the *doxa* of American culture; or, if you prefer, a major *topos* in the collective psyche of our moment; or, if you prefer, one of modernity's major *topoi* (which, because it helps to structure economic relationships, might be better called an ideology); or, if you prefer, total banalization in which the conceptual grounds of such terms as 'invention' and 'innovation' have been hollowed out, since the overuse of inspiring rhetorics sound, in the end, duplicitous, a sly way to hide the instabilities of the marketplace that may drive a company to mediocrity, mismanagement and corruption – consider the fate of Enron.

A brief analysis that reveals the workings of these texts might help readers see both the overlapping semantic clusters and the multiple levels of meaning. Invention/innovation as a semantic cluster piles up ('intelligence', 'smarter', 'insights', 'learn', 'imaginative', 'ideas', and so on) as a kind of *energia* in this small collection, revealing itself as driving an always-about-to-appear utopia of emancipation. I am speaking of the optimistic belief that ingenuity has the power to cut through limitation and deliver progress – and all this, of course, is the promise of modernity. It would seem, then, that the semantic clusters of progress ('improve', 'next wave', 'generate what's next', 'melts boundaries', 'new frontiers', 'to dare', and so on) and invention/innovation are so closely wedded that one cluster automatically slips into the other – which is another way of saying that the collective psyche has become accordingly conditioned.

A major problem of progress and invention/innovation, however, is their destructive power ('out with the old, in with the new', as was stated earlier). These texts, it appears, neutralize that power by summoning another semantic cluster that might be labelled 'service to the human community'. Some of this work gets done via puns such as those of Verizon and GE: 'Make progress every day' and 'We bring good things to life'. In this sense, Verizon's verbal logo might be read as hiding the rupturing power of progress by making progress a common 'everyday' occurrence, and GE's as suggesting a certain animism (things becoming living things) in addition to assuming the role of provisioner to the human community. In this semantic cluster of 'service to the human community' are such terms as 'we', 'you', 'community', 'patient', 'human health', 'people', and so on. In other words, in this semantic cluster modernity and progress do not displace; in fact, they come to our rescue, thus stabilizing the utopian promise.

Consider how the concept of risk taking plays out the tensions between the semantic clusters of 'invention/innovation' and 'service to the human community'. Risk taking celebrates the bravado of challenging personal and social limits. It also celebrates the very spirit of inventing/innovating. Do we not look for 'risk taking' CEOs to head up our most 'dynamic' and 'innovative' firms? But to what extent is risk taking another name for distortion? Recall here another point made by Bender and Wellbery (1990), that is, that the classical era – hence, its rhetorical theories – valued harmony and proportion. Late modernity does too, of course, for risk-taking is not all that we look for and reward. Nevertheless, it is interesting how, in the U.S. at least, we celebrate an individual's or a nation's willingness to take risk. And yet we are all too aware of how risk taking can slide quickly towards harmful destruction. Take El Paso Corporation, whose earlier statement claims that they do *business in a bold, imaginative manner*. The company engaged in risky profit making that created an artificial energy crisis in the state of California between 1 November 2000 and 31 March 2001. In 2003 El Paso made a $1.7 billion reparation settlement with the states of California, Nevada, Oregon and Washington, and in 2004 further settlements were made with Arizona. The scandals of 2000–2001 were accompanied by fraudulent salary increases and other lucrative bonuses made to the firm's top four officers. In 2005 it was revealed that these bonuses were awarded on the basis of aggressive profit figures when, in fact, the company was experiencing serious losses. We might further note that this risk taking occurred in the context of deregulation.[2] If 'service to the human community' can, though certainly not in all instances, be aligned to government regulation, risk taking is encouraged by deregulation, which is argued by libertarians as freeing up the innovative capacities of capitalism. The point is that the tension between these two rhetorics says much about government–corporate relations and, in addition, constructs the face that many corporations project to the public.

So Bender and Wellbery's point regarding the shift that I described earlier from *inventio* as skill to invention as pervasive need parallels another shift: from valuing harmony and proportion to valuing risk taking and distortion. And given California's encounters with El Paso and so many other recent corporate scandals, do we not sense how boldness and distortion, or risk taking and grotesquerie are inevitably paired? Right in the very depths of the mainstream we implant firmly into the collective psyche (via all the ideological apparatuses available – schooling, the speech making of our political, scientific, corporate and civic elite; and the incessant noise of television commercials) not just the first element of each of those pairings (boldness and risk taking) but, simultaneously, the second one as well: distortion and grotesquerie. You cannot have one without the other. Where lies the balance? (A Citigroup billboard in my Chicago neighbourhood used to say: 'It's okay to buy generic, just make sure your life is anything but. Live Richly'.)

Finally, invention/innovation or the production of the new is part of the mystique or rhetoric of the companies listed earlier, but it is also the basis of their livelihood. They can't just 'talk the talk' but must also 'walk the walk' – or else lose market share. They are in the business then, of producing around the theme of invention/innovation both rhetorical *copia* as well as material *copia* – that is, producing the moral conviction that progress does, indeed, serve the human community and simultaneously producing real goods that confirm that conviction. These productions must go hand in hand, and the reason why can be explained by considering the common phrase 'tomorrow's technology today'. There is no such technology, of course; there is only today's technology pretending to be tomorrow's. But producing the mystique of the future in the midst of our ragged present is a necessary fantasy, for it helps to produce hope, optimism, and finally real goods, which seemingly prove the worth of the whole system, and thereby hide or make bearable the insufficiencies of the present. Late modernity requires invention/innovation to undergird every body of knowledge in order to guarantee that we do not run out of future. If we were to run out, despair might set in. Of course, we never seem to transcend our stubbornly disappointing present, but the urgency to do so leads to the overproduction of a specific fetish – namely, the future – via words, words,

words, images, images, images, things, things, things (*copia*). By inventing a future and imagining even more of it, late modernity derives its special *energia,* its rapid pace, all of which helps to postpone the arrival of that strange apocalyptic moment of no more future.

9/11

It is in this light, then, that I wish to consider 9/11. At the core of so many of our Hollywood disaster and action films is an image of apocalyptic malevolence. Malevolence never wins because humankind is too inventive/innovative; hence, the future and the continuation of human hubris are guaranteed. Consider the grand edifices of science fiction spaceships and how vulnerable they suddenly become in the face of a malevolence that may be literally galactic. Their hyperbolic engineering suddenly creaks and groans or is swept aside with ease as the malevolent force approaches. Or consider a related hyperbolic image that appears in many action films: a man rushes towards the camera while a huge fireball or some other monstrous thing threatens to sweep over him. The malevolence's ability to fill up the screen is a sign of the inescapable doom that is approaching directly at the audience. These images should remind us of Benjamin's famous reading of Klee's painting *Angelus Novus* where 'the angel of history' beats its wings towards a future that is threatened by history's death and destruction that keeps piling up. Compare Benjamin's dour reading of Klee's image to a reading of our movie hero who will somehow dodge the disaster as it approaches at an ever-accelerating rate. Indeed, he will rise up unfazed to continue his just mission as if this latest trauma were routine and not apocalyptic. Here, the impending apocalypse is defeated by coolheaded invention. In other words, our hero's ability to remain rational, optimistic, even jocular and foxy in the midst of utter chaos echoes the flexible, triumphant spirit that makes modern progress so indomitable. Like the Energizer bunny, 'it just keeps going and going', always beating its own drum. Such rousing ideology ably feeds the dream life of the collective and, in so doing, keeps at bay depression, both socioeconomic and personal.

Much of the fantasy life, then, of late modernity tracks between these hyperbolic images: on the one hand, human inventiveness/innovativeness will solve all problems, and so there is no natural cap to growth, no limit to an ever-expanding future; on the other, apocalyptic malevolence is nipping at the human project because our very own inventions/innovations are linked to some innate perversity or blindness in the human condition. Even if the malevolence comes in the form of a meteor, which is an impending apocalypse not of our own doing, the apocalyptic signature remains – something much larger than ourselves is threatening to do us in. In short, limit, finally, is going to exert itself over the hyperbolic condition called humanity. Much of the iconography, then, that tells us something about the meanings and directions of late modernity vacillates between the poles of optimism and doom, between limitlessness and limit. Each pole hyperbolically answers the other's excess, and, according to my analysis, it is their pairing that functions as part of the dialogical structure of late modernity.

Consider this possibility: the World Trade Center and the experience of 9/11 are material objects and events that moved through the filters of these interpretive frameworks. How so? Let's start with the building of the World Trade Center. In a revealing article, the *New York Times Magazine* published an account of the movers and shakers who first imagined the WTC and the architects and engineers who realized it (Glanz and Lipton 2002). Starting in 1955, David Rockefeller, one of the world's richest men, needed a new tower to house the Chase Manhattan Bank. Putting it in Lower Manhattan would secure property values in an area that had been deteriorating for some time due to the shift of the city's financial centre to Midtown. At first, the building was to be 'the sixth-tallest office tower in the world', but the project steadily grew. By 1960 it was projected to offer 'five million square feet of office space' on a 13.5 acre site. Rather quickly it encountered resistance from the state of New Jersey, which wanted something for itself; from local merchants whose cut-rate stores were going to be removed; from entrenched Midtown real estate tycoons who feared that an excess of office space would drive down the real estate market; from the populist mayor John V. Lindsay who felt the city was being shortchanged by the financial deal that had been cut with the previous mayor; and from architectural critics such as Louise Huxtable of *The Times* who denounced the project as 'gigantism' that could become triumphal or tragic.

The movers and shakers countered the opposition at every stage by, essentially, increasing the size of the project. New Jersey got what it needed and the mayor, because of the size increase, secured for the city a larger revenue stream. Any group that resisted its now spectacular size could be effectively dismissed as 'standing in the way of the inevitable march of progress'. The plans that emerged called for 10 million square feet of office space, more space than could be found in all of 'Houston, more than in Detroit or downtown Los Angeles'. When it came time to make architectural decisions, the project rocketed even higher. Clearly, the architectural and technical innovations that were being contemplated were analogically related to other hyperbolic feats of the time. For instance, the director of the project told the architect: 'President Kennedy is going to put a man on the moon. You're going to figure out a way to build me the tallest buildings in the world.' The result was 'two 110-story towers, each with floors an acre in size'. Later, when the engineer was brought on board, the goal was to abandon the prior era, which he called the 'cage of the past', meaning 'not just the structures he wanted to leave behind but also the older engineering minds that, he felt, were trapped by history'. Almost everything about the project called for the rupturing of the old and a need to innovate: new construction methods, new ways to bear the enormous loads and to dampen the effects of wind, new fireproofing materials, and so on. The towers, then, represented architectural excess and engineering innovation, but also an excess of urban political clout, that is, the ability of political will when fused to the will of capital to dismantle competing wills and shift the geography of power in a city that arguably represents the greatest concentration of the world's wealth.

But at a more global level, the WTC represented the hyperbolic conditions of international capitalism. The philosopher Slavoj Zizek, in one of those numerous statements by famous thinkers that circulated on the web shortly after 9/11, captured much of what was at stake: 'The WTC towers [symbolize] not so much the old-fashioned notion of the "center of financial capitalism," but, rather, the notion that the two WTC towers stood for the center of the VIRTUAL capitalism of financial speculations disconnected from the sphere of material production.'[3] Notice his organizing *topos,* 'old' material capitalism has been replaced by 'new' virtual capitalism. The shift from old to new echoes my earlier statement about limit encountering its rupture, more specifically, that old-style capital rooted to industrialization has been superseded by a faster/vaster way of making profit, for instance, buying and selling currencies as their values fluctuate (see Stiglitz 2002). Making money from money rather than goods and services can occur instantaneously via computer from any point on the planet. A kind of radical wealth making that has been liberated from material production and long time-lines has made older forms of wealth making conservative. In short, the WTC represented a rhetoric of excess – that is, the hyperbolic hypermodern – across a number of planes: urban politics, architecture and engineering, and most especially as one of the world's major nodes for organizing vaster and more nimble forms of wealth making.

In sum: to say that the WTC was hyperbolic across a number of domains is not just to speculate but to reiterate a common understanding. Further, to say that the WTC symbolized the hypermodern is to say that it represented the rupturing of some of modernity's existing limits and the establishment of new ones. The WTC was, so to speak, at the tip of modernity, forecasting and materially enabling its own future rupturing. Deeply enmeshed in the dialogical structure of late modernity, its performance of the hyperbolic hypermodern was, in effect, a siren call issuing an invitation for its hyperbolic destruction. It is not as if the 'call' were preventable, for the call is part of the necessary logic and trajectory of the material and subjective realities of what constitutes the broad patterns of modernity. Of course, WTC's destruction did not come from within the churning of modernity, as described by de Certeau. That is, a technology or an advanced version of capitalism did not supersede another, for each monument of modernity – at least figuratively and sometimes literally – must give way to the next, and rapidly so, in order to maintain, ironically, the status quo. No, the destruction was not another affirmation of limitlessness; rather it affirmed its hyperbolic partner: limit; the end of future-think; apocalyptic malevolence; Siva, the auspicious one, who destroys form (the individual body as well as the cultural logic or *doxa*) after its potential has been spent.

In my account of modernity, then, hyperbolic spectacle begets hyperbolic spectacle. More often than not the spectacle affirms narratives of progress, but the innate unease that helps to structure modernity occasionally surfaces as apocalyptic destruction. That is, the WTC was bound to be superseded, but no one knew if this would occur affirmatively or negatively. The defining moment, of course, occurred on 9/11 (11 September 2001), and it is to that moment that I now turn.

Interestingly, al-Qaeda's own need to perform hyperbolic spectacle for global television was consistent with what has become general military strategy whether enacted by the U.S., Israel or the Palestinians. That is, the greater the hyperbole and symbolic quotient, the stronger the political message. Although both the conservative and liberal establishments in the U.S. would label as cynical this apparent equalization of United States and al-Qaeda methods, it is hard to dispute the idea that hyperbolic spectacle for mass consumption has become a favoured technique for making political statements. For instance, U.S. military strategy currently relies on overwhelming force, in short, high-tech firepower to annihilate resistance, make conflict short term, and save the lives of American combatants. The eerie night bombings during both Iraqi wars (rocket flares, occasional bright explosions, stealth planes, and military experts showing and explaining pictures of smart bombs at work) established this spectacle of American (and to a lesser degree Western) might. These 'shock and awe' shows, yes, served a military purpose, but they were also spectacular propaganda that have cemented the Cold War victory by clearly stating to the rest of the world that the new political and economic order could sweep away resistance. The 'old world order' had to be rebuilt into a new incarnation, and hyperbolic military devastation – or its threat – became a powerful tool for initiating that change.

Curiously, the public has seen very little real death and never established its numbers on the Iraqi side perhaps because we are unsure of audience reaction when spectacle as empty space for fireworks becomes, instead, a death-filled space. However, one of the things that should concern us about a military strategy of hyperbolic devastation is that when war becomes real war for one group and war-'lite' for another, the latter group is in danger of becoming cruel because it never comes face to face with its own actions, never receives them in return. In short, it is tempted to play the same video game forever. A dangerous and insidious strategy this one.

What intention can we discern behind a war strategy that relies on the hyperbolic, a strategy that brings together like no other the dialectic of modernity where invention/innovation literally births the apocalyptic? I am thinking particularly of al-Qaeda's intentions, but also, by extension, those of the Americans, Israelis, Palestinians and so on. To pursue the hyperbolic as strategy is to pursue the trump card that will out-trump all other trump cards, the card whose finality and completeness puts an end to the entire card game. In other words, the goal that underlies the sort of hyperbolic action described in this essay is that of domination without reply. In order to understand this effect with some accuracy, we might pay attention to the idea of astonishment. What does it mean, this desire to astonish? I would suggest that the goal is to break down the reigning logics of the viewer, to cast the viewer somewhere else, towards, perhaps, stupefaction and speechlessness where the mind, albeit momentarily, is stripped of available meanings and explanatory narratives. To the extent that the viewer does not know what to say, does not understand, the normative structures have been overthrown. The collapsing WTC towers literally instilled those kinds of reactions, as we will see shortly. But the psycho-social motive behind the creation of an astonishment that overwhelms speech and comprehension is the desire for a power that enacts a kind of cleansing that washes out the known and never replaces it. Apocalyptic malevolence insofar as it aspires to or achieves this kind of astonishment is, in the end, an enactment of brutal purity.

It is difficult to know whether al-Qaeda expected literally to topple the WTC towers, but, as television showed us the second plane and later as each tower collapsed, we were guided into successive levels of astonishment. It was at this moment that we can understand how astonishment can produce silence or speechlessness, and the point here is not just a symbolic or theoretical point. It is a point about human corporality. The following quotation from Fire Chief Walter Kowalczyk, recounting his experience of 9/11, summarizes my analysis:

> As soon as we came through the Brooklyn-Battery Tunnel, the devastation was almost immediate. In my career, I have managed many multiple-casualty incidents from plane crashes to severe train derailments, so managing high-scale incidents never scared me. However, as you're driving down West Street and you have to maneuver the vehicle to avoid driving over what appeared to

be body parts as well as debris, my mouth went dry. I had the sensation that I had a job to do. I had to ensure the safety of the E.M.S. [Emergency Medical Service] work force. But how do I do this if I can't talk?[4]

Kowalczyk, an experienced emergency officer, someone accustomed to dealing with the hyperbolic, encountered a scene whose proportion reduced him to near silence. His condition is what astonishment intends. Perhaps what his example suggests is that when mind and emotions are in normative conditions the body functions as expected, but when astonishment washes over mind and emotions, it takes the body with it.

Another way to approach the astonishments of 9/11 is to consider how most of us experienced the event through the medium of television. Let me borrow here the term 'televisual chaos' developed by communications theorist Christopher Smit (personal communication). Televisual chaos as a theoretical concept seizes with uncanny precision the very uniqueness of television as a medium. Smit talks of how the television industry understands itself as having an unparalleled ability to be immediate or spontaneous and exploits those abilities most saliently in 'live' broadcasts. Of course, rarely is immediacy or spontaneity deeply evident because some sort of script informs its 'breaking news': the script of the director and producer, whose voice may be literally plugged into the ear of the news reporter; the script of capitalism evident both in how commercials structure the airtime of the report and ideologically control the industry; and the sociocultural scripts or *doxa* that define what counts as news and overlays all subject matter with its reigning interpretations. These 'scripts', of course, fail to imprint themselves fully on the audience; nevertheless, as part of the forces of production they encourage us to qualify any claim concerning the immediacy or spontaneity of television. But at the moment of televisual chaos, which in the case of 9/11 was also a moment of astonishment, something powerful occurs. Explanatory narratives, for a short while at least, seemed unavailable. Were these scenes occurring in front of us bizarre accidents or terrorist plots? If the latter, who was performing them? Sense making was not available. The old narratives and logics were being ruptured. Invention/innovation, as described in the previous section, is jolted. Broadcast networks, awestruck, floundered for explanations, and this is one of the reasons why, as widely reported, internet use spiked as people searched online for answers.

It is hard to say how long the televisual chaos lasted. The inability to speak or comprehend is largely a subjective experience, meaning that for some an explanatory narrative became available rather quickly – in just a few seconds, perhaps. For others, it may have taken much more time. The difference in reaction time is insignificant. The point is that during moments of televisual chaos narratives, explanations, comprehensions are hard to manufacture. The reigning logics are momentarily assaulted, astonished. However, the moment of televisual chaos, which, in effect, is the broadcast industry's equivalent of astonishment, is also a dangerously in-between time, for silence will soon be overrun by the hyper-production of invention/innovation. In other words, silence is followed by rumour, interpretive panic, scapegoating, and so on. Al-Qaeda's hyperbolic actions engendered hyperbolic responses in the form of ideological assertions that Americans were now united in grief and patriotism. 'The world will never be the same', 'America at War', 'the cowardice of the terrorists', comparisons to Pearl Harbor, the proliferation of American flags, the public slamming of interpretations that did not express horror, grief, nationalism and righteous vengeance – these were the shapes that the tyranny of collective fear quickly took. In other words, the shock to the system was not sufficiently gargantuan, much less apocalyptic, to do away with the old formulae. Indeed, the old formulae were not blown away but, instead, have become more entrenched – the U.S., for instance, has become even more reluctant to lean on Israel to solve the Palestinian question, which means that Israel's domestic and foreign policies are threatening to become Euro-America's, albeit on a larger, more dangerous scale: more surveillance at home, more incursions against elements that threaten until we too start chasing and swinging at phantoms. (I write this in July 2006 after Israel's hyperbolic response to Hezbollah's kidnappings of a few Israeli soldiers, a response whose real intention, backed by the United States, is to wipe out the whole of Islamic fundamentalism.)

In some ways, al-Qaeda has read late modernity quite correctly. Modernity pries open a vista concerning human possibility. That vista promised transparent justice, emancipation, the banishment of toil and pain, self-realization, control over vicissitude, a more equitable distribution of wealth and pleasure, and so on. These promises needed to be self-evident and materially realizable rather than mere conjectures; hence, science and technology were and still are recruited as visible, material successes of the project's benefits. Moreover, these promises became bourgeois revolutions and a variety of colonialisms, but the inconsistencies and hypocrisies that quickly emerged (for instance, laws and constitutions that favoured the already empowered) meant that it was easier to theorize than to realize the project.

I have pointed to the hyperbolic hypermodern as that innate point in modernity where limit encounters its rupture. Unfortunately, some people are ruptured more than others. Indeed, modernity aims its project particularly at those lives whose pasts are to be vanquished in the name of a higher modernity; moreover, it too often fails to replace that loss with sufficient social capital that might help those lives move with flexibility in the present and future. These are the specific failures of government policies that create a brew of dehumanization that has instigated a long history of indigenous revolts, working-class and peasant skirmishes, the rioting poor, religious fanaticism, criminality, terrorists of all sorts taking up wildly differing positions, rogue states, ethnic cleansings, and so on. These failures, of course, emerge from very local conditions, but they are also evidence of a more disturbing, long-term process, namely, modernity's and capitalism's uneven realization.

To repeat: Al-Qaeda has read late modernity rather astutely. It is not that their methods or solutions are acceptable – of course not; rather, they have let loose a special tremor in the psyche of modernity, exposing once again modernity's long-standing self-doubts behind its grand surfaces. The meaning of this tremor demands our attention. For where has late modernity gotten us? Does the hyperbolic hypermodern sustain life? The answer is decidedly 'yes', if you are fortunate to be on the crest of 'tomorrow's technology today'. Here, food and lifestyles are easily purchased. But there are too many who resemble the *maquiladora* workers along Mexico's northern frontier whose wage scale enables the manufacture of 'tomorrow's technology today' but not its purchase. Al-Qaeda belongs to the underlying impatience with these global conditions and lets it loose in the control centres that continue to claim that these human tragedies will be solved through more of the same.

Al-Qaeda's is an apocalyptic fervour, a face-off with Western secularism, but also a fiercely teleological, an 'all or nothing' proposition regarding the approach of an end-time (the no-more-future described earlier). This perspective, however, obscures al-Qaeda's dependence on and embrace of late modernity's global markets, communications industry, technology and weaponry. In other words, al-Qaeda cannot be imagined as somehow backward or outside the orbit of late modernity and the West, for if it were profoundly outside the reach of global capitalism and modernity, it would be no enemy at all. Being firmly inside their reach, however, is to be subject to their unequal distributions, for late modernity and capitalism are disorganized and fissured. And one common response to unequal distribution is to fight for the local determination of global modernity and capital as opposed to being determined by them from afar. In this special, richer sense, then, the face-off is completely from within late modernity, and it concerns the unresolved disturbances that are always there. To view al-Qaeda this way is to understand that the apocalyptic madness of fundamentalism, despite its archaic origins, is in deep relationship with that other apocalyptic madness, namely, late modernity's hyperbolic self-doubt. This self-doubt is, in effect, an empty slot ready to be filled by any number of golems lurking behind the shining, technological surfaces of late modernity: fear of nuclear holocaust, global warming, DNA engineering, overconsumption of natural resources, super-resistant disease strains, and so on. 'Golems' is the right word for them, for each represents a human artifice that has been endowed with hyperbolic power, namely, apocalyptic malevolence ironically derived from being almost nonexistent, more a vague threat than something real. Indeed, in 2006 al-Qaeda barely exists as an organization, but therein lies its power. Its ideology spreads despite late modernity's fantastic bulwarks of technology, knowledge and control. In this sense, al-Qaeda is but one voice in a larger network of displeasure, and as long as its minimal actions continue to thwart America's hyperbolic reactions, that is, continues to be unsolvable, it grows in size – like a golem – in the collective psyche of late modernity.

Conclusion

Most analyses of the terrorist wars are framed through the idea of the nation-state: Palestinians are struggling, it is said, for self-determination and their own state; Muslim fundamentalists are struggling against Saudi Arabia, the U.S., Britain and so on; Israel replies to Hezbollah in defence of its sovereignty and its right to exist and, similarly, 'America is in a fight for its survival'. When we allow the category of the nation-state to drive analyses, both the left and the right become concerned with security landscapes; national self-interests; just vs. unjust interventionism; presidential authority vs. checks and balances; and whether or not the spread of democracy and human rights constitutes *the* historical trajectory. But I have chosen modernity as a category of analysis mostly because the very concepts of the nation-state, of democracy, rights and the rule of law are themselves largely the projects of modernity. Indeed, in my view modernity's vast engineering has at least two facets: a technological project and a political one. Both continue the dream of the Enlightenment, of revolutionary emancipation; both aim at the accumulation of human freedom, itself a hyperbolic fantasy about transcending limit, necessity and mastering death – or at least their postponement. Both technological innovation and rights, then, attempt to dismantle limit in order to assemble the new, the transcendent. And in so doing, it occurs to me that modernity and particularly rights discourses are about the unsustainable over production of life and life chances. Clearly, modernity occurs beyond any territorial organization even if specific territories or nation-states are more or less identifiable with it. Modernity, then, is a more elusive concept, which means, I suppose, that a nation-state type of analysis has more immediate relevance. That is, the nation-state, as a material entity and as a *doxa* or *topos,* is more recognizable and, therefore, has the power to concentrate public fears and desires. However, if, as many claim, the nation-state is undergoing serious strain, I am wondering if the fault line runs deeper – into the psycho-social-material phenomenon that includes it. It is this perspective that guides the difference of this essay. Finally, a rhetoric culture perspective begins when we are willing to treat the nation-state and modernity as themselves rhetorical categories produced through daily discourse, and when we are willing to entertain the idea that such apparently inviolable determinations as 'the security of our nation', 'the survival of civilization', 'the holiness of our book' are utterances that hope to abandon their origins in human motive and rhetoric in order to project themselves towards some other origin, namely, the hyperboles of truth. In this sense perhaps all discourse that forgets its rhetoricality is hyperbolic.

Notes

1. Consider the consequences and origins of such common American expressions as 'you owe it to yourself', 'treat yourself well, you deserve it', and the U.S. Army's famous 'be all you can be'. These expressions help to solidify the importance of self, particularly the realization of one's full potential/capacity. Realizing one's total beingness as species and individual are critical so that we 'don't miss out on life'. As such they are examples from everyday discourse that have emerged from the deep structures of modernity: that is, they represent a philosophy of immanence that has partially replaced philosophies of transcendence.
2. See articles in *The New York Times* (24/9/2002; 27/9/2002; 13/12/2002; 28/12/2004; 13/3/2005).
3. Zizek titled his posting 'Welcome to the Desert of the Real!' (15 September 2001). By 2002, he had extended those insights into a book with the same title.
4. See 'Capturing for History Many of a Tragic Day's Triumphs and Problems', *New York Times*, 30 January 2002.

References

Augé, Marc. 1995. *Non-Places: Introduction to an Anthropology of Supermodernity*, trans. John Howe. London: Verso.
Bauman, Zygmunt. 1993. *Postmodern Ethics*. Oxford: Blackwell Publishers.
Bender, John and David Wellbery. 1990. 'Rhetoricality: On the Modernist Return of Rhetoric'. In *The Ends of Rhetoric: History, Theory, Practice*, eds John Bender and David Wellbery, pp. 3–39. Stanford, CA: Stanford University Press.
Benjamin, Walter. 1968. 'Theses on the Philosophy of History'. In *Illuminations: Essays and Reflections*, trans. Harry Zohn. New York: Schocken.
Berman, Marshall. 1982. *All That Is Solid Melts into Air: The Experience of Modernity*. New York: Penguin Books.
'Capturing for History Many of a Tragic Day's Triumphs and Problems', *The New York Times*, 30 January 2002.
Casey, Edward S. 1998. *The Fate of Place: A Philosophical History*. Berkeley: University of California Press.
'Company News; El Paso Settles Allegations of Price Manipulation'. *The New York Times*, 28 December 2002.

Dear, Michael J. 2000. *The Postmodern Urban Condition*. Oxford: Blackwell Publishers.
De Certeau, Michel. 1988. *The Practice of Everyday Life*, trans. Steven Rendall. Berkeley: University of California Press.
Elshtain, Jean Bethke. 2003. *Just War Against Terror: The Burden of American Power in a Violent World*. New York: Basic Books.
Fish, Stanley. 1999. *The Trouble with Principle*. Cambridge, MA: Harvard University Press.
Gaonkar, Dilip. 1990. 'Rhetoric and Its Double: Reflections on the Rhetorical Turn in the Human Sciences'. In *The Rhetorical Turn: Invention and Persuasion in the Conduct of Inquiry*, ed. Herbert W. Simons. Chicago: University of Chicago Press.
Glanz, James and Eric Lipton. 2002. 'The Height of Ambition', *The New York Times Magazine*, 8 September 2002.
Glater, Jonathan D. 2005. 'Sorry, I'm Keeping the Bonus Anyway', *The New York Times*, 13 March 2005.
'Golem'. http://en.wikipedia.org
Habermas, Jürgen. 1998. *Between Facts and Norms: Contributions to a Discourse Theory of Law and Democracy*, trans. William Rehg. Cambridge, MA: MIT Press.
Hardt, Michael and Antonio Negri. 2000. *Empire*. Cambridge, MA: Harvard University Press.
Koolhaas, Rem, Sefano Boeri, Sanford Kwinter, Nadia Tazi and Hans Ulrich Obrist. 2000. 'Harvard Project on the City; Arc en rêve centre d'architecture'. *Mutations*. Barcelona: ACTAR.
Lanham, Richard A. 1991. *A Handlist of Rhetorical Terms*, 2nd edn. Berkeley: University of California Press.
Lewis, Michael J. 2002. 'The "Look at Me" Strut of a Swagger Building', *The New York Times*, 6 January 2002, Sec. 4, p. 1.
'Making Money on Fiber, the El Paso Way'. 2002. *The New York Times*. 27 September 2002.
Mamdani, Mahmood. 2004. *Good Muslim, Bad Muslim: America, the Cold War, and the Roots of Terror*. New York: Doubleday.
McComiskey, Bruce. 2002. *Gorgias and the New Sophistic Rhetoric*. Carbondale: Southern Illinois University Press.
Oppel, Richard A. and Lowell Bergman. 2002. 'Judge Concludes Energy Company Drove up Prices', *The New York Times*, 24 September 2002.
Oppel, Richard A. and John M. Broder. 2002. 'Seeking Huge Electricity Refund, California Is Told to Pay Instead', *The New York Times*, 13 December 2002.
Podhoretz, Norman. 2004. 'World War IV: How It Started, What It Means, and Why We Have to Win', *Commentary*, September 2004.
Rawls, John. 1999. *A Theory of Justice*, revised edition. Cambridge, MA: The Belknap Press of Harvard University Press.
Stiglitz, Joseph E. 2002. *Globalization and Its Discontents*. New York: W.W. Norton and Company.
'The Terrorism Index'. July/August 2006. *Foreign Policy* and The Center For American Progress. http://web1.foreignpolicy.com
Viroli, Maurizio. 2002. *Republicanism*, trans. Antony Shugaar. New York: Hill and Wang.
Zizek, Slavoj. 2001. E-Mail Posting: "Welcome to the Desert of the Real!" 15 September 2001.
——— 2002. *Welcome to the Desert of the Real: Five Essays on September 11 and Related Dates*. London: Verso.

CHAPTER 9

Rhetoric in the Moral Order
A Critique of Tropological Approaches to Culture

James W. Fernandez

■ ■ ■ ■ ■ ■

We begin argumentatively! There is hardly any other option given the 'observer effects' that characterize investigation and inquiry of any kind, and particularly in the human sciences, that intends to be offered up in the *agora*. Life in such public culture, as the Sophists well understood, is argument, *controversia*, and especially figurative argument, argument by analogy, *allegory*. We argue that moral order should still be a productive interest in anthropology even as concern for 'moral economy' and 'distributive justice' is being replaced by the idioms of the commoditized market economy, the stimuli of individual choice therein, and bottom-line profitabilities. We address the work of three clusters of human scientists tropologically informed and alert to issues of moral order who are concerned with what we can call the *play of tropes* in culture and whose work is thus relevant to the ambiguities of the *moral sentiments* and hence to the complex dynamic of the Moral Order in the face of the vicissitudes of life. It argues that paying attention, as the student of rhetoric pays attention, to the Moral Imagination's role in Moral Order is central to the ethnographic task and to our understanding of social dynamics over time.

The Moral Imagination and the Moral Order

We will reference for our purposes that definition of the moral which grounds itself in social interaction and derives the word, *moral*, from its classical root, *mos*, 'a way of comporting oneself'. It emphasizes the complexities and contrarieties of comportment challenged recurrently by the vicissitudes of the sentiments of solidarity or lack of them. That is to say, as the signs of social interaction in the world shift their valency the springs of comportment need to be recurrently 'figured out' (in the rhetorical sense of the word 'figure' as in 'figure of speech') as *aides-pensées* and as actual guides to comportment. This 'figuring out' is most often done through moral casuistry in the form of moral narratives of various kinds. Since Aesop, at least, stories about social interaction, whether in animal guise or not, are told to make moral points. This understanding of narrative has characterized the Bakhtinian era (Bakhtin 1984) where so much emphasis has been put upon the place of narrative in the social world as a source of moral energy and of possible moral closure on the dilemmas of comportment.[1] Ethical deliberation at least, if not much more of life, has come to be seen in storytelling terms. And it is accepted that useful comment, that is, comment with moral closure, on the dilemmas of social interaction can be found in narrative art.

A complete narrative, understood etymologically as 'progress in knowing', has movement forward in it. It has what might be called 'coherence and momentum', to recall the frequent professorial critique of the lack of these qualities in student essays. Narrative shows us 'being in becoming', we might say, as in its unfolding the being of the characters is tested and confirmed by their overcoming (or not) of obstacles, among which often are the uncertainties and mysteries surrounding their knotted circumstances. This unfolding leads finally, as the plot moves forward, to denouement, the untying of the complexities and the overcoming of the obstacles and, hence, the becoming, that is the affirmation or transformation of character in moral or immoral terms. Effective and affective narrative regularly offers this transformation in time.[2] If the topoi of movement forward or movement back is thus fundamental to narrative these topoi in any narrative are given the complexity of cultural circumstance and cultural elaboration and it is this elaboration that challenges ethnographic understanding. It challenges our understanding of how moral order is achieved or lost in local terms. Constantly in storytelling moral closure, which is to say justifications and adaptive rectifications of comportments in respect of moral order, is sought, and pertinent modes of being and ways of becoming, operative social interactions in the presence of the vicissitudes of life, are recounted.

Of course, to state this enduring narrative realization in so stark and formal a way is to miss the moving complexity of cultural entanglements which compose the vicissitudes of everyday life. I would like, therefore, in respect to the figuration of thought and its relation to action, to examine three exemplars of the treatment of the figuration of the moral imagination: the work of the dialectically anchored, anthropologist-ethnographer Thomas Beidelman in his ethnography *Moral Imagination in Kaguru Modes of Thought;* the work of the cognitive linguist George Lakoff and his colleagues over several decades, and particularly his *More than Cool Reason* and his more recent *Philosophy in the Flesh;* and, third, the kind of understanding found in arguments by Emily Martin characteristic of an anthropologist of her persuasion aware of the ideological, that is to say moral, work done in the body politic by certain tropological orientations and commitments.

Figuring out an Ethnography of Moral Order in a Myriad and Contradictory Social Reality

There are few anthropologists who have compiled as extensive an ethnographic work in articles and monographs as Beidelman among the Kaguru, particularly in the 1960s and 1970s. *Kaguru Modes of Thought,* first appearing in the late 1980s, is his first book-length treatment of this culture.[3] The author describes it as the product of more 'seasoned judgment' and thus a 'less youthful' treatment of his subject than his earlier work, more seriously and fully aware of the 'essential pathos and ambiguity of social life' that all cultures contain and which they seek to face through the moral imagination (1986: xi). His main argument, conditioned by that mature judgement, is that 'it is in the realm of the imagination that a people confront these disparate and conflicting features of their thought and experience' (1986: 5). Insofar as the Kaguru and many other African peoples are concerned this imaginative confrontation takes place mainly in the various forms of folklore and folk narrative: proverbs, maxims, folktales, legends and myths.

Beidelman takes as his task that of teasing apart the complexities of these narratives and the way they confront the dilemmas, contradictions and ambiguities of social life so as to aid people in their comportment. Of course that aid is itself most often set out in quite ambiguous terms. That is to say, while these folk narratives provide characters with whose thoughts and actions the audience can empathize, sympathize or reject, just as often the thoughts and actions of the heros, villains or fools portrayed offer no easy polar or oppositional choices and excite the moral imagination by subverting any direct and ready application of moral principle. The narratives thus cultivate a sense of the challenging ambiguity of everyday life. Indeed, one might argue (Karp in Beidelman 1993: ii) that Beidelman's work focuses not on successful moral practice but on subversion and failure and blight. In respect to the straightforwardness of moral conduct the narratives and implied statements of belief he has elicited focus on the 'pathos', as the author says, and not upon the 'ethos' of everyday life. Focusing on these negative case materials, the author seeks to reveal the more profound challenge to the moral imagination which lies in the pathetic.

In any event it is in this narrated lore that the anthropologist has most direct access to the images by which cosmologies are both constructed and criticized. They are a choice means by which an anthropologist's own imagination can be guided in his or her empathetic interpretations of that life. For it is a part of the balance of Beidelman's judgement that the anthropologist's own interpretations, confronted by the ultimately irresolvable contradictions of the social life under his inspection, are also an exercise of the moral imagination (1986: chapter 1)! In respect to the 'Moral Space' of the house and the bodily etiquette appropriate to it (1986: chapter 4) the author points up the tensions and contradictions between the conduct appropriate to the private intimacies of the house, on the one hand, and public obligations, on the other.

At the same time he points up the importance and challenge of these private conducts to the individuals' and families' sense of its public moral identity. In Chapters 10 ('Speculation about the Social Order: Stories and Society') and 11 ('Humans and Animals: Stories and Subversion') Beidelman focuses on storytelling not as charters for right action but as explorations of the problem of right conduct ... explorations usually provoked by subversive behaviour in which, for example, sexual etiquette and morally respectful relations between generations, siblings, and brothers and sisters is violated. For in the end Kaguru life, like life in any culture he would posit, has many puzzling features not susceptible to an easy moral casuistry. For Kaguru, particularly, there is 'the puzzle of matrilineality', where children must learn to love and respect their mother's brother more than the father that engendered them. And the father himself finds his love for his offspring subverted by the claims upon them of his brother-in-law.

There are two methodological, which is to say analytic, issues that Beidelman confronts: (1) the evocation of the emotions through the moral imagination and (2) the interlinkage of elements within the imagination to the terrain of social action. There is almost always an emotional charge as the proverbial wisdom of lore and story is brought forth into social life for meditation and comment. Proverbs, themselves, for example, are often introduced during heightened moments of argument and contribute to the agonizing, even agonistic, atmosphere of these moments. And tales, myths and legends heighten awareness in their presentation of a panoply of characters which are provocative of sympathy and antipathy, in any case empathy of a positive or negative nature. The emotions aroused by these presentations of imagined comportments and meditations upon them are influential, one deduces, in conditioning if not directing actual comportment in the extant social world. They are effective in stimulating thought about the moral order if not commitment to just the right behaviours that can properly instantiate that order!

Central to the power of these Kaguru narratives is the fusing of different domains of experience accomplished by metaphor, their chief rhetorical device. Though Beidelman does not, to any great degree, enter into an analysis of the systematicity of these linkages he seems to posit in the notion of 'evocation' and, with virtually a nuclear reaction model in mind, a release of affect and feeling from the very act of linkage itself.[4] But an analytic systematics of narrative or of tropological analysis is not a dominant or even an especially salient concern of this ethnographer and his ethnography, whose focus is on the details of ethnographic interpretation itself, which is to say, on the challenge of understanding how informants in their folklore activate often subversively and by indirection the moral imagination, making use of it in making their way through, as the ethnographer understand it, the puzzling complexities of their social order. Powerful simplicities of interpretation, if any simplicities are to be found beyond these complexities, are inevitably strained by the very thick layering of social life and social experience of which the ethnographer has become aware in his participant observation. The local moral imagination constantly runs up against and is challenged by the subversiveness and contrariness of the moral order at once confronted and recreated in local lore and narrative.

The Perversion of Parsimony

An ethnography of the Kaguru kind which seeks to be true to its subject matter is caught up almost from the first moment in the complexity and contradictions of lived interaction, both observed and testified to by informants and that experienced, day in and day out, by the ethnographer. The second approach, which focuses on the *experiential gestalt*, as it is called by these cognitivists, of 'being in the world', is enabled, by virtue of that focus, to much more readily discover the simplicities upon which the moral imagination or (preferentially in their parlance) the Moral Metaphor System, is grounded. Or at least Lakoff and Johnson in their discussion of Morality (1999: chapter 14) from the first moment and up front tell us that 'the range of metaphors that define our moral concepts is fairly restricted (probably not more than two dozen basic metaphors) and that there are substantial constraints on the range of possible metaphors' (1999: 290). These constraints and limitations arise because the set of metaphors are all grounded in the experience of 'well being' (or ill being) and particularly physical well-being in our diurnal, annual, life-cycle-experienced world of gravitational of ups and downs, of lights and darks, of health and disease, of cleanliness and impurity, of prosperity and impoverishment etc.

We can not enter here into the cognitivists' working out of the moral metaphor system and their argument for the metaphorical nature of moral understanding except to indicate (1) that they believe that what is revealed is a 'widespread if not universal folk theory of what well being in physical terms is', although in the same breath they recognize that this theory has not really been tested cross-culturally (Lakoff and Johnson 1999: 311–12; see also 325, 332); and (2) that they, like Beidelman, recognize that the system is not perfectly self-consistent with itself. Their approach, in other words, not only itself envisions contrarieties and dilemmas that any metaphoric system of understanding generates but that itself as system inevitably throws up moral choices to be made, advertently or inadvertently. In respect to point (1), of course, it is just here, as regards cross-cultural implications, that tropologists in anthropology have been most uncomfortable with the cognitivists' theory (Quinn and Holland 1987). For example, by their understanding one of the most important metaphors for moral well-being and moral judgement turns out to be the wealth and accounting metaphor. Moral bookkeeping and moral judgement as book balancing and the paying of moral debts may be, as it is, a convincing and resonant set of metaphors in Western culture, to be sure, and with the creation of a world marketplace and the globalization of acquisitive and market-minded mentalities it may approach universality among certain classes. But it is hard for an anthropologist to argue that it is a universal in culture, and, as an aside, with the contemporary scandals among accounting firms in mind, the negative valences of accounting itself as a trope could well come to the fore as predominant. This would make of it a trope of falsification or of dubious or ironic use in moral 'calculation'. The culture-centric nature of the limited set of metaphors identified in the moral metaphor system of the cognitivists is one thing, and in any case the theory is recognized by the cognitivists to be in need of cross-cultural testing, but the content and self-consistency of the system proposed is altogether more interesting.

Here we have an issue which brings the cognitivist approach into more direct comparison with the ethnographic. The cognitivists' theory recognizes and works out the details, in a particularly clear way, of the kinds of dilemmas that moral systems anchored or grounded in metaphor get themselves into and the consequent choices posed for moral casuistry. For the metaphors put forth as cultures struggle with the vicissitudes of life are themselves never fully compatible. One is obliged by a rule of retribution to pay or repay moral debts, for example, while, by the rule of 'absolute goodness', one is obliged to forgive debts. One has to make a choice and the cognitivists' approach to the moral system is particularly pertinent to anthropology in pointing out just what some of these choices are and, indeed, their argument recurrently points up such challenging situations of contrariety. It points up the many different metaphorical models for distributive justice, for example, with 'no overarching neutral conception of fairness available to resolve the conflict' (Lakoff and Johnson 1999: 297): moral authority as dominance (Moses) or moral authority as submission (Christ or St Francis) (1999: 301); moral character as an essential (ascribed) or as an acquired condition (1999: 307); absolute empathy as against egocentric empathy (1999: 309–11). In sum, this metaphor-based system of understanding morality and moral judgement does not obviate the choices which accompany life's vicissitudes.

But the question arises whether this tropologically oriented system of analysis is itself free of certain implicit choices of its own that are less clearly recognized and which are subject to anthropological appraisal. For example, the metaphor (other than the wealth and accounting trope) which overall ties together the moral system of the metaphors of Western culture is the 'Family' or 'Family of Man' metaphor which grounds moral behaviour and moral casuistry in family experience, and more particularly the disciplinary atmosphere of the family, whether one of strictness and unquestioned authority or one of nurturant openness. This is the 'Strict Father' vs. 'Nurturant Parent' models which Lakoff finds primary and pervasive in moral reasoning not only in the home but also especially in politics. Here there is a clear choice and for the cognitivists the choice seems clearly in favour of a moral guidance in parenting and politics, and in the conduct of human relationships generally, a guidance based on greater openness and nurturance, based, that is, on the parental nurturance model although not, as they insist, to the point of pathological permissiveness.

The cognitivists in discussing the metaphor of moral order do not hesitate, then, to express moral repugnance for that order based on the strict father model even to the point of finding the idea of moral order itself unacceptable especially insofar as it is strictly (in a *pater potestas* way, one can say) identified with the natural order of things and thereby rendered absolute and free of needful casuistry.[5] But it is quite unclear if there is an alternative to that metaphor insofar as considerable time is also spent in the argument in pointing out the mappings in the physical sphere – the primordial gestalt of uprightness, stability and strength, that is to say the logic of physical top-down dominance out of which the idea of Moral Order is constructed. Hierarchy may be morally repugnant but is it avoidable? The ambiguity of argument on this issue is such as to suggest that what we are being offered is a platitude of repugnance along with an attitude of complicity with the 'fixedness in nature of hierarchy' from which emanate many of the 'naturalizing' judgements which support existing power relations in cultures.

We encounter this same problem where Lakoff and Turner in an earlier work, *More Than Cool Reason: A Field Guide to Poetic Metaphor* (1989), take up a widespread Western trope, that of the Great Chain of Being. Though usually taught as a guide to Western thinking from Plato to Pope, the Great Chain of Being is, the authors argue, in fact a still current cultural model so 'widespread, largely unconscious and so fundamental and indispensable to our thinking that we hardly notice it' (Lakoff and Turner 1989: 167). Indeed, as it turns out, it is indispensable to our understanding of ourselves, our world and our language (Lakoff and Turner 1989: 167–169) The indispensability of this widespread trope lies in the fact that it embodies a basic dynamic of understanding by which (1) the experience of being is arranged on a hierarchical scale of greater complexity and power ranging from inanimate being on the lowest rung with animate being above themselves arranged according to their sentient complexity and power, with self-conscious human beings and their superior divine beings on the very highest rungs. It is indispensable (2) because, using the cognitivists' scale of basic metaphoric operations, we are able to understand some of the attributes of being of higher-level complexity and power by predicating lower-level and more understandable attributes upon them. In the simplest (anthropomorphic or zoomorphic) case this would mean predicating animal-like – pig-like or lion-like – attributes upon humans, or vice versa human-like attributes upon animals.

The authors use this model to give insightful explanations of generic-specific predications involved in proverbial wisdom. As it turns out, the Great Chain is a crucial model for understanding the logic of metaphor itself as a predicative process operating up and down on such a hierarchical scale of simplicity and complexity. The Great Chain is, therefore, more than a metaphor or, as the authors say (Lakoff and Turner 1989: 172), 'not strictly a metaphor' or 'not just a metaphor' but rather a recurring conceptual complex made up of a metaphor, a common-sense theory and a communicative principle. It is thus a fundamental cognitive tool of great power and scope.

It is just here, as far as anthropological ethnography is concerned, that this tool of understanding provokes misgivings. This is seen when the authors examine in the closing pages the 'Social and Political Consequences of the Great Chain of Being' and its hierarchies of domination of lower forms by higher forms. And here the ambiguity we have pointed up re-asserts itself. For, particularly as this Great Chain has been 'elaborated'[6] in the West, the Great Chain has had profound social and political consequences in that it teaches both what the hierarchies should be and, as these hierarchies are laws of nature, that it would be not only wrong but unnatural to try and subvert them. This has, as the authors indicate, profound implications in justifying class and caste systems, domination and subordination in race and gender relations, the exploitative relations of man over nature and authoritarianisms of many other kinds. These uses provoke the authors' moral reaction and rejection although it is not clear that since the Great Chain is, as they say, 'more than a metaphor' but is actually built into the conceptual logic by which metaphor operates, that the moral imagination can do anything about that except resign itself in despair. A concluding paragraph captures that fateful ambiguity.

> For whatever reason, perhaps because in our early cognitive development we *inevitably* [authors' emphasis] form the model of the basic Great Chain as we interact with the world it seems that the Great Chain is widespread and has strong natural appeal. This is frightening. It implies that those social, political and ecological evils induced by the Great Chain will not disappear quickly or easily of their own accord. (Lakoff and Turner 1989: 213)

It is of interest to ask, in respect to the apparent moral energy of this argument coupled with an underlying ambiguity about 'inevitability' in which moral choice is obviated, as to whether because of its lodging in the biology of cognitive process we have the option to find some other metaphor more suitable to our moral imagination. Here in respect to this ambiguity we turn to consider a recent critique by Emily Martin (2000) of the definitive turn in the human sciences towards neural structures of the brain for foundational explanation free of the dilemmas of moral choice. This, indeed, is seen in the recent work of the cognitive linguists, and is particularly apparent in the work of Lakoff and Johnson we consider here (1999). For, somehow, despite the manifest exercise of their moral imaginations concerning the hierarchical implications of the Strict Father Model and the Great Chain of Being metaphor, the reader feels an underlying and pervasive sense of the inescapable realities of neural structuring of conceptualization which is inevitably hierarchical in nature. Beyond or behind the moral imagination, in other words (whose workings, incidentally, are otherwise illuminatingly analyzed by Johnson, Lakoff and Turner), is the greater reality and the 'inevitabilities' of the neuron-computational machinery. Under this paradigm tropological science, the study of the 'play of tropes in society', necessarily gives way to neuroscience, the study of the determinative neuromechanisms. The complexities not to say contrarieties in the cognitivists' ethical cum biological narrative here would surely be a support for Beidelman's view of the 'inevitable' pathos present when ethnography examines in depth the struggle of cultures, including intellectual cultures, wrestling with their foundational ethos.

A Reponsibility to Social Being and Becoming

Emily Martin, as always in her papers, is interested in 'the ideological work' done by certain choices of tropes, say the choice of the neural mechanism as the explanatory engine of all behaviour, and the relationship of such choices to (1) the current cultural context in which they may be strategic and adaptive, and to (2) anthropology's enduring task to focus ethnographically not only on the complexity of social behaviour in its actual cultural context, but on the socially self-serving nature of apparently foundational arguments in culture. In the case of her argument examined here she finds the reduction of human social life to the structures of reason embodied in the neuromechanism as a compensatory turn to interior stability amidst the manic irrational energy of our present exterior world of an ultimately uncontrollable and unpredictable marketplace, entrepreneurial to the point of self-indulgent irresponsibility and self-contradictory to the point of irony. (This particular article was written before the collapse of the dot.com bubble and the scandal of the Enron Corporation, two manic enterprises, victims of illusory expectations and/or the depredations of the energy robber barons[7] maniacally and gluttonously engaged in creating offshore empires hidden from a reasoned accounting practice.) She points out that, in a moral economy like the present – one that increasingly removes from the individual the former governmental and institutional protections of his long-term well-being, removes, that is, social safety nets of every kind, leaving him or her like miniature corporations, every boat on its own bottom, to sail on very uncertain seas – a turn to the certainties and logic lodged in the neural mechanism has clear compensatory benefits. It represents a convenient truncation or obviation of the moral imagination as it reorders to elite advantage the moral economy.

Martin, entering into a moral mode of reasoning, compares the present political economic context and its compensatory thought about human nature with the eighteenth century and the compensatory thought of the Moral Philosophers. They too were faced with a time of insecurity, the collapse of the *Ancien Régime* with all its securities of religion and aristocratic right and rank. They too turned to philosophize about the interiority of human nature, discovering there the universality of 'enlightened reason' and an apparatus of sentiments that, freed from the superstitions, privileges and other constraints of the past, would, if understood properly, and with the benevolent oversight of an 'invisible hand', enable self-rule and social order. Not so long ago, of course, we contemporaries have heard in the halls of the American Congress the argument that if the burden of government controls were only lifted from the backs of business, financial acumen, the present manifestation of universal reason in human nature, coupled with the age-old discipline of self-interested competition, Darwinian in nature, would bring unparalleled prosperity and brilliance to our polity! As irony ever follows after self-interested reasoning one remarks that such a lifting of burdens certainly has brought prosperity to the managerial elite!

Without wishing to overstretch the comparison of the Enlightenment and Universal Reason of the Moral Philosophers with the 'enlightened argument' of our contemporary money managers – that is to say, the neoliberal free market argument of the present-day business gurus anxious to be given the green light to social betterment through self-improvement – we may wish to pursue Martin's argument further, which is to say her own moral philosophy about anthropology's task, and do so by brief reference to another, not unrelated moral philosophy, which is rhetorically very much part of our times and which is also of inevitable interest to anthropology. I refer to the human ecology movement and its particular efforts to relate nature to culture and to relate Darwinian views of human evolution to an ethical commitment to a holistic view of nature and mutual respect for quality of life. This is the concordance of life forms that E.O. Wilson, in a Latin leap, calls the *consilience* of life (Wilson 1998). His ecologist's preservationist arguments constitute an unusually salient instance, as we can see, of the moral imagination in action in respect, we might also say, of his particular sense, quite different from that of Lakoff and Turner, of the Great Chain of Being.

■ ■ ■

Of course that particular effort of the moral imagination to relate Darwinian evolutionism to the ethics of social interaction with the environment is not new. There was something of that sensibility in Darwin himself. It was most certainly present in the great palaeontologist, Darwin's bulldog T.H. Huxley, whose final efforts are contained a collection of essays labelled *Evolution and Ethics* (1893). Indeed, there is much evidence of the moral imagination at work in his continuing struggle to relate evolution to ethics and, as it were, return to some wholeness of perspective, to a more benevolent human condition otherwise tending to fall into the Hobbesian, not to say Darwinian part-ness where every man's hand is set against every other's. In the mid twentieth century at least it was, as we recall, the Jesuit palaeontologist and moralist Teilhard de Chardin, much admired by Huxley's grandson Julian Huxley, who sought to create a more holistic evolutionary humanism by relating the canons of Darwinism to an exceptionalism in humans derived from our cephalization, which is to say our consciousness of self, or self-awareness, a self-awareness which carried with it moral choice. The appearance of mind in this sense, he argued, was an entirely new element in evolution and instead of the evolutionary radiation of species, in humans we have increasing convergence and 'complexification' of social interrelationships suggesting the possibilities – congenial to his professional Christianity – of increasing perfection and unity of communicative interaction in this round world where what goes around eventually comes around.[8] His was an argument of moral imagination indeed. In any event Teilhard is another notable instance of a thinker fundamentally committed to evolutionary science who yet, like the two Huxleys and like Wilson, seeks to relate it to moral matters and to the spiritual, not to say teleological-ethical commitments involved in 'becoming more human'.

Subsequently we have seen other notable efforts to make whole in a moral way, whether by a hermeneutic or a scientific circle, the difficult if not opposed relationship of natural selection with spiritual self-awareness, and competition and issues of survival with ethical intention. We see this in the recent very large idea of unitary co-evolution associated with the work of Gregory Bateson (1972, 1980), for example, or in the Gaia Hypothesis of James Lovelock (1979; Margolis 1997). These symbiotic or unitary arguments in search of what Bateson calls the 'necessary unity' of mind and nature are surely exercises in the moral imagination under the aegis of one of the grandest tropes of all, Gaia, that is to say, Mother Earth! They are each attempts, like Huxley's much earlier attempt, to interconnect the biophysical and mental worlds and to see in that connection a systematic self-adjusting or self-correcting relation, the kind of self-regulation based on moral reflection that is life's most essential characteristic.

All these imaginations were and are in one way or another in struggle with the moral – or perhaps better said, the amoral – implications of the Darwinian message. They are, therefore, among other things exercises, in presence or in absence, of the moral imagination. No one would doubt either, though we only glancingly consider Marx, the energizing power of his moral imagination, an imagination whose concentrated consciousness-raising about the involuted and self-serving excesses of capital and the exploitations of class became, to say the least, a dominant leitmotif of the social imagination if not moral imagination of the last century and a half.[9] And surely Marx had important and morally energetic things to say about the evolution of political economy! We do not have time to offer in this argument evidence of the connections between Huxley's argument and all these latter-day inquiries into the very general topic of 'Evolution and Ethics'.

The Ethnographer's Imagination and the Moral Imagination

In reviewing these exemplars of tropological awareness we see moral imagination active in a variety of ways. In Beidelman we see a moral imagination working in pathetic mode contemplating the irresolvability of the contradictions in the social contract and as these are reflected in the moral code. In the case of the cognitive linguists we see the moral imagination resolving its problems by contemplating the psycho-biological inevitability of hierarchy. In Martin we see a moral imagination offended by the neuro-reductionism in much recent cognitive and cultural science and the violence it does to the complexities of the social nature which is our humanity, in particular its obviation of the challenges to our creative powers in figuring out in rhetorical ways a way through just these complexities of the human condition. In the evolutionary ecologists we see a moral reaction to the extraordinary compartmentalization of modern life, and the separation of nature from culture, in an attempt to 'return to the whole moral order'. Whatever the moral judgements contained in these contemporary explanatory narratives of our condition, in every case we find an ongoing play of tropes. It is in this play, in the end, that the sense of moral order or disorder emerges or is abridged. It is this play of mind or 'play of tropes' that we argue to be basic in the moral imagination that leads us into deeper understandings – understandings, among other things, of the dynamic of the elaboration of the tropes into full narrative argument.

■ ■ ■

No doubt there are reasons for hesitation in evoking the moral imagination in social science explanation, quite beside the fact that in a secular, constitutionally non-religious society like the American one it is felt that moral principles should be mainly left to the individual or the group of believers and that they are not the pragmatic or political issues on which one can dispute fruitfully. There is a feeling, as far as social science is concerned, that morality talk conceals much more than it reveals, however one seeks to show its constant presence even, as we have seen, in social science explanation itself. We see that concealment most obviously in political movements such as Moral Rearmament or the Moral Majority, and other faith-based organizations such as the Salvation Army which also engage in politics. The judgementalism that arises from moral principle tends too easily to ignore or override more complex and hidden matters such as prevailing hegemonic power. In the United States the so-called Culture of Poverty was extensively debated, beginning in the 1960s, and in the end it was a concept that seemed to assign so much to morals, values and ingrained behaviors as to ignore the delimiting structures of racism and the perpetuation of class privilege that sustained minority poverty and explained dysfunctional – from the majority point of view – behaviours. Morality as an explanation for behaviour, it has often been argued, mystifies more than it clarifies, and privileges more than it explains in respect to truly thorough and penetrating social science explanation.

The answer to this well-founded misgiving is simply that one does not seek to explain anything as complexly over-determined as human behaviour by simple and direct reference to the causal force of morality and moral principle itself. That would be the mistake of moral revitalization movements. But rather one seeks to elucidate how by the play of the imagination difficult moral issues are grappled with, moral principles are energized and, as we see, how they come to capture the imagination. Calling attention to the moral imagination in the end is calling attention to the imagination's role in resonating with and affecting human sentiments and responding to and influencing social order and disorder.

One can ask: is there not a better formulation? On Marx's example we might just as well, or better, have referred to the Victorian ideology, or the ideology of Social Darwinism when speaking of Darwin and Huxley. I do not wish to deny the importance of that concept in the last several centuries nor its productiveness in the investigations into political economy, and into the interface between society, particularly, political economy and the language issues we have been interested in. Indeed it could well be argued that the prevalent and preferred term in the treatment of the role of figurative language in society and rhetoric in culture, which in the end is our subject matter, *is* ideology.[10]

Several things, then, can be said in favour of and several against the idea of 'the moral imagination' as an analytic category in relation to ideology. First, as the dictionary tells us, the word 'ideology' carries a negative weight as 'a prescriptive doctrine not supported by rational argument'. This is certainly the case in the best-known use of the term, Marx and Engels', *The German Ideology*. Special precautions must be taken to prevent these negative associations from prejudicing inquiry. If we do not take care the term 'ideology' will tend to privilege those who employ it in their study over against those they study, that is the individuals, groups, classes, who are identified with such an 'unsupported' scheme of ideas as a guide to their conduct in the world. There is, correspondingly, the tendency in studying ideology of studying the other without implicating the self who is doing the studying, producing invidious analysis of the kind, 'I have well-supported beliefs, while you have an ideology.' Indeed one might argue that the use of the term 'ideology' as a purportedly objective term of anthropological science shows a lack of moral imagination.

In any event the study of the moral imagination more readily implicates, one may argue along with Beidelman, the investigator as observer, for who would want to assert that they themselves were such automata, such creatures of culture, as to be without moral imagination? And who would want to deny that their (that is the observer's) moral imagination stands in no relation with that of the observed? Of course, by that very fact of *implication* the worry arises that objectivity will be lost, insofar as one in late modern times may still hold to the possibility of an objective posture of inquiry.[11] The investigator interested in the moral imagination, it may be felt, will find himself more directly embroiled in the strong currents, which is to say the rhetoric, of moral judgementalism and revivalism so ever-present in dynamic societies, particularly those of the secularized modern world, a world, ironically, so cast off from the canonical moral anchorage of the patristic and theocratic world.

In any event, that awareness of the underlying topoi and their expansion into the different tropes and different weighting of tropes that animate the imagination, and the insights obtained into the commitment or lack of commitment generated, is part of the value, I believe, of maintaining the moral imagination as a useful concept in our inquiry into the other; an inquiry into the other which takes both ourselves and these others as beings in becoming animated by moral considerations of the imagination.

But quite beside this question of methodological posture and engagement or distancing from the other, already, after all, well treated in the anthropological literature of postmodernism,[12] the argument is to be made that by giving interpretive credence to the role of the imagination and the images it both generates and is stimulated by we are provided with insight into visions of orderly and disorderly worlds, into this old Radcliffe-Brownian term 'moral order' which society after all and in the end is. That is to say that we are given insight into *relationships* – the basic subject matter, in the end, of any envisioned social science. This is as true of the moral philosophers of the eighteenth century as of the contemporary thinkers considered in this paper, whether Darwin or Huxley, Teilhard de Chardin, Bateson or Lovelock, Beidelman, the cognitivist linguists or Emily Martin. For the moral imagination has above all to do with visions of the perfection or imperfection, of the well-being and ill-being, of human relationships in the world and of the obligations, accountabilities or liabilities these visions carry.

Notes

1. Just to take two examples of the range of work influenced by Bakhtinian studies of the narrative dynamics of the dialogic imagination that embodies the moral (or social) imagination in storytelling: Jameson (1981), Basso (1984).
2. See Paul Ricoeur's discussion of the 'chronologicizacion', in Ricoeur 1983–88.
3. This book has appeared in a second but not revised edition with an insightful Foreword by Ivan Karp (Beidelman 1993).
4. For a discussion of the emotional release attendant upon the realization of domain linkage see Fernandez (1974, 1986).
5. 'The Moral Order metaphor does not merely legitimize power relations and establish lines of authority. It also generates a hierarchy of moral responsibility in which those in authority at a given level have responsibilities towards those over whom they have that authority… The consequences of the metaphor of Moral order are sweeping, momentous and we believe *morally repugnant* [emphasis mine]. The metaphor legitimates a certain class of existing power relations as being natural and therefore moral' (Lakoff and Johnson 1999: 303–4).

6. The authors make a distinction, apparently, between elaborated and unelaborated Great Chains, reserving their criticism primarily for the latter although it is difficult to see that the Great Chain in any form would be more or less free of feelings of domination and subordination.
7. Often taken as a good measure of 'robber baron' ethics is the ratio between upper-echelon executive salaries and ordinary worker salaries in American corporations. This has grown in America over the last twenty years from some 45 times as much executive compensation in the early 1980s to some 450 times as much at the end of the booming 1990s. Such self-regarding greed has rarely been seen in the modern world, since the nineteenth century at least, even among such famously elitist economies as Brazil and Mexico. Cf. P. Krugman, 'Enemies of Reform', *The New York Times,* 21 May 2002.
8. Teilhard, a Jesuit, was criticized and brought under pressure by his own church for a too great optimism in this matter and for his neglect of ever-present evil and human imperfection. He rather belatedly, apologetically (and very briefly, three pages only and as an Appendix at the end of *The Phenomenon of Man* 1965), takes up the question of 'The Place and Part of Evil in a World in Evolution'. He discusses four evils: disorder and failure, decomposition, solitude and anxiety, and growth. These are all seen, to be sure, not from the perspective of the Ten Commandments but from the perspective of optimizing the expected evolution of increasing intensity and convergence of human interrelationships.
9. In mind here is the division of the moral imagination into subtypes: the social imagination, the religious imagination, the cultural imagination, the psychic imagination and the corporeal imagination.
10. For example, see its varied use in the recent collection edited by Schieffelin, Woolard and Kroskrity (1998). Especially important and clarifying is the Introduction by Woolard (1998: 3–47) in which she reviews the quite varied usages (four groupings) to which ideology as been put in the social science literature, most often negative. By pointing up that most usages have to do with the relation of social and political position to language she argues for creating a space (such as the collection she introduces) in which the various understandings of that responsive relationship can be explored thus opening up a bridge between linguistic and social theory. See also the pioneering consideration of this issue, influential in Woolard's review, by Paul Friedrich (1989).
11. See, in this respect, Renato Rosaldo's argument in *Culture and Truth: The Remaking of Social Analysis* (1989), that the postmodern bringing into question of the possibility of objectivity 'creates a space for ethical concerns in a territory once regarded as value-free. It enables the social analyst to become a social critic' (1989: 181); a phrasing 'to become a social critic' which we would put rather as 'to employ his moral imagination'.
12. And particularly in respect to the distancing from common occupancy of time and space with the informant (participatory co-evality), the well-known essay of Johannes Fabian, *Time and the Other: How Anthropology Makes Its Object* (1982).

References

Bakhtin, M. 1984. *The Dialogic Imagination: Four Essays,* ed. M. Holquist, trans. C. Emerson. Austin: University of Texas Press.

Basso, K. 1984. 'Stalking with Stories: Names, Places and Moral Narratives'. In *Text, Play and Story: The Construction and Reconstruction of Self and Society*, ed E.M. Bruner, pp. 19–55. Washington: American Ethnological Society.

Bateson, G. 1972. *Steps Towards an Ecology of Mind: Collected Essays*. New York: Ballantine Books.

——— 1980. *Mind and Nature: A Necessary Unity*. New York: Dutton.

Beidelman, T. 1986. *Moral Imagination in Kaguru Modes of Thought*. Bloomington: Indiana University Press.

——— 1993. *Moral Imagination in Kaguru Modes of Thought*, with a new foreword by Ivan Karp. Washington: Smithsonian Press.

Fabian, J. 1982. *Time and the Other: How Anthropology Makes Its Object*. New York: Columbia University Press.

Fernandez, J. 1974. 'The Mission of Metaphor in Expressive Culture. With Comments and Rejoinder', *Current Anthropology* 15(2): 119–45.

——— 1986. 'The Argument of Images and the Experience of Returning to the Whole'. In *The Anthropology of Experience*, eds Victor W. Turner and Edward M. Bruner, pp. 159–87, Urbana: University of Illinois Press..

Friedrich, P. 1989. 'Language, Ideology and Political Economy', *The American Anthropologist*, 91(2): 295–312.

Huxley, T.H. 1893. *'Evolution and Ethics' and Other Essays*. London and New York, Macmillan & Co.

Jameson, F. 1981. *The Political Unconscious: Narrative as a Socially Symbolic Act*. Ithaca: Cornell University Press.

Lakoff, G. and M. Johnson. 1999. *Philosophy in the Flesh: The Embodied Mind and Its Challenge to Western Thought*. New York: Basic Books.

Lakoff, G. and M. Turner. 1989. *More than Cool Reason: A Field Guide to Poetic Metaphor*. Chicago: University of Chicago Press.

Lovelock, J. 1979. *The Ages of Gaia: A Biography of Our Living Earth*. Oxford and New York: Oxford University Press.

Margolis, L. 1997. *Slanted Truths: Essays on Gaia, Symbiosis and Evolution*. New York: Copernicus.

Martin, E. 2000. 'Mind–Body Problems', *American Ethnologist* 27(3): 569–90.

Quinn, N. and D. Holland. 1987. 'Culture and Cognition'. In *Cultural Models in Language and Thought*, eds D. Holland and N. Quinn, pp. 1–42. Cambridge: Cambridge University Press.

Ricoeur, P. 1983–88. *Time and Narrative*, 3 vols. Chicago: University of Chicago Press.

Rosaldo, R. 1989. *Culture and Truth: The Remaking of Social Analysis*. Boston: Beacon Press.

Schieffelin, B., K. Woolard and P. Kroskrity. 1998. *Language Ideologies: Practice and Theory*. New York: Oxford University Press.

Teilhard de Chardin, P. 1965. *The Phenomenon of Man*. London: Collins.

Wilson, E.O. 1998. *Consilience: The Unity of Knowledge*. New York: Knopf.

Contributors

■ ■ ■ ■ ■ ■

F.G. Bailey is Professor Emeritus of Anthropology at the University of San Diego.

Ellen B. Basso is Professor Emerita of Anthropology at the University of Arizona.

Megan Biesele is Director of the Kalahari Peoples Fund and holds adjunct professorships of anthropology at Michigan State University and the University of Nebraska at Lincoln.

Michael Carrithers is Professor of Anthropology at Durham University, U.K.

Ralph Cintron is Associate Professor of English and of Latin American and Latino Studies at the University of Illinois at Chicago.

James W. Fernandez is Professor Emeritus of Anthropology at the University of Chicago.

Brigitte Nerlich is Professor of Science, Language and Society at the Institute for Science and Society, University of Nottingham.

Jean Nienkamp is Associate Professor of English at Indiana University of Pennsylvania.

Stevan M. Weine is Associate Professor of Psychiatry at the University of Illinois at Chicago.

Index

∎ ∎ ∎ ∎ ∎ ∎

!Xu (God) 82
//Gauwa (God) 82
1968 35
9/11 15, 16, 97, 138, 145, 148–153
A Midsummer Night's Dream 109
accountability 39
Action Signal of Atonement (*Aktion Sühnezechen*) 47
Adam 9
address 6, 8, 15
addressivity 6–7
Adenauer 43
adolescence 28
adolescent survivors 62
adolescents 63
Advancement of Learning, The 18
afford, affordance 42
African-American 128
After Nature 53
agency 8, 118
agency-cum-patiency 8
agents, complex 19
Agger, Inger 56, 57
agora 156
Aichinger, Wolfram 98
AIDS 73, 89
Al Qaeda 148, 149, 151, 152
Allan 99
allegory 156
amae vocabulary 122
ambiguity of social life 158
Amsterdam 26
analogy 49, 156
Anatomy of Dependence, The 122

Angelus Novus 145
animals, farm 13
anthropology 156
anthropology, symbolic 88
anti-Semitism 128–9
apocalypse 152
Appadurai, Arjun 126
Aristotle 20
Arminius 44
army 88
Assmann 36, 38
astonishment 149–150
audience 46
Augé 139
Austerlitz 54

Bacon, Francis 18
Bailey, F.G. 4, 5, 13, 14
baita (upland shack) 107 *passim*
Bakhtin, Mikhail 7, 53, 59, 157
Balkans 57
Basso, Ellen 15
Bateson, Gregory 167, 170
battle, metaphor of. *See* war.
Bauman 139
BBC 100
Beidelman, Thomas 158–160, 167, 169, 170
Bender 141, 144
Benedict, Ruth 123, 124
Benjamin, Walter 145
Berlin Wall 36
Berman 139
Biesele, Megan 5, 12, 13, 15

Billig, Michael 11
biomedical system 13, 78, 79
Bird-David, Nurit 38
Bismarck 44
Blair, Tony 88, 101
Blumenberg, Hans 9
body. *See* mind / body.
Boeing 142
Bolsheviks 44
Booth 116
Bosnia 12
Bosnian refugees 63–68
Brenneis, Donald 49
Britain 153
Brooklyn Bridge 139
BSE (mad cow disease) 89
BSE panic 91
Buddha 1, 9
Bude, H. 35
Burke, Kenneth 8, 9, 19–20, 32
Burleigh 39
Bushmen. *See* Ju'/hoan San.

cancer 72–83
capitalism, late 139
capitalism, virtual 147
carcasses 90
care, heroic 77
care, total 77
Carrithers 4, 5, 11–12, 14, 46, 49
Casey 139
catastrophizing 89
CBBC 100
Certeau, Michel de 138–140, 148
chaos 81
character, defined 39
Chardin, Teilhard de 166, 170
Charon 13, 69, 73, 74, 81
Chase Manhattan Bank 146
chemotherapy 75, 78
Cheney, Jim 132
Chicago 53, 63–68
chicken 89
Christ 22, 35, 162
Christian Democrats 113
Christian thought 41
Christianity 37
Chrysanthemum and the Sword, The 123

Cicero 6
Cintron, Ralph 4, 5, 15
Citigroup 144
civility, affinal 126–133
 - Jewish experience of 126–129
 - ordeals of 126–129
CNN 63
cognitive restructuring 76
cognitivism 49
cognitivist explanations 57
cognitivists 160–164
Cold War 41, 43, 48
collective symbolic coping 94, 95
combat, metaphor of. *See* war.
commercialization 89
commodification 141
communication, ritualized 123
communicative silencing (*kommunikatives Beschweigen*) 35
Communist party 47
community-based services 56
complaint discourse 70
concept, essentially contested 4
Conrad 95
consilience 166
Constable landscapes 98
consumers 89
contadino (peasant) 108
containment policy. *See* slaughter policy.
controversia 156
coping, collective 96
Costall 42
coup, against Hitler 37
Cousins 74
Creighton 124
crisis 89, 90
Crocker 88, 98
Crowden 100
CT scan 76
Cuddihy, John Murray 126–129
culling 87
cultural rhetorics 31–32
culture 4–6, 49
 - defined 3
 - of poverty 168
 - as quality space 37
 - rhetorical edge of 6
Cumbria 98

daffodils 98
dance, healing 71
dAquili 77
darkness, image of 37-38
Darwin 170
Darwinian thought 166-167
Davis-Floyd, Robbie 69, 70, 73
Dear 139
death 71, 74, 78, 81, 82, 148
death, acceptance of 76
 - good 13, 81
 - as journey 9
 - mastering 153
Deauville 55
deception, positive view of 135
demystification 79
deregulation 144
Derricote, Toi 128
Detroit 146
dialogic theory 53, 59, 60, 61
diaries 21-33
Dieckmann, Christoph 35
diffuse, the 12, 53-58
DiGiacomo 74, 78
disaster, national 89
discourse 4
 - affinal 129
 - deceptive 129
disease, economic 89
disease, rhetorical and cultural 89
disinfectant 93
distortion, vs. harmony 144
doctor / patient conversation 79
doctor / patient dialogue 84
doctor / patient relationship 79
doctor's role, and women 74
Doi, Takeo 122, 134
Donaldson 89
Döring 89
dot.com bubble 165
doxa 141, 142
Dubiel 42
Duke Energy 142
Dumont, Louis 4
dying 78, 82, 83

E. coli 89
ecological psychology 42

economic miracle (*Wirtschaftswunder*) 42
eggs 89
eironeia, Socratic irony 116-117
El Paso Corporation 142, 143
election 92
Emerson 60
Emigrants, The 54, 62
emotion 22, 23
 - as intersubjective 121
 - rhetorics of 121
emotions, evoked in moral imagination 159
Empire State Building 139
enargia (ocular demonstration) 138
End, The 57
enemy, disease as 92, 93
energeia (vigor in expression) 138, 142
energy, healing. *See* n/om.
Enlightenment 153, 164-165
Enron 165
epidemic 89
equality, ideology of 126
eradication policy. *See* slaughter policy.
ethical deliberation, as storytelling 157
ethnic cleansing 140
ethnographic imagination 167
ethos 20, 30
European Parliament 89
euthanasia 69, 77, 81, 82
evaluation, moral 14
evangelicalism 22
Evangelische Akademie Berlin-
 Brandenberg 37
Evans-Pritchard 119
Eve 9
evil 37-51
Evolution and Ethics 166
expectation 2, 10, 15, 31
experience vs. rhetoric 47
experts 91

fairness 162
family, metaphor of 162
farmers 13, 89, 91
 - as prisoners 101
father, strict, metaphor of 162
fear, collective 151
fear of outsiders (*taijinkyofusho*) 124

Female Quixotism 23
Fernandez, James 4, 7, 16, 17, 34, 37, 45, 98, 118
figuration 156, 157
figurative thought 34
figure 16
First World War 45
Fisher 78
floods 89
FMD. *See* foot and mouth disease.
folktales 158
foot and mouth disease, (FMD) 13, 87–104
   - in contest with 102
   - as fire 101
   - as hand to hand combat 102
   - on journey 102
   - as plague 101
   - as rhetorical and cultural disease 89
Fortune 500 companies 142
Foucault 32
Fox 82
France 55
Frank, Anne 22, 25–33
Frank, Margot 26, 29
Frank, Otto 25
Frankfurt 26
Frazer, James G. 123
Freud 123
Freudian thought 41
Frevert 36, 38
Friedrich 48
Fröhlich 35
frontline 92
fuel protests 89
Fulbrook, Mary 35, 36
fundamentalists, Muslim 153
future, as words and images and things 144–145

Gaia 167
Gallie, W.B. 4
Gandhian *satyagraha* (struggle for truth) 117
GDR (German Democratic Republic) 36
Gee, James Paul 32
Geertz 81
general election 89
General Electric 141–142
genocide 54
genres, oratorical 129
Gergen 39
Germans 25–31
Germany 5, 34–51
Gestapo 26
Gettysburg Address 8
Giordano, Ralph 41
global warming 89
globalization 89
gloom 55
GM food 89, 96
GM tomatoes 94, 95
God 71, 82
Goffman 116
Golden 90
Golden Bough, The 123
Golden Calf 101
Goody, Esther 48
Grand Hotel des Roches Noires 55
Great Chain of Being 163–164, 166
   - as metaphor, theory, and principle 163
growth, and testimony 56
Guardian 91
Guardian Unlimited 97
guilt 124

haji (Japanese: shame) 124
Hamaguchi 124
Hamburg 57
Hamilton 90
Hamlet 116
Hanusch 37, 40, 47
Hardt 57
Hariman, Robert 12
harmony 144
Harré 88
healers 70
healing and religion, linked 82
hecatombs 40–41
Hemingway 20
Heraclitus 1
Herz 36
Herzfeld, Michael 115
Hezbollah 151, 153
history, contemporary (*Zeitgeschichte*) 38
History of the Human Heart, The 23

Hitler 11, 12, 37–39, 41, 44
Hodgkins disease 78
holism, in biomedicine 77
holistic model of medicine 74
Holland 98
Holland, Dorothy 161
Holocaust 13, 35, 55
holocaust (of animals) 87–104
holocausts 139
honorific language 130
house, moral space of 159
Houston 146
Huber 118
human rights and mental health 56
Hutcheon 116
Huxley, T.H. 166, 170
hyperbole 15
 - as constituent of modern reality 140
 - as corrective satire 140
 - as distortion of communal bond 140
hyperbolic grief 151
hyperbolic hypermodern 139 *passim*

IBM 142
ideology, as moral imagination 169
ideology, semiotic, among Kalapalo 132
Illness Narratives, The 80
image-beliefs 96
image/story 41–43, 50
imagery 34
images 14, 90
inchoate 43, 45
inchoate pronoun 37
indexing code, acknowledging otherness of other among Kalapalo 129
individual, self-realized 141
industrialization 89
industrialized states 45
inner / outer, as cultural ideas in West 126
inner / outer distinction, in Japan 134
inner conflict, necessary experience of 135
insight 58
interaction 7, 8
interaction, constant, among Kalapalo 129
interactions, face to face 48
internal rhetoric, primary 19–20
intersubjectivity 7
inventio 141

invention 139
 - as fantasy 144
 - as pervasive need 141
 - as skill 141
invention, as prevalent in modern psyche 141 *passim*
invention/innovation 144, 145, 150
Iraq 15
Iraq wars 148
irony 114–118
irony, apotropaic 116
 - combative 115–118
 - subversive 116
Irony in Action 119
Isocrates 8, 18
Israel 148, 151, 153
Italy 13–14 , 107–119

J.P. Morgan Chase 142
Japan 122, 124–126
Jensen, Soren 56, 57
Jewish experience of modernity 126
Jewish leaders 127–8
Jews 25–31, 40, 41, 44
Johnson 88, 90, 160
Ju'/hoan San 5, 12–13, 69–84
judgment, moral 14
justice 46
 - distributive 162

Kaiser, the 44
Kalahari 5, 12, 70
Kalapalo 129–133
Kaluli 80
Kennedy, J.F. 146
killing fields, British 95
Kitzinger 95
Klee, Paul 145
Klein 78
Kleinman, Arthur 79, 80
Kockleman 121
Kohlstruck 35
Konner 73
Koolhass 139
Kosovo 12
Kowalczyk, Walter, Chief Fire Officer 149
Kronberger 92
Krupat 122

Kubler-Ross 83
Kulenovic 63–68

Lakoff, George 8, 88, 90, 158, 160–164
lambs, killing of 95
Langer, Suzanne 81
language, ordeals of 122, 123
Laub, Dori 57
Laughlin 77
Lee 26
legends 159
Leudar 42
Lévi-Strauss 80
Linde, Charlotte 39
Lindsay, John V. 146
lintel 107 *passim*
Lippmann, Walter 44–45, 48
Lira, Elizabeth 56
listeria 89
logos 20
Los Angeles 146
Losa (community) 107 *passim*
loss 10
Lovelock 167, 170
Lowe 89
Lübbe, Hermann 35
Lyng 78, 79

Machiavelli 118
mad cow disease. *See* BSE.
MAFF (Ministry of Agriculture, Farming and Fisheries) 88
Malinowski 81
Man and Superman 90
managerial elite 165
manga 125
maquilidora workers 152
Margolis 167
Maritime Alps 107
Mark Anthony 117
Martin, Emily 164–167
Marx 139, 169
Master of Tricks 71
matrilineality, puzzle of 159
Mattingly, Cheryl 40
McManus 77
Mead, George Herbert 21
meat 89

media 89
- discourse 96, 97
media, mass 57
medical rhetoric 70
melancholy 54, 58
Mennonites 77
mental health and human rights 56
Merck 142
metaphor 9, 12, 34, 36–39, 41, 48, 49, 87–104
- absolute 9
- chief rhetorical device of Kaguru narrative 160
- conceptual 102
- defined 37
- as grounded in well being 160
- systems, moral, contradictions in 161
Mexican border 152
military operation 102
mind / body, Cartesian separation 73
Ministry of Agriculture, Farming and Fisheries. *See* MAFF.
mockery 111–112, 115
model, brotherhood 110
model, intentionalist 108
model, interactionist 108
model, market economy 109
model, market, as abstraction 109–110
model, qualified intentionalist 108
modernity 139 *passim*
- bankrupt 140
- as rhetorical category 154
Montaigne 1
Moodie 94
moral aesthetic 14, 15
moral closure 157
moral community 110
moral imagination 16, 17, 119, 156–170
- as necessary to social science 170
Moral Imagination in Kaguru Modes of Thought 158–160
Moral Majority 168
moral metaphor system 160
moral order 156
moral pedagogy 14
moral philosophers 165
Moral Rearmament 168

moral sentiments 156
morality 109, 160
 - as mystification 168
 - *paesano* 110
 - and social science 168
More than Cool Reason 158, 162–3
Morita, Shooma 124
Morpurgo 100
Mort 89
mos, a way of comporting oneself 157
Moscovici 88
Moscow 128
Moses 162
Muecke 116
Müller 44
Müller, Anne 48
Müller-Gangloff, Erich 36–51
murder, as schema 41
museumize (*musealisieren*) 36
musicality 133
Mussolini 113
mutability 49
mythoi 142
myths 158, 159

n/om (healing energy) 70, 83
n/om kxaosi, 'owners of n/om', shamans 70–71, 83
Namibia 69
napalm 101
narrative 12–14, 25, 34, 38–51
 - of death 78
 - dialogic 53, 61
 - doctors introducing structure into 56
 - as ethical deliberation 157
 - as exploration of the problem of right conduct 159
 - healing 71
 - as instrument 57
 - minimal 40
 - polyphonic 60, 61, 62
 - prototype 41
 - skeletal 41
 - thought 34–51
narratives of destruction 90
narratives of diffuseness 54
nation-state 153

 - as rhetorical category 154
NATO 41
natural countryside 94
nature / culture 10–11
nature vs. nurture 11
Navaho 2
Nazi Germany 26
Nazis 25–31, 34–51
Nazism 45
Needham 82
Negri 57
Nerlich, Brigitte 13, 89, 90
Netherlands 26
neurasthenia (*shinkeishitsu*) 124
neuro-reductionism 167
neuromechanism, as compensation to uncertainties of market 165
neuroscience 164
New Jersey 146
New Life 90
New Light 22
New York City 138, 139
New York Times Magazine 146
NGOs 57
Nienkamp, Jean 7, 9, 11
North 92, 95
North Yorkshire 89
Northumberland 88
Nossack, Hans 57
novels, romance 22, 23
nutrition, in healing 79

observer effects 156
Olbrechts-Tyteca 20, 109
oncologist 13, 72–83
O'Neill 98
Orleans 92
Our City of Refuge 62
Out of the Ashes 100
overcoming the past. *See* Vergangenheitsbewältigung.

paesano (fellow countryman) 110
Palestinian question 151
Palestinians 148
Pappenheim, Bertha 127–129
parent, nurturant, metaphor of 162
past, the 38

pathos 10, 20, 22
patient 70
Pearl Harbor 151
Perelman 20, 109
performance 7, 37–39, 48
person, rational, self-interested 109
personification 44–45, 48
Philammon 24–25
Phillips report on BSE 91
philosophy 77
Philosophy in the Flesh 158
Phoenix 101
pigeonholes 8–9
plague 89
plague pits 100
Plato 163
plot, defined 39
poems, concerning FMD 99, 100
politeness 15
politeness, levels of, in Japan 125
political potential of catastrophes 103
political repression, testimony of 56
politics and rhetoric 91
polyphonic voices 60
polyphony 60
populism 44
Premack, D. 14
prestation 110
primates, social 7
Prince, The 118
privacy, European-American rhetoric of 134
progress 143
prolepsis 38
pronoun, inchoate. *See* inchoate pronoun.
Protestant Christians 47–49
proverbs 159
psychiatry 56
psychotherapy 124
public / concealed contrast, in Japan 124
public culture 156
public knowledge 90
public practices 36
public speaking 6
public thinking 90
purification 94
pyres 90, 95, 100

Quinn, Naomi 49, 98, 161

racialism 127–129
reactions 4
reality 9, 10
  - deflection of 20
Rebel 122, 135
reciprocity 122
redemption 41–43
refugees, Bosnian 53–68
refugees, German (*Heimatvertriebene*) 44
Reilly 95
Reliant Energy 142
religion 22
  - and healing, linked 82
  - and medicine 80
repression 42
Reynolds, David 125
rhetor 8, 47
rhetoric 6–9
  - as communicative culturally prescribed activity 119
  - culture 7–11
  - of excess 140–141
  - vs. experience 47
rhetoric, as terministic screen 9
  - defined 3
  - energy of 7
  - ideological 122
  - internal 11, 18–33
  - Marxist 113
  - mere 6
  - palaestral (as wrestling school) 13, 107–119
  - romance 22–25
  - as vicissitude in itself 13
rhetorical self 26
rhetorical situation. *See* situation, rhetorical.
rhetorics, dominant 123
Rieff, Phillip 122
risk taking 143, 144
Roberto (pseudonymous character) 107 *passim*
Rockefeller, David 146
Rogers, Daniel 22
Rogers, Martha 'Patty' 22–25
Rose, Wendy 122

Rosenberg 70, 90
Rowe 90
ruins 55
Russians 40, 41, 44

salmonella 89
Sapir 88, 98
Sarajevo, University of 63
Saudi Arabia 153
schema 4, 14
 - narrative 41-42
Schieffelin, Edward 80
Schlink, Bernhard 50
Schütz 48
Schwab-Trapp 36
Sebald, W.G. 53-55, 58, 59
second guilt, the (*die zweite Schuld*) 41
Second World War 11, 45, 55
Seifert 92
self-consciousness 21
self-constraint 15
self, reflective 29-30
self, rhetorical 21-22
self, rhetorical, defined 20
set, of people 5
Shakespeare 109
shamanic function of doctor 80
shamanism 132, 133
shamans. *See* n/om kxaosi.
shame 13, 123 *passim*
 - Japanese 134
 - kinds of 124
 - as morality 124
 - summary of differences in 135
Shaw, George Bernard 89
shock 10
shock and awe 148
Shore, B. 49
shut-in syndrome (*nikokomori*) 124
Siegel 74
signore, meaning glossed 111-112
Silence of a Dale 90
silence of the lambs 95
silence, brought about by astonishment 149-150
silent spring 95
Simonton 74
simplification 48

sin 41-43
sincerity, modernist 133
single self, ideology of, in West 126
situation, rhetorical 8
slaughter policy 87, 88, 91-93
slippage 49
Smit, Christopher 150
sociability, smile of 122
Social Aid Foundation 56
social bias, in human intelligence 48
social psychology 88
social sciences 4
Socialists 113
sociality 49
society, as set of people 5
solidarity 110
 - break in, during FMD crisis 102
 - created by war metaphor 92
Song Texts from the Masters of Tricks 71
Sontag, Susan 63
Sophists 116, 156
spaces, social 55
speech about affines, among Kalapalo 129-133
speech, as heteroglossic and polyvocal 122
speech, deceptive (*augunda*) 129-130
speech, ritualization of, as commitment to common project among Kalapalo 130
spirit world 70
St Francis 162
stamping-out policy. *See* slaughter policy.
stance 121
Star of David 26
Stasi (East German secret police) 36
Steen 96
Stein 73
stereotypes 48
stereotyping 44
Stiglitz 147
story seeds 38-51
 - defined 38-39
story, enacted 45-47
story. *See* narrative.
Storytelling. *See* narrative.
strategy 118
Strauss 49
Strecker, Ivo 60
Streeck, Jürgen 40

structure, as imagined 109
structure, as replaceable 109
structure, doctors introducing, into narrative 56
structure, plurality of 14
structure, social 4
structures, as resources 118
Styx 69, 73
subconscious 18–19
suppression, self 123
surgery 77
survivor 54, 56
swine fever 89

taijinkyofusho (fear of outsiders) 124
technocratic medicine 73
technocratic model of medicine 74
technology 139
teknonyms 130
televisual chaos 150
Tenney 23, 24
terminality 78, 81
terministic screen 18, 20
testimony 53–68
 - dialogic theory of 59
testimony school, Latin American 56
Texas 69
texts of self 122
The Saving Lie 119
thumb piano 71
Todd 78
topoi 142
topos 114
Totem and Taboo 123
traces 55
trance, healing 71
transaction 113
trauma 53–68, 89
trauma, community 89
traumatic stress theory 57
trickster 12–13, 132, 133, 136
tropologists in anthropology 161
truth and beauty, in narratives 58
truth and sincerity, ideology of 126
truth as revealed 132–133
Turner, Victor 16, 80, 88
Twin Towers. *See* World Trade Center.
Tyler 122

UK 13
unintended consequences 45
United Nations 8
United Nations War Crimes Tribunal 57
United States 148
Universal Declaration of Human Rights 8
unmastered past 11–12, 49, 50
utopia 142

vaccination 88
values 4, 14, 24
values, *paesano,* as *topos* 114
van Daan 28
Vergangenheitsbewältigung (overcoming, or mastering, the past) 34–51
verification in conversation, among Kalapalo 129
Verizon 142
vicissitudes 9–11, 15, 39, 156
 - defined 2, 3
 - of everyday life 157
Vico, Giambattista 8
Vietnam 99–101
violence 53, 54
virtue, Christian 37
virus. *See* FMD.
vitamin C 76
voice suppression 123, 126, 134
voices 19–32, 60
 - of testimony 58
voicing 122
Volk (German people) 41, 44, 47, 48
Voloshinov 121
Vygotsky, Lev 22

Wagner 88, 92, 94–96, 102
war 54
war metaphor 92
 - declaration of, on Iraq 8
 - as metaphor 13, 87–104
 - on terror 153
Ward 89
Weber, Max 45
Wehrmacht 36
Weine, Stevan 12
Weinstein, Eugenia 56
Wellbery 141, 144

Wertsch 22
West Germans 36–51
Whately, Richard 18, 22
Whitefield, George 22
whore 5–6
Wilson, E.O. 166
wisdom, perennial 10
Wolf, Eric 45
Woolf, Virginia 9
Wordsworth, William 98

World Trade Center 5, 97, 138–154
- designing and building of 146–147
- as establishing new limits of modernity 147
Wundt, Wilhelm 123

Yorick's Sentimental Journey 23

zero hour (*Stunde Null*) 42
Zizek, Slavo 147